Fast Track to
PASSIVE
INCOME

THE INDISPENSABLE GUIDE TO BUILDING A
SECURE PASSIVE INCOME FOR RETIREMENT

RON FORLEE

ISBN: 978-1-925952-30-8
Published by Vivid Publishing
A division of Fontaine Publishing Group
P.O. Box 948, Fremantle
Western Australia 6959
www.vividpublishing.com.au

A catalogue record for this
book is available from the
National Library of Australia

To my mother, the late Mabel Forlee,
and my wife Cindy Forlee who passed away in 2018.

The two most inspirational women in my life
who will always be remembered.

CONTENTS

ACKNOWLEDGMENTS

This book would not have been possible without the support and encouragement of certain people who have in many ways contributed to my life. I express my gratitude to:

My late mother Mabel who supported and encouraged me to live my dreams but also taught me the importance to help less fortunate people;

My late wife, Cindy who always loved and supported me throughout our 38 years of marriage and showed me the importance of being happy and positive; and

My children Taryn, Jared and Charisse who have loved and supported me in every possible way.

Ron Forlee

PREFACE

As I'm getting closer to retirement, I realise that many of my friends do not have a passive income. Their superannuation may not meet their future financial obligations and they may not be able to enjoy the same level of lifestyle they currently have. Creating a passive income stream is an alternative way to earn money rather than a traditional wage, salary, pension or superannuation. By creating a passive income, you gain financial freedom, and real estate is a great way to generate passive income.

Real estate is one avenue to create passive income stream, as both rental income and the value of your property are almost guaranteed to increase at least in line with inflation. Generally, the rent you receive escalates annually providing you with more passive income and the increase in the value of your property provides you with additional money to grow your investment portfolio.

Traditionally most investors who invest in real estate for a passive income take out a mortgage, and it may take several years when the rental income exceeds the mortgage repayments where they are positively geared. This book has been written for those who would like to speed up this process. It demonstrates and outlines strategies of real estate development and wholesale investing by which a passive retirement income can be achieved earlier.

One of the strategies explained this book, involves developing several building units (whether residential or commercial) selling some of the units to reduce the development loan and retaining a few so that they are positively geared. For those who do not to want to undertake the risk of developing, other strategies demonstrate where to find discounted real estate opportunities. This book covers how you can benefit from the tax incentives provided by the government and how to form partnerships or to create a syndicate to reduce development risk and to grow a healthy income-producing real estate portfolio faster than traditional real estate investment.

While this book has been written from an Australian context, the principles and strategies can be applied to many other countries. The concept of real estate development, financial leveraging and market demand for real estate are similar in most OECD (Organisation for Economic Co-operation and Development) counties.

The content of this book takes into account the 2019 Australian federal election and the recommendations of the Royal Commission into Misconduct in the Banking, Superannuation and Financial Services Industry, such as fees paid to mortgage brokers. Had the Labor government won, areas of negative gearing would have needed redrafting. This book is aimed at those seeking or creating positively geared property as it is prone to fewer risks and provides a more secure passage to early retirement. Therefore, I do not support a negative gearing strategy unless you have a stable job with a steady salary.

Since I started writing books on real estate development and investment in 2004, I have received numerous emails from my readers thanking and complimenting me on the subject and contents of my books. I'm truly humbled and thankful for their interest. This book is the fourth and I do hope that you enjoy reading and learning from the content herein and that it will lead you towards the creation of a healthy real estate portfolio with a passive income to be enjoyed in your retirement.

In addition to book writing, I'm now providing mentorship programs on property development through my company AYR International Pty Ltd. These programs are based on the culmination of over 40 years as an architect and property developer. One of the motivating reasons for providing these mentorship programs is to educate people interested in property development to undertake developments for the right reasons. I believe that developers should make money as they are taking significant risk, but that this should not be the sole motivating factor. As developers, we are decision-makers who create built environments for our future generations. It is therefore, our responsibility to create environments that are ecologically sustainable and can be enjoyed by all.

Ron Forlee B.Arch.
Email: ronf@ayrinternational.com
December 2018

CHAPTER 1

WHY START A REAL ESTATE PORTFOLIO?

INTRODUCTION

Creating a real estate portfolio can be challenging. There are some tasks you must get through, and you need the capacity and financial resources to deal with unexpected issues arising from your investments. Many ordinary investors are creating extraordinary wealth through real estate. With the right mindset, strategy and meticulous research come confidence to invest in real estate. However, where does a first-time real estate investor start?

Real estate investment has always been popular in Australia. It is an asset class that historically, over the long term, has produced healthy returns for some people. Real estate has made more people wealthy compared to shares, and it can significantly affect the wealth of the small investor as there is the potential for capital growth and – even more beneficial for the investor – the capital growth is created using bank loans.

One of the main reasons for building a real estate portfolio is to build up your wealth with the purpose of achieving financial independence and to have a passive income in your retirement. Buying investment properties and creating a portfolio is not a short-term investment. In the short- term, there may be little or no profit from rent after expenses like mortgage, insurance, rates and maintenance are taken into account. However, in the long-term, your investment in real estate will show a profit as prices rise and your original mortgage is reduced therefore increasing your equity position and net worth.

THE BENEFITS OF HAVING A PORTFOLIO

Having a real estate portfolio has many benefits to an astute investor seeking financial freedom. By creating a portfolio of properties, spreading capital across more than just one property in different locations with varying asset types can reap significant wealth. Placing money in a bank savings account may protect your money, but growth is likely to be modest compared to the potential profits in the real estate market. By having a real estate portfolio, not only can you invest to protect your capital but also position your portfolio to earn sizable profits. The points listed below describe the benefits of having a real estate portfolio made up of diversified property assets with various types of properties and varied locations.

Passive income

Being financially free means you have enough income to support your lifestyle. One way of achieving financial freedom is to have a passive income, which is an income that is received regularly but with minimal effort needed to sustain it. One of the easiest and indeed the most popular way of generating a passive income is through real estate investments. You do not have to be born into a wealthy family to achieve financial freedom through real estate ownership. Provided you plan early – and stick to your plan – you can acquire a portfolio of properties that produce a steady stream of income.

Furthermore, the value of your real estate assets will increase each year when rent and demand in your area increases. Many retired people live off the rental income from properties they own. Younger people can also earn extra income from passive investments in housing if they start early.

Leveraging through equity growth

Many smart people in Australia own two or more properties. These owners start building wealth through leveraging their initial investment property. They buy their own home, and after a few years of ownership, they discover their property's value has increased significantly. Instead of selling, the owners take out another loan from the bank against the increased equity in their home. With this cash, they place a deposit to buy another property. Later they find that both properties they own have continued to grow in value, and they approach the bank again for a loan against their properties' equity and buy a third property. They repeat the process until they are ready to retire or continue to grow their portfolio as a hobby.

Direct control over your investment

Compared to shares or managed funds, with real estate, you are the owner of the whole investment, so you have total control over it. When you invest in shares, you generally will need a broker to handle your trades for you unless, of course, you have the know-how to manage the trades yourself using one of the many software packages on the market. Also, the value of your shares is reliant on market conditions and the actions of other people running that company over which you have no control. With real estate, you directly own the asset once you have settled a property in your name, and you have complete control over it if you can meet the mortgage payments. It means that you can influence the value of the property by adding value to it by way of renovations or rent increases.

Pride of ownership

As property is a tangible asset, it can always be viewed by you and others. Having a portfolio of properties gives you a sense of pride when driving by. It also gives you a sense of security as you see your assets grow over time. When thinking long-term about your portfolio, don't only think of ownership during your lifetime but of the investment legacy you can pass onto your children. Depending on the ownership structure under which you own your properties, you can pass your investments onto your children either before or after you pass away. Your portfolio can also be used to raise capital for your children when they attend university or start their own business.

You can use your super

One way of building a real estate portfolio in a shorter period is to use your superannuation (pension) and the yearly contributions you make to a self-managed super fund (SMSF). This option has been around for some time, but only recently has it become feasible to invest in property via an SMSF due to changes in the Australian law regarding borrowing within your super fund. An SMSF is tax-effective as the Capital Gains Tax (CGT) on sale is just 10% and zero if you're over 60. As each investor has a different profile in terms of income and asset holding, it is advisable to seek professional advice on SMSFs, as you must abide by the rules, which are quite complex and prone to changes by the Australian Government.

INVESTING IN AUSTRALIAN REAL ESTATE

Investing in rental property has proven to be a successful model for many Australians over the years. The difference between an investment property and your own home is that you earn an income from the former. While there are various strategies you can employ to make money from property, there are two ways to make a profit. The first is from rental income, the second from capital growth. Rental income places money directly in your pocket. When rental income from a property exceeds its costs, the remaining rent is profit that puts you in a positive cash-flow position. The other way of making money relies on properties increasing in value over time. As your loan is a fixed amount to buy a property, the increase in value over time is all yours, increasing your equity. Therefore, when you hold property for the long-term, you can see big improvements in value, making a significant gain to you personally.

Although inflation has been quite low in Australia for the last 20 years, we have still seen significant growth in property prices. Over the longer term, returns on property are about one or two points higher than the Australian inflation rate, but because of the secure nature of property, banks are prepared to lend money against it. This means that 80% of your real estate investment may be the bank's money, but you earn an above-inflation return on your overall investment. Property has historically increased in value, typically faster than inflation.

In the long-term, real estate investment can deliver good returns. We only need to go back to the GFC (Global Financial Crisis) in 2008 when we saw superannuation balances tumble while real estate prices increased. Historically this growth in real estate prices has been driven by continued population growth and immigration combined with a chronic undersupply of housing. The housing supply remains tight in many areas particularly capital cities, which means that prices in the real estate market are less likely to crash. However, you need to do your research carefully, as in some areas of the market do experience oversupply, which will dampen its value.

REAL ESTATE COMPARED WITH OTHER INVESTMENTS

Real estate is classified as a medium-risk investment, like shares and certain bonds. More conservative investments such as savings accounts, cash trusts and government bonds carry less risk but do not show the same capital growth as real estate. With higher-risk investments like futures and options, your potential returns are much higher but so is your exposure to volatility.

One of the main differences between investing in real estate when compared to shares or bonds is that real estate is an investment in the 'bricks and mortar' of a building and land. This makes real estate highly tangible whereas shares you cannot see. This tangibility gives the investor a considerable pride of ownership, but there is also a downside as requires hands-on management and more work compared to other investments.

Other investments each have their level of risk and rewards. It is typically the case that the more money you can make from an investment, the higher the risk that you might not get all your money back. It is recommended to have a mix of different types of investments to spread your risk. Broadly, investments fall into three categories: growth investments, defensive investments and alternatives as described below.

Growth investments

Growth investments are long-term investments, which in the early stages can be affected by the highs and lows of the market. Real estate falls under this category, and so do shares and managed funds.

- *Shares*

  Shares can help grow the value of your original investment over the medium to long-term. Also known as equities or stock, shares have historically delivered higher returns than other investment types. However, they carry more risk in the short term because share prices can be volatile, moving up and down on a daily basis. When you buy shares, you are buying a small part of a company that is looking to raise money to fund their growth through the stock exchange. Buying shares in a company gives you the right to a portion of the profits that the company makes (dividends) and is dependent on them performing well. Money is made on the share market in two ways (a) through dividends or (b) by selling your shares for a profit. These transactions are done via online trading or through a stockbroker. Like house prices, share prices are generally expected to grow over time, which creates a 'capital gain' on your money when you sell.

- *Managed funds*

  Managed funds give investors access to professional fund managers who conduct in-depth qualitative and quantitative research of the chosen investment market. Managed funds can also provide investors with a diverse range of assets. Managed funds can be either 'listed' and tradeable on the stock market or 'unlisted' and bought and sold directly through a fund manager. If 'listed' the value of the shares is dictated by supply and demand, which is in turn dictated by performance and valuation. Joining a managed fund allows you to pool your money with other investors. Experienced fund managers will then spread the investment over a range of assets such as property, bonds, cash or shares. The benefit of managed funds is that you do not have to worry about tracking your varied share portfolio and can leave it instead to the experts. In Australia, there are four different types of managed funds:

  – Capital Guaranteed Funds will guarantee the earning amount which is safer and lower-risk.

  – Diversified Stable Funds invest in assets with a stable return, such cash and fixed interest.

– Diversified Growth Funds invest in a combination of properties and shares.

– Diversified Balanced Funds spread their investment across property, shares and fixed interest.

When compared to direct real estate investments, you relinquish that direct control when investing in shares and managed funds. Depending on the type of shares, your investments and capital growth can be severely affected by the volatility of the share market.

Defensive investments

Defensive investments are conservative, lower-risk investments that focus on consistently generating income, rather than capital growth.

- *Cash and savings*
  Savings accounts with Australia's major banks and credit unions are one of the most common and least risky ways to invest your money. These investments include everyday bank accounts, high-interest savings accounts and term deposits. In general, they carry the lowest potential returns of all the investment types. Also, they offer no capital growth. They can deliver regular income and can play an essential role in protecting wealth and reducing risk in an investment portfolio. The Australian Government guarantees the deposits of Australian deposit-taking institutions (i.e. banks) for deposits of up to $250,000 per person per institution giving comfort that money will be safe.

- *Fixed interest*
  The best-known type of fixed interest investments is bonds. A bond is like an 'IOU' issued by a government, council, or company. You lend them your money for some years, and they promise to pay a guaranteed interest rate defined as a coupon. Considered as a defensive investment, bonds generally offer lower potential returns and lower levels of risk than shares or property. Like cars, they can also be sold relatively

quickly, although you should note that they are not entirely risk free. The risk level depends on the credibility of the issuer. Unlike term deposits, you can sell your bonds early. However, the price you will get may go up or down.

Alternatives

Alternatives is a broad term used to describe investments that fall outside the standard asset classes which include cash, shares, bonds and property. Alternatives include commodities, currency and derivatives.

- *Commodities*

  Commodities do not pay interest or dividends, but they do increase and decrease in value, which can result in a capital gain if you sell at a higher price than that at which you bought. Their value often moves in the opposite direction to other asset classes. For example, when share prices go down, gold tends to increase in value, and vice versa. So some investors buy them as a way of protecting their money.

- *Currency*

  Besides being used to buy general goods and services, foreign currency can be used as an investment as well. Currency investors look for higher interest rates overseas or hope that exchange rates will move in their favour and result in a capital gain. Both investors and managed funds may also use currency to protect, or 'hedge', other investments overseas.

- *Derivatives*

  Derivatives are complex investments and are generally only used by more sophisticated investors, such as managed funds. Derivatives can also include options and futures. This can be a confusing and complicated area of investing, however, derivatives are built on a relatively simple concept, i.e. allowing people to protect themselves, or 'hedge' against future price movements.

- *Other alternatives*

  These alternatives can include things such as gold coins, private equity, hedge funds, artworks, fine wine, exotic cars and stamps. The reasons for investing in these alternatives are varied, but, as with all investments, their value can go up or down.

REAL ESTATE AS AN INVESTMENT

Now let us look at real estate as an investment in more detail. For most people, the most significant single investment that they will make in their lifetime will be when buying their first home. Below are some areas to consider when investing in property.

- **Single large purchase**

  Buying a property is a significant purchase requiring many thousands of dollars. It is typically the most substantial investment that a person may have aside from superannuation. When investing in the share market an investor can spread their investment over several companies, however, diversification is hard with real estate, and your investment capital will be tied up in a single asset. If anything goes wrong with a property or the real estate market moves negatively, your whole investment capital is at risk.

- **Management costs and time**

  When compared to other investment types, real estate is expensive to buy, sell and maintain. It is not unusual for purchase costs to be around 5% of the value of the property and selling costs approximately 2%. There are also costs such as management, maintenance and repairs, and lost rental income if the property is vacant. On top of these costs is the time needed to maintain the investment. You need to find a property manager, screen potential tenants, approve repairs, deal with a body corporate and regularly deal with the accounting and taxes of the property. Property is more time intensive when compared to other assets.

- **Gearing**

  Any investment that involves borrowing means a higher risk or return, especially when it involves a single asset. Gearing is risky, particularly with property, where it is common for people to borrow up to 95%. Gearing can significantly increase returns but also increases losses as well should the market drop.

BENEFITS OF INVESTING IN PROPERTY

In general, real estate can be considered a fairly low-risk investment given Australia's political stability. It can also be less volatile than shares. Some of the advantages of investing in real estate include:

- **A safe investment**

  In broad terms, the real estate market is more stable than the share market, partly due to the time and work that is required before purchasing a property – including research, due diligence, legal checks, inspections, settlement periods and so on. For this reason, real estate is less prone to short-term speculators than the share market. Also, around 68% of people who own real estate are homeowners, rather than investors, making real estate more steady and secure than the stock market where prices rise and fall more often. It does not mean real estate prices do not fluctuate, however, properties in well-located areas, underpinned by strong demand, rarely crash overnight. Another significant factor contributing to the safety of real estate is the fact that a property can be insured against almost all risks, unlike many other investments. You can take out property insurance against fire and natural disasters and landlord insurance is available against damage to your property, loss of rent, and so on.

- **Tax benefits**

  As the demand for real estate increased in Australia, the Australian Government realised that they had a growing problem which they could not meet. They then introduced tax relief measures to encourage investors to invest and develop new properties, primarily residential. As a result, Australians enjoy some of the most favourable tax law advantages of any other country when it comes to real estate investment. An investment property can obtain a number of deductions that can be claimed on your tax return, such as loan interest paid, repairs and maintenance, rates and taxes, insurance, agent's fees, repairs, and building depreciation. Tax deductions can also be claimed when the property is negatively geared – where the costs of maintaining an investment property exceed the income gained from it.

- **Regular Cash Flow**

  Another benefit of investing in real estate is the rental income received from tenants. Rental income will generally offset the loan repayments for negatively geared investments or will provide an additional cash flow for a property that is positively geared. This cash flow can be guaranteed for real estate investments with good long-term tenants and low vacancy rates. Also, legislation protecting both the landlord and tenants means that rent increases can be negotiated.

- **Capital growth leverage**

  It is common that the bank provides most of the funds to purchase a property, meaning there is considerable leverage, and your capital growth returns can be significant. The history of real estate investment is one of consistent capital growth over time. In Australia, history has shown that real estate properties have doubled in value on average every ten years, which means the likelihood of your property increasing in value is strong.

- **Inflation Hedge**

  Historically, real estate values have shown to keep up with, or exceed, inflation. Property returns are directly linked to the rents received from tenants. Some leases contain provisions for rent increases to be indexed to inflation. In other cases, rental rates are increased whenever a lease term expires, and a new tenant moves in. Either way, rental income tends to rise faster in inflationary environments, allowing an investor to maintain the property's real returns.

- **Demand**

  In Australia, there seems to be an ongoing housing shortage. Reports of the National Housing Supply Council indicate that the public and private sectors are not building enough homes. This means that the demand for rental properties should keep rents growing and house prices stable. According to the fourth Intergenerational Report, released in March 2015, Australia's projected population will be rising from 24 million to 39.7 million by 2054–55. According to a report by the Housing Industry Association (HIA) in October 2015, Australia's long-run average annual rate of new home building could be almost 30,000 dwellings short of what is needed to meet future demand.

- **Long-term investment**

  Investing in real estate is a long-term wealth creation strategy that can provide investors with consistent returns over the long term. Most people like the idea of an investment that can provide them with funds for their retirement. Housing is one sector that has rarely seen a decrease in price, making it a good potential option for long-term investments. With real estate, you do not have to sell your rental investment to realise the capital gains you have made. So when your real estate portfolio increases in value, so does your access to this value.

- **Third parties adding value**

  Real estate values also increase through government and private investments in a property's neighbourhood or location. Government spending on infrastructure such as roads, rail and airports can increase value in a specific suburb or regional town which may have previously had accessibility problems. Investment in new projects such as universities, hospitals, factories, shopping centres, and so on can provide employment opportunities and increase housing demand and in turn, increase the value of existing properties.

- **Government incentives**

  Besides the Government's tax benefits and the increased value due to Government spending on transport and social infrastructure such as schools, libraries, community centres, the Government will also provide additional incentives for property buyers. The better-known incentive is the $7,000 First Home Owners Grant, and in some states, there are incentives for off-the-plan and new properties. Another incentive for investors by the Government is the National Rental Affordability Scheme (NRAS), which offers $9000 per annum to investors as a tax deduction for investing in affordable housing.

- **Positive asset base**

  There are many other benefits of having an investment property. If you need to take out another loan or invest in something else, you have the ability to show your potential lender that you can maintain a loan without defaulting, which will be highly regarded. Banks prefer property assets as security as they can mortgage their loan on the property. A property is a useful form of security when taking out another home, car or personal loan, so building a real estate portfolio against your existing property assets is a lot easier than against other investments.

- **Ability to add further value**

  Because a property is a tangible asset, an investor can do things to a property to increase its value or improve its performance. For example, adding another room, adding a new kitchen, making cosmetic renovations, and thus signing up new leases with better tenants, will enhance its value. Redeveloping a property and adding a new home or granny flat due to increased density allowance by the local council, can also significantly improve an investors equity position. An investor has a higher degree of control over the performance of a real estate investment compared to other types of investments.

- **Low entry level**

  Many investments require significant existing wealth, but with property, this is not a pre-requisite allowing one to enter the market with less capital. Banks will lend at least 80% of the value of the property. Depending on an individual's circumstances, an investor with an average salary and some increased equity in their existing home or savings may be able to invest in a new property. This makes real estate investment within reach of most Australians, but that doesn't mean that all Australians will be eligible to invest as they would have to demonstrate that they have financial resources to repay a bank loan.

RISK OF INVESTING IN REAL ESTATE

All investments carry a certain level of risk, and that includes real estate investments. Without risk, there is no reward, and successful real estate investors identify, manage and mitigate as many of these risks as possible. Listed below are risks typically associated with real estate and ways to manage these risks.

- **Market risk**

  Market risk affects all investments including real estate. The real estate market moves in cycles which can is described as rising, booming, slowing, falling and recovering. These cycles are affected by factors such as the state of the economy, interest rates, availability of finance, inflation, demand, pop-ulation growth, urban development and government incen-tives. To mitigate this risk, real estate investors should view their investment on a long-term basis, which means the market has time to recover and correct itself, should there be a dip. In normal circumstances, the investment should be held for a minimum of five years to recoup acquisition costs and allow time for reasonable capital growth. Also, it would be best if you formed an opinion on where the market is in its cycle, and what the short to medium term outlook on price movements is likely to be. In this way, doing your research and talking to local estate agents and property advisors could pay dividends.

- **Liquidity risk**

  It is difficult to sell a property quickly should the need arise, which is not the case for shares or government bonds. It can take months to sell which includes marketing time plus the settlement period. To mitigate liquidity risk in real estate investment, you should invest in capital city suburbs with a known demand and constrained supply. Also, you should also ensure you have sufficient equity (at least 15% to 20%) in your property from day one in case you have to sell at less-than-market to facilitate a quick sale. The more equity you have, the better leverage you have to drop your price to get out of a financial emergency.

- **Interest rate risk**

  Interest rates have a significant impact when owning a property. Should interest rates rise, investors need to be able to bear the cost of the increased payments. In an investment property, the interest rate risk instead lies in variable rate mortgages as the cost of debt capital can materially increase especially when the Reserve Bank increases the cash rate. The interest rate risk can be mitigated through the use of fixed-rate mortgages and prudent cash-flow management. Also, it would help if you inform yourself on the current state of the interest rate cycle. There is no shortage of experts providing commentary on the level and direction of interest rates from the press and online.

- **Rental risk**

  Rental risk is when your property does not generate the rental income to meet ongoing operating and holding costs. The reasons could be many, such as a glut of rental properties in your area, not being able to find a tenant, or your existing tenant refusing to pay. Whatever the reason it means added financial stress. To mitigate rental risk, you should research the rental demand in the area before purchasing and aim for suburbs where the vacancy rate is 3% or less. Good suburbs are localities that have all the necessary established transport and social infrastructure such as schools, shops and so on. Local real estate agents, property managers and property research companies will be a good source of information on vacancy rates and rental yields. Taking out landlord and property insurance will help to cover yourself in case of non-payment of rent or your tenant damaging your property. Also, when setting your operating budget, allow for a vacancy period of between two to four weeks to ensure you can cope financially.

- **Personal risk**

  Personal risks relate to personal issues or events that could adversely affect your real estate investment. Most real estate investors take advantage of the tax benefit by negatively gearing, which means they are contributing their cash to cover the loan interest shortfall and operational costs. The personal tax advantages of this structure still require that investors be out of pocket until the property is sold. Unemployment, long-term sickness and changes to your family situation such as divorce, a long-term illness, and moving from a dual income to a single income, are examples of changed personal circumstances that can cause significant financial difficulty, which can undermine your investment objectives. Mitigating against the variable personal risk is impossible. However, there are some precautionary steps you can take such as: (a) prepare a budget and run 'what-if' scenarios to see how and whether you could cope financially if something unforeseen were to happen, (b) only buy a property if you can positively gear the investment, and (c) insure yourself against accident, sickness and unemployment risk whereby you would get either a lump sum or a regular income to help meet mortgage repayments. It would be best if you also took out life insurance to at least the value of the mortgage, which would pay-off your loan and leave your family debt free should the worst happen.

- **Knowledge risk**

  You should not invest in real estate unless you have gained enough knowledge about it and understood its risks and rewards. You need to know what you are committing to and be satisfied that this type of investment meets your criteria. You will have to invest time, effort and money and make sacrifices to give your investment a chance to be successful. Making a bad investment decision can become a costly exercise. Mitigating this risk is not difficult. The first thing to do is to read and research the industry extensively. Follow the market in your local newspaper to get a feel for prices and activity. Speak to experts and get an unbiased view about real estate investment. Attend real estate seminars but be cautious as often they include a sales pitch about exclusive property deals or proven training programs. The Internet is a great place to pick up information and many property sites and property research companies have free newsletters and market research you can subscribe to. Furthermore, before fully committing to a purchase, it is vital to undertake due diligence of the property.

- **Negative value risk**

  A negative value is when the market price of a property you purchased is lower than the original price you paid. This could happen if you purchased a property at the peak of a property boom, and it devalues when prices start falling post-boom. A typical case was the recent mining boom when property prices in mining towns were achieving double-digit returns on rental properties. With the mining downturn, the value of these prop-erties fell into negative value territory, and if the property was highly geared, investors selling these properties found that they still owed money to the bank. To mitigate this risk, you should time your purchase during the pre-boom peak and sell at the peak. Alternatively, carefully invest in areas where there are fewer peaks and troughs such a major capital city. Avoid regional mining towns and Greenfield suburbs where transport and social infrastructure has not been established.

- **Call risk**

  Call risk is applicable to investors who have a share portfolio which is geared with a lender. Call risk is not generally found in real estate investment but can apply to property investors who are highly geared with a specific lender. Australian commercial property investors have periodically been subjected to the property equivalent of a margin call, which forces the investors to reduce debt exposure through the redemption of assets. After the Global Financial Crisis (GFC) many property inves-tors who were highly geared were forced by their banks to sell their properties as their values had dropped. When an invest-ment property is mortgaged with the same bank as your own home, there is the risk that the bank could sell both properties if you run into difficulty with paying either of the mortgages. To mitigate this type of risk, it is better not to have all your properties to one lender, and it will also help if the ownership of the property is under a different name or a special purpose vehicle such as a company that is owned by you.

- **Governmental risk**

  The risk of the laws changing may affect any of your investments. This could be particularly relevant to superannuation, as the rules tend to change continually. In some other cases, the Government may decide to replan your area and divert a major arterial or build a freeway next to your property. These changes can severely affect the value of your investment. It is probably the hardest risk to deal with because it involves politics. Mitigating this risk will help by reading newspapers and keeping up with any proposed changes in the area where your property is located. Financial planners keep up with the latest legislative issues, and it is worthwhile to appoint one. Subscribing to various investment media and attending professional development seminars may help as well.

While there are additional risks in real estate such as credit risk, sovereign risk, and severe climate risk, in general, the benefits of property investing in Australia outweigh the risks. Astute investors who have made millions out of property investing are passionate about real estate and keep up with changes in the industry by continually reading and researching.

TYPES OF REAL ESTATE INVESTMENTS

When you are looking at building a real estate portfolio, one of the essential criteria aside from location, is to analyse the type of property to invest. You need to ask yourself which property type will suit your investment strategy as each property type has a different set of drivers influencing its performance. For example, the income and the valuation of residential properties differ from those of commercial properties.

In broad terms, real estate investment can be broken down into two main categories, namely residential and commercial. Residential property is made up of houses, villas, townhouses, apartments and holiday homes, whereas commercial property can be defined as offices, retail and industrial. Furthermore, within these categories, other factors drive their performance. For example, under residential, an investment in a house may differ to an apartment within the same location. Later in this book, we analyse each specific property type in more detail.

One of the major differences between residential and commercial properties is how they are appraised or valued. With residential, the value is generally based on a sales comparison with similar properties or market approach whereas with commercial properties value is based on their income and are not compared to other similar commercial properties. With the latter, no matter how expensive it is to build or how shabby the building looks, the actual income of the commercial property derives its value.

Commercial real estate investment will suit investors who are willing to take more significant risks for bigger returns and who appreciate a hassle-free longer-term tenant. On the other hand, residential investment might deliver lower returns and demanding clients, but it is the safer option. Before deciding to buy a commercial or residential property let us look at their advantages and disadvantages.

Residential property

Residential properties can be defined as houses, villas, townhouses, apartments and holiday homes that could be rented out to third parties. The length of their stay is based upon the rental agreement or lease agreement between a landlord and a tenant.

Advantages

- *Vacancy*: Residential property is less likely to stay untenanted for long periods. Residential leases are also shorter than commercial ones, however, residential properties are generally easier to rent due to a larger rental market.

- *Greater rental market*: Residential homes are easier to rent. With the turnover in housing being high, you can usually count on an ample pool of potential tenants. Regardless of the economy, residential tenants are available as most people like to live and rent in places close to their friends, families, work, educational institutions, and so on.

- *Ease of finance*: Financing residential property is usually fairly straightforward. A smaller deposit is needed, which can be important especially if it is your first investment property. Depending on your credit rating and income, you can even borrow 100% of the purchase price. Interest rates on residential mortgages also tend to be lower.

19

- *Consistent cash flow*: Investing in rental properties also guarantees available cash flow given that they are easier to rent. When a tenant leaves, there are always new tenants coming in. Most residential tenants pay their rents on a weekly or fortnightly basis.
- *Ease of selling*: If needed, it is easier to sell houses than a commercial building because buyers in the housing market are more numerous than commercial buyers who are mainly investors.
- *Less complicated leases*: Rental leases are relatively standard, short and easy to understand. Therefore, land-lords and tenants should not have difficulty in under-standing these documents.
- *Capital appreciation*: Historically residential properties tend to double in value every 7 to 10 years whereas the commercial property market can be less predictable.
- *Land value ratio*: Residential properties have a higher land-to-building ratio than commercial properties, so usually offer higher capital growth because land values go up, but buildings depreciate.

Disadvantages

- *Lower return*: Due to the competitive market, residential properties typically deliver a lower yield when compared to commercial properties which, depending on their location, may have a monopoly, especially if demand increases.
- *Outgoings and maintenance*: With a residential property all of the maintenance costs and repairs is the responsibility of the landlord. If the property is older, it may require more repairs and maintenance which could affect the returns from the property.
- *Management*: Residential properties usually require much hands-on management. Landlords can get a call or com-plaint at any time of day or night, so it is best to employ a property manager who specialises in residential leasing – it is worth the money spent.
- *Late payments*: The problem with some residential tenants

is that they don't pay their rents on time which means if you are on a tight budget it could affect your repayments to the bank.

- *Bad tenants*: If tenants are not carefully screened, a property owner could end up with a bad tenant who when given notice due to non-payment of rent will refuse to leave, making the eviction process difficult.

Commercial property

Commercial property is used for businesses such as retail outlets, offices or industry. Generally, commercial investments involve stricter lending conditions and a more substantial deposit than residential property.

Advantages

- *Outgoings*: Commercial tenants are generally responsible for outgoings like rates and taxes, insurance, water rates, land taxes and so on whereas with a residential property this is the responsibility of the landlord.
- *Greater care*: Commercial tenants will also tend to maintain and take care of the property better as the look and con-dition of the property are essential to their business and their staff. Some tenants will make improvements that will enhance your property.
- *Longer leases*: Leases tend to be much longer which could be anything from 3 to 20 years, and they are often secured by bank guarantees, which translates into guaranteed long-term cash flow. Five-year leases with built-in rent escala-tions and options to renew are not universal but certainly quite common.
- *Flexible lease agreements*: Another advantage for com-mercial leases is that you can add clauses and conditions when necessary, benefitting you and the tenant. Com-mercial leases are also powerful when it comes to leasing payments. Rents that are unpaid rents can result in rent penalty and consequently eviction.
- *Bad tenants*: Both residential and commercial property

owners can experience bad tenants, except that the latter has the upper hand. When it comes to eviction, the landlord has the right to remove the tenant by performing specific actions for example by changing locks and seizing the premises in accordance with the lease document.

- *Escalation and rent reviews*: In most commercial leases rent is escalated annually either by the CPI or by 4%, whichever is higher, and reviews every 3 to 5 years keep it in line with the current rental values in the area.

- *Higher returns*: The return on invested capital on commercial properties ranges between 7% and 10% net after all costs. With residential property, the returns are 5% or less, plus investors must pay all outgoings and other expenses.

- *Less management*: Hands-on management is less than with residential properties. Most commercial leases are written to include the requirement that the tenant is responsible for interior repairs, maintenance, glass breakage, and so on.

- *Tenant fit-out*: Depending on the type of space such as retail and higher-grade offices, the tenant generally will fit-out the space to suit their requirements. Some landlords may give a one-off fit-out allowance or a period of free rent to attract a tenant.

- *Creating value*: Because a commercial property's value is based on its income stream, an investor has the opportunity to create value by enhancing that income stream. This means that the investor is not relying on general market appreciation to increase the property's value, but can take steps to improve its value by renovation or redevelopment.

Disadvantages

- *Strict lending criteria*: Financing commercial property can be more complicated than with residential. Lenders have more stringent borrowing criteria for commercial properties. Most banks are willing to lend around 75% or more for a residential property whereas with commercial property they start at 60% or less.

- *Longer vacancy periods*: Commercial properties can have a vacancy for long periods, particularly in tough economic times. Also, commercial leases will typically require that a tenant exercise an option to renew well before the lease expires anything from 6 to 12 months before the expiry of the lease so that the landlord has ample time to look for a new tenant.

- *Longer lead times*: Leasing a commercial space can take longer when compared to residential. After a tenant is identified and basic terms agreed upon, it is usually necessary for the landlord and tenant's lawyers to negotiate the terms and conditions of the lease. The cost and complexity can vary depending on whether you are dealing with a local or a national tenant.

- *Complex lease agreements*: Commercial lease document usually are long with many clauses. With residential, the leases are more standard and most residential property managers would provide one or they can be bought on the Internet as well.

- *Economic downturn*: As most commercial tenants run their premises for business purposes, a drop in the economy may result in loss of income and eventually loss of businesses. When this occurs, they vacate or are forced to vacate leaving the onus on you to find new tenants. Therefore, commercial vacancies can cost an investor a lot more, compared to residential.

- *Knowledge and cash reserves*: With commercial property, investors need to have greater knowledge, experience and market knowledge of the commercial property industry plus have enough cash reserves to sustain any vacancies.

Both residential and commercial properties tend to have their strengths and weaknesses. In general, most property investors start investing in residential before stepping into the commercial sector. Although there are differences between the two, you should not necessarily conclude that one is better than the other until both have been studied and analysed in line with your investment criteria which is based on your current financial situation and personal goals.

A FASTER ROUTE TO A PASSIVE INCOME

The above topics covered a great deal on real estate investment and the capital growth potential in buying established properties. This capital growth takes anywhere from five to ten years, where the growth in value plus your equity can increase at least in line with inflation. Instead of waiting for this capital to grow over time there is a quicker process in increasing your equity position and the number of assets in your portfolio, and that is through property development or selective buying of discounted properties. With real estate development, the increase in equity is created with your efforts in developing the property. This is called the developer's margin or equity creation and the additional equity is generated when the total development cost is deducted against the value of the project on completion. When investing in discounted property, an investor focuses on finding opportunities to purchase properties at a discount relative to market prices or wholesale from a builder or investor.

If you are seeking a faster route to financial independence, it is advisable that you endeavour to hold on to as many of the properties that you intend to develop or to purchase and add them to your real estate portfolio. Whether you hold these property assets under your personal name, family trust or a self-managed super fund (SMSF) is entirely up to you and your personal financial circumstances.

CONCLUSION

Historically, Australians have always embraced real estate development and investment, either as a career, part-time income earner or as a hobby. When compared to other investments such as shares, real estate over the longer-term has produced higher returns to investors. It has the potential to provide both capital growth and cash flow from rental income.

If you are looking to create a passive income for your retirement or to attain financial independence, building a real estate investment portfolio is one of the better solutions. Real estate investment should not be viewed as a short-term investment but as a longer-term strategy for a period of at least five years before you can see an increase in capital growth and improved rental returns.

CHAPTER 2

BENEFITTING FROM TAX AND GEARING

INTRODUCTION

If you decide to purchase an investment property, your personal financial status, employment and income will determine what you can afford as well as your long-term investment goals. Before you decide to invest in any property, it is essential to consider any risks involved, to grow your knowledge and always get advice from experts so that you have a clear understanding of both the benefits and risks involved. Always make informed decisions rather than emotionally based ones.

In Chapter 1, it was pointed out that investment in property has long been a popular way for Australians to build wealth due to the potential tax advantages that can result from well-managed real estate investment. One of the great benefits of real estate investment is leveraging and then taking advantage of negative gearing, tax deductions and depreciation allowances in the hope that the value of the property will grow over time. While there are many potential tax benefits of real estate investment, there are also some pitfalls to avoid as an investor. If you sell a property, you must take into consideration the capital gains tax. In this chapter, we explore these tax benefits against the potential drawbacks.

LEVERAGING

Leveraging, also known as gearing occurs when you use debt to fund an investment. There is no other investment that allows you to significantly gear or leverage borrowings as easily as real estate. For example, some lenders will give you a loan with only a 10% deposit. If you take out a loan to purchase an investment property, you can offset interest on the loan and most property expenses against rental income, for tax purposes. Provided your property is available for rent, the interest incurred on money you have borrowed for the property is tax-deductible, including money used to purchase the property, undertake repairs and improvements, or deal with tenant-related issues.

The kind of security put up for the loan does not affect the deductibility of the interest at all. For example, if your investment property loan is secured by your home, it does not change the tax deduction available on the interest. However, the tax deduction is only available to the extent that the borrowed monies are used for income-producing purposes such as rent. If the monies were applied for both private and income-producing purposes, apportionment of the interest would be necessary to determine the tax-deductible portion. For instance, if a loan was drawn down to purchase a home and a rental property, only the interest that is attributable to the rental property will be tax-deductible. Similarly, if a loan was taken out to purchase a single property that is used partly for rental and partly for private purposes, only the interest related to the rental portion will be deductible.

In most circumstances, people would purchase their own home first, and when the equity portion of their home has grown over the years, they will take out another loan to purchase an investment property. If they are smart, they maximise the loan on the investment property to take advantage of the tax deduction on the interest charged over the investment property.

NEGATIVE GEARING

Negative gearing is when the annual cost of your investment is more than your return (income) from that investment. Put simply, negative gearing is when:

- You borrow money to acquire an investment
- The interest and other costs you incur are more than the rental income you receive from the investment (in other words you make a cash loss), and
- This cash loss is offset against income from other sources, thus reducing your taxable income, and hence the amount

of tax you have to pay (compared to the tax you would pay without the investment).

As mentioned above, the Government allows you to deduct the costs of your property from your gross income. So say your income is $75,000 a year, but your property costs you $20,000 a year, your taxable income will only be $55,000.

In the above circumstance, there are tax advantages, but the investment is still making a loss. Hopefully, the loss will be more than made up for by the property's increasing value (capital gain). You probably won't see a return on your investment until you sell the property, and only if it is for a much better price than you originally bought it for.

Also, the term 'negative gearing', while used extensively in Australia, is ambiguous. A bank would not grant a loan of greater amount than the value of the asset being acquired (plus other security), so it's unclear in what respect gearing itself could ever be negative. The only item which is 'negative' in negative gearing is net income, and this could conceivably be negative without borrowing. Nevertheless, negative gearing, for decades, has made it easier for investors to accumulate properties and let them grow in value over time.

In Australia, negative gearing has been around since the 1930s when the Commonwealth Parliament passed the Income Tax Assessment Act. The act does not mention the phrase 'negative gearing' at all, but what it does is establish the principle across all types of business and income-earning activity where income that is taxable, and the expenses earned in assessing that income are deductible from that income. When this principle is applied to real estate investment, the situation known as negative gearing occurs.

If you decide to negative gear your investment property it is vital that you do your research and carefully select the area and location, you would like to invest in. Below are some key points to consider:

- Invest in areas of good capital growth potential. An investment property with capital growth will more than make up for its short-term cash loss;
- Ensure that you are willing to accept wealth in the form of non-spendable capital gains (or future profits) in the short or medium term.

TAX DEDUCTIONS

Whether you are negatively geared or getting a positive income stream from your property, you can claim expenses relating to your rental property for the period your property was available for rent. All of the following expenses can be claimed:

- Advertising for tenants, agent's fees and commission
- Interest payments, loan fees and bank charges
- Council rates, land tax and strata fees
- Depreciation of items such as stoves, fridges and furniture
- Repairs, maintenance, pest control and gardening
- Building and landlords insurance
- Stationery, phone costs and any travel to inspect the property
- Body corporate fees and charges
- Legal and accounting fees and expenses
- Government land tax
- Stationery and postage
- Travel undertaken to inspect or maintain the property or to collect the rent
- Water charges
- Capital works and improvements (refer section under 'Depreciation' below).

This is not a full list of what you can claim. It is strongly recommended to get professional advice from a tax expert before submitting your return. Bear in mind that there are also expenses for which you are not able to claim deductions, some of which include:

- acquisition and disposal costs of the property
- expenses which were not incurred by you, such as electricity charges paid by your tenants
- expenses not related to the rental of a property, e.g. expenses connected to your own use of a holiday home
- borrowing expenses or interest on the portion of the loan you use for private purposes, such as buying a new car.

DEPRECIATION

In addition to the tax deductions listed above, many property investors forget about claiming depreciation especially in properties that are older. Tax depreciation (also known as property depreciation) is the decline in value of property assets over a period of time. It is a legitimate deduction against assessable taxable income, generated by a residential or commercial investment property. Different items within a rental property have different rates of depreciation based on the practical life of the item, and the Australian Taxation Office (ATO) sets out a comprehensive guide regarding what it considers to be appropriate. These depreciation benefits can be easily calculated by engaging a qualified quantity surveyor upon purchase of the property to prepare a depreciation schedule for it. Quantity surveyor's fees are 100% tax deductible.

The preparation of a Tax Depreciation Schedule should always include a site inspection where the Quantity Surveyor will take detailed photos and notes documenting sufficient evidence to prepare the report. The report will consist of a value of each and every qualifying plant and equipment item within the property, the cost of construction at the time the building was built, and a projection of the deductions claimable by the owner per financial year over a 40-year period.

The ATO recognises that the value of capital assets gradually reduces over time as they approach the end of their effective life. If you own an investment property (new or old, large or small), two areas of depreciation are available (a) Plant and Equipment and (b) Capital Works on the Building, explained further below.

- *Plant & Equipment*

  The ATO has identified a number of removable assets that depreciate at a faster rate than the building itself. Dependent on the size, age and condition of the property and fittings, as much as 35% of the construction cost of a property can consist of plant and equipment, and as such, they will often form a sizeable part of a depreciation claim. These items include hot water systems, floor coverings and swimming pool plant, door locks, TV aerials and smoke alarms etc. If a furniture package is provided as part of the rent, then these items also depreciate.

- *Capital works*

  The materials of any building depreciate in value over time. This loss in value is, therefore, tax deductible which includes the structural elements and any permanent fixtures. Not all properties are eligible for capital works depreciation, but if your investment property was built after 18th July 1985, then you are eligible to claim for Capital Works Allowance at either 2.5% or 4% for either 25 or 40 years from the date of construction. Furthermore, any renovations, additions, new fit-outs etc. within the allowable dates will also qualify for this allowance.

Claiming tax depreciation allowances on an investment property increases its value by giving investors a higher return on their investment. Depreciation allowances combined with additional negative gearing factors such as interest on a mortgage, repairs and maintenance, can help investors reduce their taxable income, pay less tax and improve cash flow.

Depreciation in commercial property

The tax depreciation described above applies to both residential and commercial investment properties generating a rental income. However, with commercial property, there are some variations as follows:

- *Use your commercial property and still claim depreciation*

  Because the ATO does not recognise your commercial real estate investment as your principal place of residence, you can run your own business from the property by leasing it. This can be done if the property is under two separate ownership entities. For example, the property is owned by you or your SMSF and your business being run under a company.

- *Depreciation can be claimed against older commercial buildings*

  In property building allowance the drop in the value of the materials that make up your property's structure can be claimed. In commercial property you can claim building allowances for the following periods if construction began from:

– 20 July 1982 to 21 August 1984: entitled to depreciate 2.5% of the construction cost.

– 22 August 1984 to 15 Sept 1987: entitled to depreciate 4% of the construction cost.

– 16 Sept 1987 onwards: entitled to depreciate 2.5% of the construction cost.

- *Lifespan*

  Annually, the ATO issues a list of the items that property owners can and cannot claim. This list is not always applicable to commercial real estate investment as claim some items deteriorate faster than in a residential property. For example, with commercial property, floor coverings can be claimed over eight years due to public use whereas floor covering in a residential property the claim is over ten years due minus wear and tear.

- *Industry specific*

  The ATO has also determined a number of industry-specific items for depreciation claims. For example, a hotel owner can claim items used specifically in the hotel industry, and where food and beverages are served, items used by its patrons can also be claimed.

There are additional areas where depreciation can be claimed on commercial property such as lifts, air conditioning plant etc. so it is best to employ the services of a quantity surveyor to assess the value of the claims to be made.

RISKS AND PITFALLS

While the potential for wealth accumulation from tax benefits through real estate investment is appealing, it is essential that you are aware of the risks involved. The risks to consider are (a) if the value of the rental property declines, the potential tax implication is that your losses might exceed your profits from other sources, which will result in a net loss, and (b) if the property is vacant or tenants do not pay the rent your financial situation will be affected. Additionally, there is also a liquidity risk if you want to sell your investment property. If your property doesn't have a buyer when you are ready to sell it, you will have to hold on to the investment or potentially reduce the purchase price to attract a buyer, thus incurring further losses.

One of the most significant risks in property development is your own personal circumstances which could affect your real estate investments especially if you are using negative gearing as an investment strategy. Your financial circumstances could change through the loss of a job or a business, or through ill health. Over the years I have seen many property people incur significant losses especially when there is a recession. My advice is that you should positive gear and not negative gear a real estate investment, meaning that the rental income minus tax benefits and depreciation gives you positive cash flow.

Positively geared property is hard to find, and will it will take a longer time to build a real estate portfolio especially if you have to wait for your other property assets to grow in value. In Chapter 3, I will demonstrate how to expedite the expansion of your real estate portfolio with positively geared property through property development.

NEGATIVE vs POSITIVE GEARING

Before deciding to invest in property, it is essential to consider whether to negatively gear (creating a capital growth property) or to positively gear (creating a cash-flow property). When comparing the two positions, there are advantages and disadvantages to both strategies and whichever one you follow will depend on your personal circumstances and investment strategy. In the following section the two approaches are compared in more detail in order to help you to form a better idea of what may suit your investment strategy.

Negatively geared property

Negative gearing is also referred to as 'capital growth property'. This means purchasing a property with the intent to negatively gear the investment in anticipation that it will appreciate in value over time. The advantage of this strategy is that if you are in a higher income tax bracket, the investment-related loss can be offset against other taxable income; therefore you pay less tax. If you decide to follow this strategy, then it is best to find an investment property located in a stable, high-growth area, which is most likely to be found near capital cities that typically perform better over the long term.

Example of a negatively geared property

The figures below are based on a property purchased for $500,000 as a House and Land package with a $400,000 interest-only home loan, fixed at 5% p.a. The property is rented out for $450 per week.

Income		
Rent	$23,400 p.a. ($450 a week)	
Annual Income		$22,360
Expenses		
Mortgage	$20,000 p.a.	
Rates	$2,100 p.a.	
Property Management	$1,638 p.a. (7%)	
Insurance	$800 p.a.	
Maintenance	$600 p.a.	
Other – Electricity, Water	NA	
Annual Expenses		$25,138
Annual Cash Loss		-$2,778
Depreciation (Year 1)		-$12,500
Annual Pre-tax loss		-$15,278

Advantages

- *Tax Deductions*: With the ATO allowing investors to claim tax deductions related to the expenses incurred in leasing a property it reduces your rental shortfall and in turn reduces your taxable income.
- *Capital Growth*: Should the value of your property increase over time the capital returns from the property will eventually

outweigh the borrowing levels and costs to create wealth for investors when sold.

- *Rental growth*: Over time, as you can charge more rent, the rental income flowing from the property into your bank account can become greater than all the costs, so you end up with a cash flow positive investment or a positively geared property.

Disadvantages

- *Cash shortfall*: You will need to have enough cash from other sources, like wages, to make loan repayments, especially if a tenant moves out and if it takes a few months to find another – as you will still have to pay all the usual costs. Budgeting for shortfalls is critical.
- *Higher financial risk*: If your circumstances change such as losing your job you will need to be able to maintain any costs involved and if not may be forced to sell. Ensure that you have a plan in place such as income protection and insurance policies.
- *Change in interest rates*: The threats of negative gearing include coping with years when interest rates are high, and property values do not increase as rapidly as you would like them to. This may result in paying out more over the years that you are paying off the property than you actually get back when it is sold.

Positively geared property

Positive gearing occurs when you receive more in rent from your tenants than what you pay out such as loan repayments, property maintenance, rates and other related property expenses. This type of investment is often referred to as a 'cash flow property' as the cash balance goes directly to you.

Example of a positively geared property

The figures below are based on a property purchased for $450,000 as a House and Land package with a $350,000 interest only home loan, fixed at 5% p.a. The property is rented out for $500 per week.

Income		
Rent	$26,000 p.a. ($500 a week)	
Annual Income		$26,000
Expenses		
Mortgage	$17,500 p.a.	
Rates	$2,100 p.a.	
Property Management	$1,638 p.a. (7%)	
Insurance	$800 p.a.	
Maintenance	$600 p.a.	
Other – Electricity, Water	NA	
Annual Expenses		$22,638
Annual Cash Loss		$3,362
Depreciation (Year 1)		-$12,500
Annual Pre-tax loss		-$9,138

Advantages

- *Increased income*: As an investor, you will benefit by re-ceiving a positive income from the property which allows you to make additional payments into your mortgage and own your home sooner, potentially enabling you to retire earlier.

- *Less financial risk*: Should your personal financial situation change for the worse then the income will cover the costs of the investment, and you are less likely to need to sell under pressure in potentially unfavourable conditions.

- *Increased real estate portfolio*: With the additional income and value you can purchase another investment property increasing your portfolio or the income to balance your portfolio, using the additional income to pay the shortfall of negatively geared investments.

- *Attractive to banks*: Your bank would see a positively geared property as less risky from a lending perspective and would be happy to provide you with another loan to purchase another investment property in the future, as your track record in reducing the mortgage demonstrates good financial planning and credibility.

Disadvantages

- *Additional payable tax*: The most significant drawback is that because the property is cash flow positive, you'll earn more income and therefore have to pay more tax.
- *Vacancy risk*: Vacancy is a problem you should take into account. Vacancy rates vary from area to area, but there are a few simple things you can do to reduce your chance of having a vacant property such as keeping your property in good condition and not overpricing it.
- *Poor area selection*: Often but not always, a positive cash flow investment can be located in a regional area (rather than a capital city), which commonly (but not always) sees less or slower capital growth. These properties may be largely dependent on a particular industry of employment such as mining, which can make it subject to greater volatility should employment factors weaken.

Having analysed both positive and negative gearing above and given the boom and bust of the property industry, the best strategy, in my opinion, is to be conservative and seek positively geared real estate investments. Generous tax concessions make negative gearing the ideal real estate investment strategy by many respected investment advisers, along with many spruikers and con artists and positive gearing is less promoted even though it has excellent advantages. As mentioned in the preface, I do not agree with the negative gearing strategy. If you are building a property portfolio you do not want to be placed in a position where one property cannot be rented for an extended time, which causes you to fall behind in your mortgage payments.

CAPITAL GAINS TAX

If you decide to or are placed in a situation where you have to sell one or two of your investment properties, it is essential to understand Capital Gains Tax (CGT) implications. CGT is the tax payable on the disposal of an asset which was acquired after 19th September 1985. You only have to pay tax on capital gains if your capital gains for the year exceed your capital losses.

In short, your capital gain is calculated by subtracting the purchase price of the property from the sale price. However, there are adjustments for capital gains, for example, depreciation that you have claimed, agents' commissions charged and improvements made to the property. If you have held a property for at least 12 months then any gain is discounted by 50% for individual taxpayers or trust, or by 33.3% for superannuation funds. Capital losses can be offset against capital gains, and net capital losses in a tax year may be carried forward indefinitely.

In real estate investments, CGT applies to the sale of any property held as an investment which includes houses, apartments, holiday homes, retail shops, offices, factories and land. However, your principal place of residence is exempt from CGT.

Calculating the CGT for a property sold

The CGT calculation is based on the sale price of a property minus your expenses.

$$\boxed{\text{Selling Price}} - \boxed{\text{Cost Base}} = \boxed{\text{Capital Gain/Loss}}$$

The cost base is the total sum of the original purchase price, plus any incidentals, ownership and title costs minus any government grants and depreciable items.

$$\boxed{\text{Cost Base}} = \boxed{\substack{\text{Purchase} \\ \text{Price}}} + \boxed{\text{Incidentals}} + \boxed{\substack{\text{Ownership} \\ \text{Cost}}} + \boxed{\text{Improvements}} - \boxed{\substack{\text{Depreciation} \\ \text{Claimed}}}$$

Where:

- *Incidentals* include stamp duty, legal fees, agent fees and advertising and marketing fees.
- *Ownership costs* include rates, land tax, maintenance and interest on the loan.
- *Improvements* include replacing kitchens, bathrooms or any other improvements you have made on the property.
- *Depreciation claimed* is the amount claimed annually during the ownership of the asset being leased. This amount is adjusted by any depreciation that has not been previously claimed.

Once you have worked out the capital gain, the figure is then adjusted according to a number of variables, including:

- Any percentage of time when you owned the property that it was rented out.
- If the property was held for longer than 12 months and then a 50% discount applies.

CGT example

The table below demonstrates two situations with different outcomes should there be a CGT event before or after 12 months of ownership. In this example, an investment property is purchased for $400,000 and then sold for $500,000. We will assume the depreciation claimed is $10,000 while capital costs are $20,000 for both scenarios. The 35% tax rate has been applied.

	Less than 12 months	More than 12 months
Selling Price	$500,000	$500,000
Cost Base		
Purchase price	$400,000	$400,000
(+) Incidentals	$5,000	$5,000
(+) Ownership cost	$6,000	$6,000
(+) Improvements	$11,000	$11,000
(-) Depreciation claimed	$10,000	$10,000
Cost base total	$412,000	$412,000
Capital Gain	**$88,000**	**$88,000**
(-) CGT Exemption 50%	nil	$44,000
Taxable capital gain	**$88,000**	**$44,000**
Tax rate 35%	$30,800	$15,400
After tax profit	**$57,200**	**$72,600**

This is only a general example, and CGT will vary with each case and the investor's personal circumstances. When a sale of an investment property takes place, it is highly recommended that you talk to an accountant about the implications of CGT and the exemptions available.

OVERSEAS INVESTMENT PROPERTY AND TAX

Since the start of the Internet which created a global society, investing in overseas properties has become more popular among Australians. More and more Australian investors are turning to property markets in Europe, Northern America, New Zealand, Asia and countries where the property markets have growth potential. Many perceive that properties in these countries are now undervalued and represent good bargains for future growth. If you are an Australian resident and still living in Australia, it is compulsory for you to declare *all* foreign income in your tax return. Below are some key points which will help investors with their investment decisions.

- **Disclosure**

  The Australian tax system requires you to disclose information regarding your overseas real estate investment in your tax return. This includes the rental income, rental expenses and capital gain or loss if the property is sold. If detected by the ATO, failure to disclose this information may attract heavy penalties and interest charges. With the sophistication in data matching and exchange agreements with foreign jurisdictions, it is safer to disclose your interest.

- **Tax on rental income**

  If you are an Australian resident, any overseas income you derive such as rental income will be assessable income in Australia, unless an exemption applies. The exemption applies if your rentable overseas property in a country where there is a double tax agreement (DTA). This means you will not have to pay tax in that country. If you've already paid a foreign tax on income from your overseas property, there is a possibility that you are entitled to a foreign tax offset (FITO), or credit. Rental income from overseas properties is included in the section of your tax return called 'foreign source income and foreign assets or property'.

- **Tax deductions**

  Any expenditure or outgoing incurred that is productive of the rental income from the overseas investment property is tax deductible. Deductions can include the local government tax on the property (what Australians call 'rates') as well as insurance, interest, maintenance, any real estate agent fees and deductions for capital works. Also, depreciation or a building allowance claim may be made in respect of such costs to reduce the assessable rental income derived. It should be noted that what is tax deductible under Australian income tax law may not necessarily be so in the foreign country and vice versa. Accordingly, it is advisable to enlist the help of a local accountant to assist you in this area.

- **Negative gearing**

  Negative gearing applies to your overseas real estate invest-ment. From 1 July 2008, any net foreign loss incurred may be offset against any Australian-derived income. If the foreign loss is not used, it may be carried forward indefinitely to offset any future income derived, regardless of whether the future income is sourced from Australia or otherwise.

- **Capital gain tax (CGT)**

  The tax on any capital gain derived from the sale of the property will be determined by the DTA between Australia and the country in which the property is located. The DTA may provide exclusive taxing rights to one country, or it may allow both countries to tax the capital gain. The CGT rules applicable to an overseas investment property will be similar to properties located in Australia. If you have sold a property overseas within a tax year or made a capital loss, you need to declare this on your Australian tax return. On your tax return, you need to fill this information in on the 'Capital gains' section. Capital losses can be used to offset capital gains you make on other assets. If you've already paid foreign tax on your capital gain, you may be entitled to a foreign tax income offset, or credit.

- **Transfer of funds**

  There are no Australian exchange controls concerning transfer-ring funds outside of Australia but check with the local author-ities in the jurisdiction to which the funds are being transferred to ensure that you are complying with the relevant country's domestic exchange control requirements.

- **Currency rates**

  It is important to convert all of your foreign income, deductions and foreign tax paid, into Australian dollars before you calculate your net income.

The Australian taxation system varies considerably with that of some other countries and tax systems can be complex and specific to each country. It is advisable to acquire professional advice before investing in an overseas property so that you fully understand implications associated with the overseas investment property.

FOREIGN INVESTORS AND TAX

Over the years, Australia's property market has and still is attracting a large number of foreign investors. The reason is that Australian property is relatively stable with strong growth when compared with other property markets around the world. While property prices in many developed countries have plummeted during times of volatility, Australian property prices have performed much better overall in comparison.

- **Definition**

  A foreign investor can be defined as a person that is not an Australian resident (non-resident/foreign national) buying property, or a business or corporation where he or she will own 15% or more of a property, or more than one foreigner will jointly own 40% or more aggregate of the ownership. Furthermore, a foreign investor or buyer usually falls into one of three categories:

  – A foreigner with Australian permanent resident status currently living overseas wanting to buy an Australian investment property;
  – A foreign national or non-permanent resident living in Australia wanting to buy an Australian property; and
  – A foreign national not living in Australia wanting to buy an Australian property.

- **Restrictions and exemptions**

  If you are a foreign investor purchasing property in Australia from overseas, you are required to obtain approval to purchase from the Foreign Investment Review Board (FIRB). The FIRB is an Australian Government entity that regulates the sale of Australian property to overseas persons and corporations. Under the current rules, unless a specific exemption applies, the acquisition of both residential and commercial properties in Australia by foreigners will need clearance from FIRB, regardless of the value of the property and nationality of the purchaser. However, some acquisitions are exempt and do not require FIRB approval. Some examples include:

  – a New Zealand citizen buying residential property in Australia;

  – a foreign national buying residential property as a joint tenant with their spouse who is an Australian citizen;

  – a new dwelling sold by a developer who has obtained prior approval to sell the property to a foreign national; and

  – a foreigner buying an interest in developed commercial property where the property is to be used immediately and in its present state for industrial or non-residential commercial purposes.

- **Tax residency**

  If you are permitted to buy Australian property as a foreigner, you need to determine your tax residency status in Australia. The tax residency rules are very complex and do not hold the same as residency for immigration purposes. You may be treated as a tax resident of Australia for income tax purposes. Under Australian tax law, if you are a tax resident of Australia, your worldwide income is generally subject to Australian tax. Otherwise, only your Australia-sourced income is taxable in Australia and most of your foreign income is not taxed in Australia, but you will be subject to Australian income tax on income sourced in Australia and CGT derived on any Australian taxable property you own. Also, the domestic law in Australia will need to be applied in conjunction with any Double Tax Agreement (DTA) Australia has with your country of residence.

These rules are very complex and professional advice is highly recommended.

- **Tax deductions**

  If you are a foreign resident and you receive rental income from a property in Australia, you need to (a) get a tax file number and (b) lodge an Australian tax return. Therefore, as a taxpayer, you must declare the rental income in your tax return, and you can claim tax deductions for many of the related expenses. When you sell your Australian property, you have to pay tax on any capital gain you make. Capital gains tax (CGT) which is further described below is the tax upon the difference between what it cost you to buy the property and what you received when you sell it.

- **Goods and Services Tax (GST)**

  Most residential accommodation is exempt from GST. Whether you are a resident or foreign owner of residential property being rented, you will not be obliged to remit GST of 10% to the ATO. Similarly, you will not be eligible to claim GST that is included in any rental property expenses. Generally, you will also not be obliged to remit 10% GST on the sale of your rental property when it is sold. However, as a foreign investor and you invest in commercial premises such as a shop, factory or office, you may be liable for 10% GST and entitled to claim GST credits, when you buy, sell or lease these premises.

- **Capital Gains Tax (CGT)**

  Irrespective of tax residency status, any investor who has derived a capital gain on their Australian property that is not their primary residence will be subject to CGT in Australia. The CGT discount of 50% discount, was available to foreign resident individuals on Australian property. With the 2012–13 Budget, the government announced changes to the application of the CGT discount. These changes came into law on 29 June 2013, where from 8 May 2012, foreign or temporary resident individuals must meet certain eligibility conditions to apply the CGT discount. For any CGT events occurring after 8 May 2012, the application of a CGT discount percentage will depend on (a) whether the CGT asset was held before or after 8 May 2012, and (b) the residency status of the individual who has the capital gain.

Australian tax law is very complicated when applied to domestic transactions, but the complexity increases significantly when multiple jurisdictions and foreigner taxpayers are involved. When evaluating Australian property as an investment, a foreign investor needs to fully understand their tax obligations in both Australia and their own country of residence, which often requires the engagement of tax specialists in both countries. The additional costs for professional advice must, therefore, be factored into the overall decision-making process.

It is also important to note that the Australian Government wants to ensure that foreign property ownership is of benefit to the local community and its people. Therefore, the Government insists that all applications from foreign nationals or companies buy Australian property being developed, to be redeveloped or existing only at plan stage before being considered by Foreign Investment Review Board (FIRB). Foreign investors who have illegally bought Australian properties risk strict penalties including three years in jail and fines of $127,500 for individuals and $637,500 for companies. Third parties, including real estate agents and developers, who knowingly help those buyers will also be penalised with fines of up to $42,500 for individuals and $212,500 for companies. The Government has also announced that foreign buyers who are forced to sell property will be prevented from profiting from the sale.

CONCLUSION

If you are investing in real estate and creating a real estate portfolio, you should be taking advantage of the tax incentives offered by the ATO. Real estate investment has some unique tax benefits over forms of investment and therefore taking advantage of the tax offerings as a way of minimising your tax can be a great way to maximise the return on your investment.

The strategy here is to leverage your asset and then take advantage of negative gearing, tax deductions and depreciation allowances in the hope that the value of the property will grow over time. While there are many potential tax benefits of real estate investment, there are also some pitfalls to avoid as a property investor. If you sell your property, then you have to take into consideration capital gains tax. If you have a real estate portfolio, work closely with a good property accountant, one that can provide you with the best advice on tax issues that relate to your personal financial position as each person's finances are different.

CHAPTER 3

SOURCING POSITIVELY GEARED PROPERTY

INTRODUCTION

In Chapter 2, we concluded that positive gearing is a far better investment strategy than negative gearing due to the potential risks in real estate and personal changes that may occur. A positively geared property is a great way to generate a passive income and financial independence, which mean having the freedom or release from the need to have to work. Creating passive income is one of the essential steps towards retirement. There are other ways of generating a passive income such as business investments or having shares, but real estate provides you with control and the ability to leverage growth, therefore, accelerating your passive income.

By learning ways to maximise profits from positively geared investment real estate, you will be on your way towards financial freedom. More and more real estate investors realise that positive gearing is the best investment option for them. Eventually, if you can have more positively geared investment properties in your portfolio, and mastered the world of positive gearing, then you have a better chance of becoming a successful property investor. One of the essential factors to consider when you are planning to create a positively geared real estate portfolio is to buy the right property. This is where proper and thorough research and preparation is necessary. You need to be careful when making a real estate investment and consider all the critical factors.

It needs to be pointed out that creating a passive income in real estate requires effort and discipline. There is no such thing as a completely passive income because every dollar of passive income must flow from some work. For example, while rental income might seem to be passive income, the task of finding and investing in property, together with managing the tenant, filling in tax returns and so on, is not passive. Positive gearing is about generating passive income for the long term so that you can become financially free. This will not happen in one transaction (although it could occur), but this will happen over time and a few investment deals.

WHY POSITIVE GEARING?

Most real estate investors do not want their investment in property to be a drain on their finances. This means that they do not want to be paying out of pocket expenses every month to maintain their home plus an investment. While neutrally geared or even slightly negative cash flow may also be acceptable, many want a cash return. In Chapter 2, positive gearing was compared to negative gearing, outlining the advantages and disadvantages of both strategies. Positive gearing had many benefits over negatively geared property, and it may be worthwhile to reiterate them.

Passive Income

Positively geared investment properties generate passive income because they produce more income after the costs and expenses. In this scenario your income from the property is more than the expenses you need to pay. If you own enough of these properties in your portfolio, you will be living a successful life in your retirement or even have enough to quit your job earlier.

Income increases over time

Rent usually increases over time, but the major expense of your mortgage will always stay the same or decrease over time. This means that as the rent increases, you are generating more money. This, in turn, makes it easier for you to pay off the property.

Less risky

Positive gearing carries less risk than negatively geared investment properties where you are losing money each month. With a negatively geared property, in order to access your money, you have to sell your property for a profit, which depends on your property's value being higher than the mortgage. With positively geared properties, you are continually earning money even if your property does not increase in value. You can, therefore, say that a positively geared property is less risky as there are two ways for you to make money through capital gains and rental income.

The tenant is paying for your property

In a negatively geared investment property, you are the one paying the mortgage that your rental income cannot cover. This means that you are purchasing the property with your money. However, when your property has a good cash flow, your tenant is the one paying off the mortgage.

KEY FACTORS IN FINDING POSITIVE GEARED PROPERTY

Finding a positively geared property is not easy and if any do come on to the market, they are snapped up by eager investors. However, if one is aware and knowledgeable of the real estate market there are positively geared properties that can be found.

Get to know the rental market

With positively geared property the key is understanding the rental market and the price point, as the rental income is the critical element that will make your cash flow work. It would help if you also analysed the vacancy rate in the location of the intended purchase. If properties in the area tend to be vacant for extended periods, then even if the rental yield is high, you could face a lower overall cash flow. Note that markets change over time and rents may increase or decrease in line with supply and demand. So be prepared and think ahead of what that rental yield will look like over the time where your investment property is located.

Gain knowledge of the market

An astute investor is one who is always in tune with the market. They keep up to date with the market and future market trends. When investing in property the same rule applies, so equip yourself with knowledge so that you are prepared and informed when purchasing. In this way you will know if the property is in line with the market. This knowledge can be obtained by reading investment and real estate magazines online or in the newspapers. In addition, get to know the local real estate agents and pick their brains or meet up with them on a regular basis to discover the latest trends in the market. It will help you understand the growth potentials relating to the local economy and what areas to avoid. Remember, agents want to make sales, so as a potential investor, they're likely to keep you posted on any suitable properties on the market or that are coming up.

Do your research

With modern technology, finding suitable properties online has made become a lot easier. It gives you the ability to shop and research any time of the day and access a number of opportunities. Doing your research for specific property types, prices, locations and styles of buildings makes for an efficient use of your time. Using electronic alerts can give you access to new listings within your search criteria delivered right to your inbox. Consider looking for lower value properties (often the best returns), blocks of units as well as motels, hotels, boarding houses and student accommodation. Also, when you find a property, log on to Google Earth to get a 3D visual.

Get to know the local rental market

One of the best ways to get a good idea of the local rental market is to speak to a property manager operating in the area where you intend to purchase your investment property. Property managers usually know the rental market better than the sales people and have a good idea of rental demand and returns. They understand where the tenant demand is, and what they are likely to pay for a specific style and location of property.

Employment, transport, shops and schools

As an investor, look closely at existing employment as well as easy access to public transportation. It is worth finding out about any future infrastructure works in planning as this can have an impact on the future value of your investment property. Also, look at shopping centres and schools close to the property, which will make it more attractive for families and ensures highly rentable properties.

Look for properties with a difference

There is saying in real estate investment, 'always buys the ugliest house in the best street', as the price will be low but by undertaking a 'make-over' of the property, you could improve its value and rental return. Also look for properties where you could add a granny flat with potential for double tenancies. With rezoning occurring in many place allowing for increased density, search for properties that have the potential to be subdivided into two or more lots. Consider an old motel that might be able to be renovated to provide individual permanent rental for students. When finding an unusual property, be creative and think outside the box regarding how you could create value.

There are three main areas where you can create a positively geared real estate portfolio namely (a) finding and purchasing an established property (b) adding value to an established property and (c) by undertaking property development. These are explored further below.

ESTABLISHED PROPERTY

Finding an established positively geared property is easier said than done. Even smart investors looking for a positively geared property are having difficulty in finding anything reasonable unless located in a mining resource area where property values can be very volatile. Other than in mining areas, positively geared properties can be found as interest rates in Australia have been at the lowest levels in decades. However, how long these low rates will last? If you are a smart investor, you will factor the risks of rates increasing sometime in the future.

What to look for in an established positive geared property?

Finding existing positive geared property requires a great deal of hard work and persistence. They are there to be found but be prepared to spend long hours on research, establish what you are looking for and then finding that specific property. Many investors give up, or they decide to use a buyers' agent to help them source a property, saving them time and energy. When searching for a positively geared property you need take into consideration the following aspects.

1. *Positively geared property advertisements*

   There are many advertisements on the Internet and in news-papers claiming that the property they are selling is positively geared. However, this does not mean that the property will be suitable for you as your circumstances may differ. This is not to say that the advertisement is misleading, as the seller or their agent may be using a range of different assumptions and calculations in the assessment. It is therefore vital to review the property against your cash flow and review the seller's assump-tions against yours.

2. *Be careful of spruikers*

   The property industry is less well-regulated than the financial services industry, and so as a property investor, you need to be more cautious when dealing with property 'advisers' or property spruikers. They invite you to a free seminar only to entice you to follow their investments strategies at a cost or buying so-called positive cash flow properties. These spruikers can be quite intentionally misleading. For example, they may include potential capital gain with the rental income, and then conflate the two income streams as the overall return on in-vestment. They assume 6% per annum capital gain, and 4% per annum yield indicating a total 10% return per annum when actually the real cash flow income is 4% in cash. Smart inves-tors never categorise capital growth as 'income' when looking at the return on their investments. Sadly, these promoters often persuade uneducated mum and dad investors to use the equity in their home to purchase an overpriced property only for these poor buyers to lose both properties down the track.

3. *Always do your own analysis*

   It is vitally important that you undertake your own analysis based on your circumstances before purchasing a potential positively geared property. The advertised 'cash flow positive' could be lopsided to sell the property in a positive light. You need to know the different aspects that make up the general return of property. When you look at the numbers of a property to analyse its cash flow potential, there will be several areas to consider:

a. *Rental yield*: The first step is to check out the percentage figure called a rental yield, i.e. the amount of rent earned as a proportion of the property's price. Know how to calculate the rental yield yourself, and the factors that influence it. Below is an example of a calculating a rental yield:
   – Purchase price $350,000
   – Annual rent $20,800 p.a. ($400 a week)
   – $20,800 divided by $350,000 x 100 = 5.9%.

b. *Specific expenses*: Some expenses are both general and specific to an investment property which can certainly affect your cash flow, so it is worth knowing which of these may be upfront and factor these into your calculations. Typical specific expenses can include rates and taxes, strata or body corporate fees, insurance and property management.

c. *Ongoing expenses*: These are expenses you may not be able to ascertain to a precise degree when you are analysing a property, but you can try to reasonably estimate ongoing costs such as maintenance, water usage, utilities, gardening and cleaning.

d. *Personal financial status*: This is an important part of your analysis and can make the difference between a positively or negatively geared property. On your side, you need to consider factors such as the ownership vehicle structure, loan amount and interest rate and the marginal tax rate applied to the ownership vehicle. Also, if you are doing your own property management and maintenance, this will positively impact your cash flow.

Where can established positive geared property be found?

When thinking about positively geared *established* property, it is important to note that some of these properties (depending on location and demographics) do not increase in value or growth at an equivalent rate to some other properties. The consensus is that properties double in value every seven to ten years, but smart property investors know that capital growth from one property to the next could vary significantly. Another point to take into account is that most positively geared property serves a specificc market, and this limits their demand. When a property appeals to a limited market, competition among buyers will be less, and it will not attract the same level of capital growth as a high-demand property. You will also find that banks are not as keen to finance specialised property because of the risks. Below is a list of the types of properties and locations where positively geared properties can be found. They can be divided into broad categories such as regional and country, Government, commercial and industrial, and alternative. However, you should carefully undertake due diligence and analysis before purchasing any of these categories of property.

- *Regional and country properties*

  Regional and country properties can be defined as properties in non-major city locations. This includes properties that can be found in mining towns, rural town centres and smaller country towns. Note that most lenders tend to err on the side of caution with these locations. Most lenders will probably only lend you 60–70% of the value of the property.

  – *Mining towns*: Mining town investments are characterised by their volatility, given their exposure to a single industry. Rental rates are known to fluctuate downward if vacancies dramatically increase due to a mine closure or staff cutbacks. When a mine is in the expansion or construction phase, you usually have the peak number of people employed, so these numbers will fall away as the mine becomes fully operational. During the expansion period, it is not uncommon to have rents jump quite dramatically over six months. The timing of entry and the phase of the mine life cycle are crucial to get right.

  – *Rural town centres*: Rural town centres can be a great place to find positively geared property. As these towns are smaller, the properties are generally a lot less expensive than in a major city, but the rents can be quite high. Research your particular town before buying by looking at the employment in the town and assess how it is spread over different employment sectors. Are there high employment rates and is the population growing? More jobs mean more people, which in turn mean higher rent and housing prices.

– *Smaller regional towns*: One can quite easily generate positive cash flows in smaller regional towns. The rental yields can be even higher than in regional centres. However, as the population will be less, the rental demand will also be less. This means it could be difficult to rent out your property. To pull this off, you will likely need an outstanding property manager, and you will need a property that the market is looking for. Every town is different so find out what exactly property renters are looking for and try to buy that property.

- *Government properties*

   These are properties that are initiated by the Government with added incentives or support. The more common investments examples nationally are defence housing, The National Rental Affordability Scheme known as NRAS and National Disability Insurance Scheme (NDIS) Accommodation. Some states would also have initiatives such the GROH (Government Regional Officer Housing) in Western Australia.

   – *Defence Housing*: These are houses and apartments which investors can purchase from the Defence Housing Authority (DHA) and lease back to DHA to accommodate defence personnel. The lease is a tripartite relationship between a property owner, the DHA and the tenant. There is excellent merit with a DHA lease as it is actually between the owner and the DHA, so rent is 'guaranteed' over a 12-year lease period. DHA properties are generally in 'central locations' with family amenities nearby. On the negatives side of a DHA lease, the premises can only be used by defence personnel and is tied up for the term of the lease. The same constraints apply to if you want to sell, which means fewer willing buyers and less capital growth. Another negative is that the DHA charges 16.5% (houses) and 13% (apartments) to manage the property, which is well above industry standards. Mortgage insurers do not support DHA properties so investors must use at least 20% of their capital to buy one. DHA homes are in locations that meet DHA requirements, but this is not always necessary, especially where there are other important growth drivers that property investors look for in a new area.

– *The National Rental Affordability Scheme (NRAS)*: NRAS is a Federal Government initiative that started in 2008 which was part of a building industry stimulus package. It offered investors in NRAS properties tax incentives of up to $9,140 a year. The rental returns and tax incentives seem high, but the question is: if they are so high why is the government not holding onto them itself? If you own an NRAS property, the property has to be managed by NRAS agents and only rent it to NRAS-eligible tenants. The property management fees are about 13% (compared with 8.5% for standard residential). The rents must be charged to the tenant at a 20% discount, and lease documents are quite complex which dilutes the extra tax incentives. Add to this, banks are not comfortable lending money against NRAS properties. Those banks that require a minimum 20% deposit because mortgage insurers will not accept the properties. This means you are constrained by the size of deposit you need, as well as in your choice of bank, property manager and tenant. However, NRAS has over the past few years have been phased out by the Government, and no further allocations are being made to the market.

– *NDIS Accommodation*: In July 2016, the Australian Federal Government launched the NDIS, a funding provision to allow 28,000 Australians with a disability to move into accessible and affordable housing, called Specialist Disability Accommodation (SDA). The SDA homes have to meet strict design criteria set out in the scheme rules in order to accommodate qualifying SDA residents with 'high physical support' needs. SDA provides the opportunity for investors to buy single residential assets directly and have them registered into the scheme. However, from a practical standpoint, there are a series of complexities that are likely to negate any broad scale direct investment by investors. These include the need for each property to be registered into the scheme under an 'SDA Provider'. For property investors who do get an opportunity to invest, it broadly means that the Government will pay the rental costs of the participant tenant, for 20 years, at yields from around 10% plus, depending on location and construction cost. The scheme is still in its embryonic stage, and there are many hurdles along the way before we see the model fully functioning.

Commercial properties

Investing in commercial property is entirely different from investing in residential property. Their potential for higher rental returns and lower tenant turnover is attractive to investors. However, if you consider that it can take 6 to 12 months to replace the tenant for whatever reason, the loss of rental income for such a long period is risky. Valuations are primarily based on the quality of the tenant and best use of the property, whereas comparable sales determine residential valuations. When it comes to commercial property, banks tend to charge higher interest rates and require more substantial equity. In most cases lenders will only lend up to 70% of the value of the property meaning that at least 30% equity is required. Commercial property comes in three main forms, office, retail and industrial property.

– *Offices*: Offices offer the lowest yield of three main types of commercial property, but are seen as a safer investment compared to retail or industrial. The reason for this is because office tenants tend to stay longer in their premises when compared to owners of a retail business, therefore offering greater security to investors.

– *Retail*: Location, position and traffic exposure is crucial to retail property. It must be easily accessible and convenient for shoppers to access. The corner convenience store is fast becoming extinct as petrol stations and chain convenience stores offer more than just the basic needs such as milk, bread and the newspaper. Whereas strip shopping (a row of shops on the main road) in general has been in decline, there are some strips which perform particularly well. If you are interested in buying retail property in a suburban shopping centre, the anchor tenant such as a major supermarket brand can be the key to the success of the centre.

– *Industrial*: Of the three commercial properties, industrial property is the most volatile when it comes to yields. These properties are often limited to one tenant. For example, it could be a warehouse for manufacturing, a storage garage or a distribution centre. Yields have been as high as 12% in the past, but they have declined in the intervening years. The key reason industrial property returns are relatively low is that they come with a higher vacancy risk. Some buildings can be vacant for a number of years, waiting for the economy to improve or to find an appropriate tenant.

Niche properties

These properties do not often come onto the market. Most are promoted by developers and are bought off plan before on-site construction begins. When any of these are offered to you as an investor carefully study the conditions of sale and see whether it fits in your investment strategy.

– *Serviced apartments*: Serviced apartments are similar to hotel suites but without the room service and housekeeping. They are popular with business people and holidaymakers for short or long stays. Investing in a serviced apartment carries more risk than buying a house or an ordinary apartment as you are relying on the performance of the operator. By definition, the resale market for serviced apartments is confined to investors, so you are restricted to a much smaller re-sale market. The demand for serviced apartments is still mostly untested in most parts of Australia.

– *Student accommodation*: With one fifth of tertiary students coming from overseas, Australia is ranked third in the world as an education destination, creating an increase in demand for student rental accommodation. There are two types of student accommodation: (a) designated student accommodation apartment blocks and (b) houses located in university precincts rented on a room-by-room basis. With student blocks, you will get a high yield, and there is usually management to handle the day-to-day duties. With homes within a university precinct, you will pay an average market price, but you can enhance your yield significantly by renting the rooms individually. When investing, you have to consider both yield and capital growth. Standard residential properties might result in better capital growth over the long term because the property could still be sold to owner-occupiers later. Whereas buyers for student apartments in student blocks are typically limited to investors, so your ability to achieve capital growth is restricted due to the lower demand.

– *Blocks of apartments*: If you can find a whole block of apartments that have not been strata-titled they can be a relatively be a good investment as you can often achieve very high rental yields. You won't have to pay your strata fees which will suck the cash flow out of almost any positively geared property and buying a whole block of units can minimise your risk. If you own a single apartment, if that apartment becomes vacant your income is zero. Whereas if you own a block of 10 apartments and one becomes empty, you still have the other nine units bringing in revenue. Many lenders will treat a block of apartments similar to commercial property. This means you will require a 30% deposit. Generally with this investment lenders will judge the serviceability of the investment based on the income of the property and not on your own income.

As mentioned earlier, with well-selected established property your income will naturally increase over time because rents go up over time. However, your mortgage will remain the same. If you are paying off both principle and interest on your loan, then eventually your mortgage repayments will cease to exist. So even by simply holding the property, you can get closer to financial freedom without much hard work. If you have purchased wisely, then your property will also go up in value over a period of time. This does not directly affect your cash flow until you see the rise in value either by obtaining cash from selling your property or by borrowing against the equity. With capital growth, you can dramatically increase your cash flow if you take the money and use it as a deposit to invest in more positively geared cash flow properties.

ADDING VALUE

As pointed out above, finding the right positive cash flow real estate investment opportunity is challenging. It takes time to research and identify the right areas with strong drivers for cash positive opportunities. In most cases, you will not see immediate positively geared property for sale. Instead, you usually have to wait a few years before a property becomes cash positive. Alternatively, you can turn a negatively geared property into a positive one through various strategies. Below are some examples where you can turn the income on an investment property into the positive territory in a shorter period through multiple applications.

Renovations

Renovating older single-family home or converting a former office block into boutique or trendy apartments can turn a negative income property into a positive one. It gives you the ability to manufacture an immediate increase in rent. Renovating is the quickest solution for improving cash flow by making cosmetic or structural changes to a property. The objective of any renovation is to improve the functional space within a property, creating a visually appealing space that results in the property looking new again, therefore, adding more value. Before starting your renovations, you need to carefully analyse how you can increase the rent of your property without making significant capital outlays. A renovation is not only improving an older home with a facelift. There are many more opportunities, and you should also look out for possibilities such as:

- Purchasing an old block of apartments, renovating the building and converting and changing them into strata units.
- Buying an old commercial building such as an office block and converting and renovating it into apartments.
- Buying old squash courts or warehouses and converting and renovating them into studio units or small apartments.

Subdivision with a secondary dwelling

Another opportunity to create positive cash flow properties is looking for properties where rezoning has taken or is about to take place. These changes usually occur within a transport node, also known as a Transport Orientated Development (TOD) zone when local councils intend to facilitate growth with higher densities in residential areas. Such rezoning allows, for example, a second dwelling to be built on an allotment. The majority of the older suburbs have a home at the front of the property and a big backyard at the rear. By creating a subdivision or a strata lot, it opens up the rear backyard as the second lot. In this case, it provides the investor with several options such as (a) using the existing dwelling for rental income while the new development gets started (b) investors keeping one rented out and selling the subdivided lot or (c) building a second home at the rear and renting it out. The best opportunities will be corner lots as they can easily be subdivided into two with the second lot or home also having a street frontage, making access and egress convenient.

Adding a granny flat to rent separately

In addition to the option above, there is another way to create a positive income property without subdivision cost, and that is by adding a granny flat. If you have an investment property on a block that is over 450sqm in size, you can build a granny flat no larger than 60sqm on the same property. These granny flats come in a modular pod that can be dropped into the backyard, or you can appoint a builder to construct one. More investors are taking up this opportunity in the areas where planning laws make it relatively easy to get approval to build a granny flat that can be rented out for additional income. At the time of writing the localities that allow granny flats Australia are NSW, Tasmania, Northern Territory and Fremantle, Western Australia. As with any investment strategy, there are risks and rewards. The most significant risk is more extended vacancy periods on both properties, particularly the main house. The other is that the rent you are receiving for the house will have to be reduced to offset the negative for tenants of having a granny flat in their backyard.

Furnishing the property

A furnished property will always attract a higher rent than an un-furnished one. A furniture package can impact significantly on your rental yield and in some instances see a negatively geared property transition to positive cash flow. A furnished property will attract potential tenants such as short-term tenants, corporates, students, divorcees or migrants who will be willing to pay more for the ease of moving straight into a fully furnished home. Essential items include beds, couch, dining table, chairs, television, refrigerator and washing machine. The rental amount will depend on the property's location, size and age, as well as the standard of the furniture. However, the furnished rental pool has a lot of short-term tenants, so you need to allow for a higher vacancy. The decision to furnish depends on where the property is located; inner city, and metro fringe suburbs are better suited to furnished properties than others.

Renting out per room

Instead of renting the whole house you can increase your rental income by renting rooms instead. A three-bedroom house may be rented out $300 per week but per room could be rented for $125 per room per week producing an extra $75 per week. This concept works well for student housing or backpackers. Before you decide to offer this type of rental, it is essential to check that local council planning laws and regulations allow you to have multi-tenancy, as these laws vary from council to council. On the legal and tenancy side, consideration should be given as to whether the occupants of the property will be classed as lodgers, boarders or tenants and different rights on the resident may be applicable. Although this strategy may produce more income, it also involves more work with each tenant.

PROPERTY DEVELOPMENT

Today more and more Australians investors are looking to create wealth in the shortest timeframe and property development is one of the faster solutions to achieving that goal. Wealth creation through property development is no longer the exclusive domain of a few individuals. Everyday Australians are discovering they can benefit from small property development as a cost-effective way to accelerate the creation of a real estate portfolio.

While one can take a conservative approach and only buy established buildings and wait for the investment to become cash positive, it is worthwhile to study property development as it has many advantages in accelerating your wealth in a shorter timeframe. Chapter 4 will demonstrate in detail the strategies in creating positively geared property through property development. Below are qualitative attributes that make property development one of the faster investment models.

Leverage potential

Generally, most property developments are undertaken with the use of borrowed funds otherwise known as 'leveraging'. This means that the total capital cost of the development is borrowed with a small amount of personal equity or realising a more substantial return than the initial deposit invested. Table 3.1 below shows this:

	Property 1 (unleveraged)	Property 2 (leveraged)
Total development cost	$200,000	$800,000
Mortgage funds	nil	$600,000
Personal equity	$200,000	$200,000
Net profit (assume 10%)	$ 20,000	$ 80,000
Less interest (5% pa spread)	nil	$ 30,000
Gross profit	$ 20,000	$ 50,000
% on equity	10%	25%

Table 3.1: Leverage potential

Increase in equity

Compared to purchasing an existing property, property development can offer you opportunities to increase your equity positions through your skills and labour. This is called 'sweat equity', and there is no outlay of personal cash. Also by retaining your development as a long-term investment, your monthly principle repayments and the increase in inflationary capital gain is continually increasing the value of your equity. This equity can be used to provide for a deposit for another development and leveraged for a larger project.

Creative financing

Yields from property development can be significantly improved by creative financing techniques and smart negotiating strategies. Astute developers, who have a strong understanding of financing new projects, have started developments with minimal personal financial input. Some creative developers I know of have managed to secure 100% financing without any security except the property they are developing.

Savings on Stamp Duty

With an established property you pay stamp duty of the full purchase price whereas with property development you pay stamp duty only on the land component. As the building is not constructed yet, stamp duty is only required on the land component of the purchase price. For example, a four-bedroom House and Land package has a purchase price of $400,000. The land component is $150,000, and the building cost is $350,000. The stamp duty payable at settlement is approximately $3450. If the property had been purchased as a completed building, the stamp duty would have been closer to $12,200.

Less upfront capital required

Most property transactions that are financed require a deposit or similar equity, generally around 20%. With a new development and depending on its scale, the deposit is required mainly when purchasing the land, which is lower in price than an established building that includes both the land and buildings. Generally, equivalent size investments show that 50% more equity or upfront cash is required on an established investment. Also, there are incidental costs, such as stamp duty and conveyancing fees, which are usually higher in a completed building.

Retained profits

Most property developers target at least a 20% development profit on the total development cost which includes land, building and soft cost such as professional and authority fees. This profit is valued a lot higher when compared to cash equity invested. For example, if the total development cost of a duplex project is $1,000,000 the target profit is $200,000 (20%), the initial equity or cash required is say $300,000 (30% over $1,000,000) then the percentage profit over equity is 66.6% ($200,000/$300,000). If one of the duplex halves is sold for $510,000, it will reduce the initial loan of $700,000 (70%) to $190,000 meaning that the second duplex will only have a debt to equity ratio of 37% to 63% which certainly places the investor in a strong positive cash position.

With less upfront equity or cash required, the use of finance leveraging, the potential free or sweat equity – not forgetting the ultimate profit – it can be seen that property development can place a real estate investment in a cash position a lot faster than is possible with an established property.

BUYING ESTABLISHED vs DEVELOPING

We have looked at the qualitative aspects of property development but let now look at how does property development compare with buying established. What are the advantages, and will it benefit you financially? The decision for most people will depend predominantly on personal choice but could involve many other factors such as the availability of personal time, personal financial situation, timing and location. Below, we will analyse the advantages and disadvantages of these two options.

Disadvantages of developing

- *Established value – budget blowouts*

  When an established property is offered for sale, there is usually a bottom-line price that the seller is prepared to accept. This gives a certain degree of comfort to the investor, as he or she is only liable for additional costs such as stamp duty and conveyancing fees. When building new, the developers know the fixed price for the land, but they can find themselves in the situation where the final cost of the building has blown out beyond their set budget. With a new building, there are always additional costs such as landscaping, fencing, floor coverings, curtains and so on, that a builder does not include in their price. As well, you can get carried away and over-capitalise on the building so that when it comes to selling, you find yourself in a situation where you cannot get a buyer to match the amount of real money you spent on the building.

- *You cannot see what you are purchasing*

   Unless you are building a replica of another development, most new buildings are developed from an idea or concept and finally drawn up into a set of working plans. To most people reading and visualising the completed home from architectural drawings is a difficult task. With an established building, you can walk through and obtain the exact feel of the plan layout and see the precise room sizes.

- *Established gardens*

   Plants and trees take a long time to grow and to get established. If you are purchasing an investment property in an older suburb, the plants and trees have had a number of years to reach maturity. However, in building a new development, the gardens will look quite stark in the initial years, unless you have a reasonable landscaping budget.

- *Disputes with contractors*

   Inept builders are constantly making media headlines, which make us aware of unscrupulous practices and create a degree of scepticism about the building industry. Disputes with builders could delay the completion of the project, which increases your holding cost and thus reduces your profit. These reports are enough to make most people shy away from tackling a new development project but fortunately, not all builders are dishonest, and most have a well-established reputation for quality work and excellent client relationships.

- *Immediate return*

  When you invest in an established property – especially if it already has a tenant with a long lease – you will be able to assess the value of your return immediately. On the other hand, when you develop a new property, the amount of your return can only be evaluated when the building or buildings have been completed and fully leased, and this could take many months.

Advantages of developing

- *Free equity*

  If you have done your homework and you are a good negotiator, there is always an opportunity to purchase land and negotiate a building contract at discounted rates when undertaking a development project. If you are an experienced developer, you can save money and put in your own sweat and undertake certain sections of the project yourself. In each situation, you are creating 'free equity'. Free equity is the difference in value between the total cost of the land plus building cost and the bank value at the completion of the home. For example, if the total expense for your new development is $750,000 and the valuation at the completion of the project is $950,000, your free equity is $200,000.

- *Design to suit the market trends*

  Depending on the age of the building some investment properties may be too old or will outlive the market needs, in terms of accommodation and architectural style. For example, the rooms are too small, there is no family room, the kitchen looks tired and is not well planned, or the colours of the bathrooms are dated. With a new development, you can plan and design the building to suit present market trends that suit today's lifestyle.

- *Exciting*

  Watching your plans unfold as the architect presents your design, selecting your finishes and watching the various stages of construction while seeing your dreams being created can be exhilarating and stimulating. The same cannot be said of purchasing an established building. The excitement is limited, and there is always the thought of renovating and adding new rooms to suit the present market.

- *New design and materials*
  Like the fashion industry, architectural trends and building materials are constantly changing to adapt to consumer tastes and fads. Lifestyles are also continually evolving. Most established buildings reflect the period in which they were built in their elevation, planning, colours and building materials. Only with substantial cost and alterations can an older home be brought up to date with the latest trends. Be careful when undertaking alterations and additions because if there is a reasonable amount of work the cost may exceed the value of building something new.

- *Longer life span*
  All older buildings have a certain amount of wear and tear and will require maintenance over their lifespan. Before buying an older building, engage the services of a building consultant to examine and uncover any structural defects, electrical faults, roof leaks and so on. A younger building constructed to quality standards is less likely to require maintenance in the short term.

- *Tax benefits*
  The depreciation allowance mentioned earlier is the proportion of the cost or the book value of a building, which may be deducted annually as a legitimate expense and is usually determined by the original price of the building set against the life of the building. The present allowance is 2.5% over 40 years. This allowance, like negative gearing, is offset against your income, but this applies only if the property is registered under your own name. Also, all new properties for sale are subject to GST. Therefore, if you are a developer that embarks on a new project every year or if your income on developments exceeds $100,000 per annum you will be liable to register as a GST vendor and add the GST amount onto the sale of

your building(s). However, all goods or services supplied to the development on which GST has been paid can be offset against the project.

- *Less upfront capital required*
  With most property transactions that are financed, a deposit or similar equity is required, and this is generally around 20 to 30%. With a development, the deposit required when purchasing the land, will be lower than the deposit for an established building that includes both the land and buildings.

The Decision

The financial decision whether to invest in an established investment property or to develop your own will be a personal choice and depend on the factors pointed out above. If you are prepared to go through the process of negotiating land deals, the design with your architect or designer, selecting and negotiating with a builder and going through a certain amount of annoyance during construction, there is nothing to beat the excitement and stimulation of creating a new development.

CONCLUSION

Given the risk profile of real estate investment, a positively geared property is key to generating a passive income and financial independence. By learning how to maximise profits from positively geared investment properties, you are on your way towards financial freedom, however, achieving a passive income from property requires effort and discipline.

There are three main areas where you can create a positively geared real estate portfolio, namely (a) finding and purchasing an established property (b) adding value to an established property and (c) undertaking property development. As pointed out above, finding the right positive cash flow real estate investment opportunity is challenging. It takes lots of time to research and identify the right areas with stable drivers for cash positive opportunities. In most cases, you will not see immediate positively geared property for sale. Instead, you usually have to wait a few years before a property becomes cash positive.

There are many qualitative aspects of property development over buying an established investment property and one of the keys aspects is that it is a quicker path to financial freedom and a passive income for retirement. However, the final decision will be based on personal choice, your financial position, your knowledge and whether you are willing to take the risk for a better return.

CHAPTER 4

THE DEVELOP AND HOLD STRATEGY

INTRODUCTION

Many property investors have become extremely wealthy through real estate investment, but the real and faster profits within the property market are in property development. Each year the BRW Rich List demonstrates that 80% or more of the country's wealthiest people make and grow their fortunes through their property holdings. The secret to real property wealth is in developing quality properties and retaining as much of your project product (assets) as you can for your long-term real estate portfolio. By holding these assets as investments, it allows you to acquire your property at the developer's wholesale cost, keeping it for further capital growth and deferring the tax on the development profit until sold.

Instead of waiting for capital to grow over time as with an established property your capital growth via equity is created during with your efforts in developing the property. Whatever you want to call it the developer's margin or equity creation, it is the amount of money created when the total development cost is deducted against the value of the project on completion. The value of the equity created during the development will depend on a number of factors such as the location, quality, planning and finishes of the project and also in mitigating and managing the risks such as council approval, the builder's program and so on.

WHY DEVELOP AND HOLD?

If you are seeking financial independence, it is recommended that you endeavour to hold on to as many of the properties as possible when you are developing, and to create a significant asset portfolio.

Whether you hold these property assets under your personal name, family trust or a self-managed super fund (SMSF) is entirely up to you and your personal financial circumstances. In Chapter 1, the benefits of creating a real estate portfolio have been explained. These include passive income, tax benefits, capital appreciation, cash-flow and so on. Outlined below are additional benefits to be gained through property development.

- **Creation of free and faster equity**

  The personal time and effort you put in property development is creating free equity (sweat equity) while your profit becomes additional equity when valued at completion. Depending on the scale of the project, the creation of this equity can be achieved within a year or two, which is a lot faster than pur-chasing an existing investment property which could take five years or more to achieve the same result.

- **Tax deferment**

  The profit you make in a development project is only taxed when sold. So if you hold the property as an investment under the same ownership entity, you are not liable for any tax on the profit. When valuing your real estate portfolio, this 'profit' is added to your equity position as long as the property is not sold. This increased equity position portrays a healthy financial position when applying for additional finance.

- **Tax-free refinancing proceeds**

  With an increase in free equity and capital appreciation, it gives you the opportunity to take advantage of this equity build-up to refinance another development. If a property is refinanced for more than the existing debt, the proceeds are funds that the investor can spend on whatever he or she deems appropriate. In addition, since this money is obtained through refinancing, these funds are not currently taxable to the investor.

- **Security**

  Banks and mortgage lenders love property as security. It is real, and they understand the value of this form of security against the money they are lending to you. Banking systems and their approval processes are so entrenched that when presented with increased equity value in your real estate portfolio and offering them this as additional security for a new purchase, the proposal usually falls within their lending policies.

DEVELOP AND HOLD STRATEGY

To develop and to hold is a powerful wealth creation strategy. The theory behind it is that the development profit that should be made when sold, plus your initial equity injection, should place your project is positive cash flow position. This, of course, is dependent on the scale, type of project, and end valuation. With most development projects such as residential duplex, town-houses and apartments where there are a number of units, there is always the opportunity to sell some of the units to reduce debt and place the holding investment units is a positive cash position.

Depending on the risk profile of a development and location, developers generally target at least a 20% or more return on a residential project and minimum of 25% on a commercial development. So, let us look at a hypothetical example. You develop a duplex of 2 villa units with a total development cost of $800,000 including land at $300,000, and the bank will lend you 70% of the development cost which is $560,000 which requires you to inject $240,000 of your own cash as equity. The market value of the two units is $960,000 which includes a 20% development profit of $160,000. With the end value being $960,000 and a new equity position at the completion of $400,000 ($240,000 cash equity plus $160,000 profit) most traditional banks will lend against this as the LVR is 58% loan and 42% equity. If the units are rented out at say $400 per week this will produce an annual income of $41,600 ($400 x 2 x 52), which, after allowing outgoings, management and vacancy periods of 22% ($9,152) will provide a net annual income of $32,448. If you secure a long-term interest-only loan of $560,000 at 5%, then your repayments will be $28,000 pa. This places your investment in a positive cash flow position of $8,504 ($36,504 less $28,000).

Item	Cost
Land purchase (including Stamp Duty and Conveyancing	$ 300,000
Development cost (Construction, professional fees etc.)	$ 500,000
Total Development Cost	**$ 800,000**
End value at completion	**$ 960,000**
Development profit on TDC 20%	$ 160,000
Initial cash equity required for development 20% on TDC	$ 240,000
Total equity position at completion	**$ 400,000**
Gross annual rental	$ 41,600
Less outgoings, management and vacancies (22%)	$ 9,152
Nett rental income	$ 32,448
Interest only loan @ 5% $560,00 ($800,000 - $240,000)	$ 28,000
Positive cash flow	**$ 4,448**

Bear in mind that when you complete your development in the example above, the $180,000 profit is not taxed until you sell the units in the future. If you intend holding the units forever, in theory, you can defer your taxes for as long as you like. Moreover, if you ever decide you need to access that equity for another property purchase, you can refinance the property and tap into that equity without incurring any tax liability. This is far smarter than selling your development, paying 30% or more in taxes.

However, it should be noted that some banks may consider the above investment a higher risk to them when it is under one ownership. Should anything happen to you, they would have to sell both of the units instead of each of them individually. They would consider this as a 'one-line' investment and will discount the lending by 20%. This is further explained under Chapter 6 'Financing your portfolio'.

DEVELOP AND HOLD ANALYSIS

Before adopting the Develop and Hold investment concept, it is a good exercise to analyse the various options such as holding the total project as a long-term investment or selling part and holding the balance. By comparing the options, you will find which option will best suit your investment strategy and personal financial circumstances. In order to get a better understanding of the various proposals, we analyse the following case study.

Case Study

Four years ago, my co-directors and I purchased two older suburban homes through our company that focuses on urban infill developments. The two sites were recently zoned R30 which allowed four units per site. After analysing the economics of the development, it made sense to amalgamate the two properties, create a central driveway and create eight villa units.

During our feasibility stage we looked at the various options:
a. develop and sell;
b. develop and rent; and
c. develop, sell 50% and rent 50% of the units

Option 1: Develop & Sell

Development cost		Projected Sales	
Total cost of land purchased	$ 838,400	Sale of 8 villas @ $450,000 each	$ 3,600,000
Total construction cost	$ 1,585,500	Less GST	$ 327,273
Total consultant fees	$ 79,275	Less sales commission	$ 90,000
Total authority fees	$ 54,764		
Total management fees	$ 95,482		
Total marketing, legal fees	$ 63,655		
Total finance cost	$ 9,000		
Total interest cost (loan $1.83m)	$ 62,707		
Development Cost incl. GST	$ 2,788,782		
Less GST	$ 171,590	Nett Sales income	$ 3,182,727
Total Development Cost (TDC)	$ 2,617,192	Nett Profit	$ 565,535
Return on TDC	22%		
Return on Equity	139%		
The issue with Option 1 is that after paying company tax, our cash position was $395,875 and with no holding assets as distinct from the other options displayed below.			

Option 2: Develop & Rent

Investment cost		Projected Rent		
(Total Development Cost)	$ 2,617,192	(Value of villas at completion)	$	3,600,000
Property Management 5.5%	$ 9,838	Annual Rent 8 villas @ $430 pw	$	178,880
Outgoings (allow 12%)	$ 21,466			
Vacancy rate (allow 5%)	$ 8,944			
Interest on loan (allow 7% fixed)	$ 128,100	Total annual income	$	178,880
Total operating cost	$ 168,348	Nett income	$	10,532
Loan at completion	$ 1,830,000			
Equity position	$ 1,770,000			
Rental return on TDC	7%			

With Option 2 the nett rental income is marginal, and any movement on interest rates or unforeseen circumstances would require additional cash injection.

Option 3: Develop, sell 50% and rent 50%

Development Cost		Projected Sales	
Development Cost incl. GST	$ 2,788,782	Sale of 4 Villas @ $450,000 each	$ 1,800,000
Less GST	$ 171,590	Less GST	$ 163,620
Total Development Cost	$ 2,617,192	Less Commission	$ 45,000
Loan after Sales	$ 238,620		$ 1,591,380
Investment Cost		**Projected Rent**	
Property Management 5.5%	$ 4,919	Annual Rent villas @ $430 pw	$ 89,440
Outgoings (allow 12%)	$ 10,733		
Vacancy rate (allow 5%)	$ 4,472		
Interest on loan (allow 5% fixed)	$ 11,931	Total annual income	$ 89,440
Total operating cost	$ 32,055	Nett income	$ 57,385
Value of existing 4 villas	$ 1,800,000		
Equity position	$ 1,561,380		

With Option 3, the nett rental income is better especially with lower debt. With still a strong equity position we were able to borrow additional funds to purchase another development property.

By analysing the above, we can draw the following conclusions:

1. Option 1 is not very viable as after the profit on tax had been paid the returns were too low for the risk involved.
2. With Option 2, we would have to inject more funds should interest rates increase or unforeseen circumstances occur.
3. Option 3 looks the better solution as we could keep at least 50% of the units without too much exposure. The monthly shortfall even with the vacancy factor is more manageable.

LONG-TERM INVESTMENT ANALYSIS

Looking at the case study above, it was concluded that Option 3 was the preferred option. Unfortunately, we sold all of the eight units and did not follow up on a 'develop and hold' strategy. Had followed Option 3 we would be in a comfortable position based on the long-term analysis tabled below.

- Value of the balance of units = $1,800,000
- Outstanding loan = $1,830,000 less $1,591,380 = $238,620
- Equity position = $1,800,000 less $238,620 = $1,561,380
- Assume interest only at 7%
- Repayments = $72,863.00.
- Assume growth of 2.5% per annum
- Reduce loan from surplus income after tax

Year	Value	Loan	Equity	Loan	Nett Rent	Rent Surplus	Nett after Tax
1	$1,800,000	$ 238,620	$ 1,561,380	$ 16,703.40	$ 57,385	$ 40,682	$ 28,477
2	$1,845,000	$ 210,143	$ 1,634,857	$ 14,710.00	$ 58,820	$ 44,110	$ 30,877
3	$1,891,125	$ 179,266	$ 1,711,859	$ 12,548.63	$ 60,290	$ 47,741	$ 33,419
4	$1,938,403	$ 145,847	$ 1,792,556	$ 10,209.30	$ 61,797	$ 51,588	$ 36,112
5	$1,986,863	$ 109,735	$ 1,877,128	$ 7,681.48	$ 63,342	$ 55,661	$ 38,963
6	$2,036,535	$ 70,773	$ 1,965,762	$ 4,954.10	$ 64,926	$ 59,972	$ 41,980
7	$2,087,448	$ 28,793	$ 2,058,656	$ 2,015.49	$ 66,549	$ 64,534	$ 45,173
8	$2,139,634	$ -	$ 2,139,634	$ -	$ 68,213	$ 68,213	$ 47,749
9	$2,193,125	$ -	$ 2,193,125	$ -	$ 69,918	$ 69,918	$ 48,943
10	$2,247,953	$ -	$ 2,247,953	$ -	$ 71,666	$ 71,666	$ 50,166

Table 4.1 Spreadsheet of long-term investment

From Table 4.1, the following list of assumptions can be made. (Note that these are only assumptions and will vary according to the depth of research undertaken. Such a spreadsheet should be reviewed annually.)

- In year 8 the loan would have been paid off, therefore, providing a passive income from the existing villas.

- Any time after year 2 there is sufficient nett equity if another development opportunity arises.

CREATING A PORTFOLIO FASTER

The examples above have shown that property development can create a positive cash flow investment if done correctly. The profits made through the process increase an investor's equity position faster than buying existing or completed buildings. There is an additional tool you can use to improve this equity a lot faster, and that is leveraging. By accessing this equity and using leverage, you can springboard into another property development and start to create a wealth-generating real estate portfolio. This process can be repeated a number of times thereby increasing your wealth exponentially. Below is an example of how leveraging could work for you:

Develop and hold strategy:

- Develop a duplex project every second year for a period of 10 years. With each development, one is sold, and the other is retained
- The equity retained from the sale plus the initial equity is used to develop each new project

Assumptions:

- Total development cost (TDC) = $800,000 ($400,000 each half)
- Equity required for development = 30% of TDC
- Construction debt = 70% of TDC
- Targeted profit margin on TDC = 20%
- Capital growth on portfolio each year = 3.3% (CPI)
- Assume interest-only financing = 5%

Leveraging on initial equity of $240,000

The spreadsheet Table 4.2 at the end of this chapter sets out the project development, debt and equity position each year if you develop a duplex project every second year over a 10-year period (meaning five small projects). The strategy is that you sell one of your units and retain the other in each of these projects. The total development cost (TDC) is say $800,000 (2 x $400,000) with 30% equity of $240,000 and construction debt of $560,000. The targeted profit margin is 20% showing the as complete value of $960,000 or $480,000 per unit.

The exercise has assumed a modest growth of 3.3% per annum – well below the average long-term growth rate of 5% shown historically in most Australian capital city markets. So, in year 1, we had two units worth $960,000 of which one is sold for $424,320 nett ($480,000 less GST and sales commission of 2.5%) leaving you with the other unit at $480,000 in value. The debt is also reduced by sale, which will stand at $135,680 ($560,000 less $424,320) leaving you with an equity position of $288,640 ($480,000 less $135,680).

The following year, the first unit held in Project No 1 is now valued at $495,840 reflecting a 3.3% growth and the debt is reduced to $125,824 ($135,680 less surplus income $9,856). A new duplex project 2 is undertaken this time with the TDC is $853,671, 30% equity at $256,101, construction debt at $597,570 and end value of $1,024,405 with a 20% profit margin. To secure 30%, the equity for this new project, the debt on Project No 1 is increased to$384,997. The process then is repeated over several times over a ten-year period.

Figure 4.1 shows a graph of your equity position starting with $240,000 cash equity and leveraging off the equity created without further capital injection, you could potentially create $3.21 million real estate portfolio with $1,87 million debt, $1.34 million equity and $17,134 positive cash flow after ten years.

Equity Position

Figure 4.1 Leveraging initial equity of $240,000 plus top-up

The second exercise (shown in Figure 4.2) is to demonstrate that by topping up with additional cash equity and using the equity created from the previous project you could accelerate a portfolio. The top-up equity is ideally suited for a SMSF. If you do use an SMSF, it is essential that you get professional advice on the structure and the entity which will hold the investment asset.

The increased equity build-up is used to purchase another property for development similar to the example above, but instead of waiting for every second year for the equity growth to increase, additional equity cash is injected so that you can develop every year. Obviously finding additional equity every year can be difficult unless you use part of your superannuation input as the fresh equity. In using this strategy with the initial investment of $240,000 and a top up equity of $ $41,320 to $53,575 (total $425,000) over nine years, you could build a real estate portfolio of $6.4million in value and an equity position of $2.9million. After paying the annual interest, you still have a surplus cash flow of $48,364 per annum.

You can now see how leverage, good cash flow property and good planning can lead to fast tracking your financial future. While conservative figures have been used in the spreadsheets, if history repeats itself with properties doubling in value every ten years (as they have done in Melbourne for the last 30 years at an average growth rate of 7% p.a., Source: Valuer-General), then your portfolio could grow even faster. However, getting that first development started is usually the hardest. You need to save that initial deposit to get going. There are other options such as a joint venture or syndicate, which is more fully described later in this book.

EQUITY POSITION

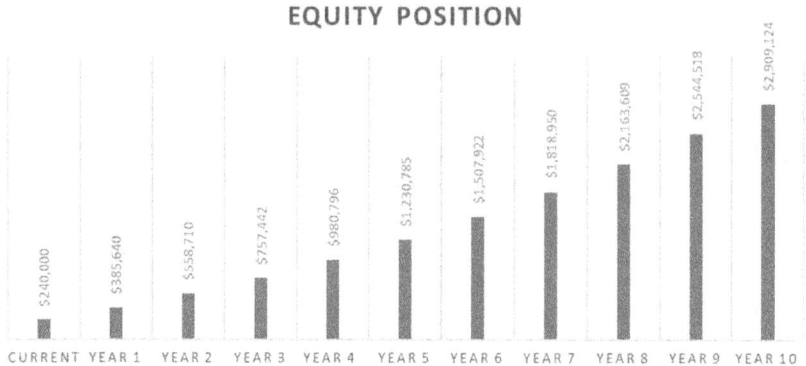

Figure 4.2 Equity position after 10 years with top-ups

These are theoretical examples using a duplex project as a model of developing, selling and holding. However, a lot will depend on your expertise, experience and cash position.

WHOLESALE INVESTING

If the strategy above is not for you as it is too troublesome or you do not have the time due to other commitments such as your own business, there is an alternative method of investing in a development and benefit from the 'profit equity'. Under this strategy, you will need to find an experienced developer where you put up some early risk equity for the development and are then able to purchase a unit at a wholesale price. If you decide to use this strategy, it is essential that you invest only with an experienced developer with a good track record and ensure that the developer provides you with some form of security.

This concept is not a syndicate but rather a direct investment in a unit that you will own. This strategy means buying brand new property at wholesale prices. So what is a wholesale property? It is a property that is sold at a discount with respect to the retail valuation price, from a developer and differs to wholesale investing in trust or 'flipping properties'.

Another format of wholesale investing is to invest in a listed or unlisted property development trust/fund. With an investment into a fund, the investor is an owner of units/shares in a fund that owns the property. With wholesale investing, the investor has direct ownership of the property and therefore has better control over their investment.

Comparing wholesale investing with retail investing

If you are buying investment property through an investment club or group, they would recommend properties to purchase at retail, and the club/group itself would charge the developer a commission from 5% to 15%. By buying directly from the developer, these 'commissions' are passed onto you. Figure 4.3 is a graph showing wholesale investing over a 10-year period which shows five properties accumulated over this period with each property positively geared. If the same strategy is followed by retail investing, only two properties would be accumulated with a gap of 8 years between purchases.

Net Worth (Leveraging)

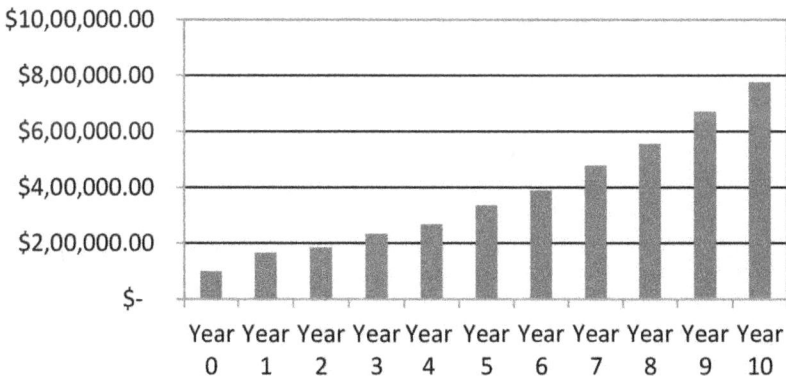

Figure 4.3 Net worth after wholesale investing over a 10-year period

The above graph is a theoretical analysis of investing only $100,000 plus establishment costs. This initial $100,000 is never topped up during a ten-year period and is continually used to purchase other properties. The analysis is based on the following assumptions:

- Each Property increasing in value at 3.1% per annum
- Rental income based on a net return of 4.7% per annum
- Loan repayments based on 5.0% interest-only loan
- Surplus income is paid to reduce the loan principal.

The graph is only a sample of wholesale investing with a minimal initial investment. The individual financial circumstances of investors will vary and may not produce the same results. An individual analysis has to be undertaken before a commitment is made to wholesale direct investing.

Using your superannuation fund to participate in wholesale investing?

If you want to accelerate the investment process faster than can be seen in Figure 4.3 and if you are still working and have a created an SMSF you will be able to purchase additional wholesale direct properties by adding your annual superannuation payments to your SMSF. However, before you adopt this strategy, it is advisable to talk to your accountant or a superannuation expert. Below is a hypothetical sample of wholesale investing using your SMSF.

Net Worth (Leveraging)

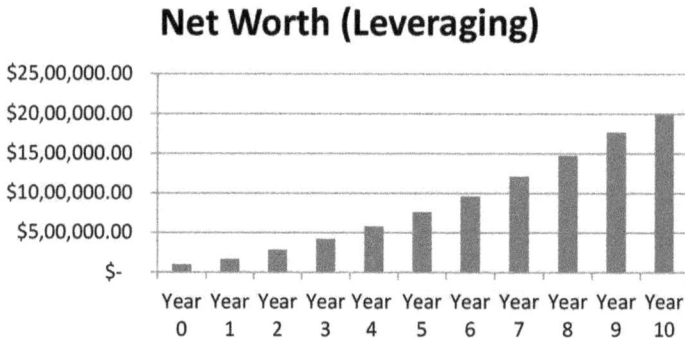

Figure 4.4 Net worth after SMSF topped-up wholesale investing over 10 years

The graph in Figure 4.4 is like the previous scenario, which started with $100,000 initial investment and then contributed $30,000 per annum which is allowable for a person earning $100,000 per annum.

In the Chapter 5, the wholesale strategy is expanded further along with discounted investment real estate strategies. It is another format for investors who are not keen to undertake development risks.

RISK MANAGEMENT IN A DEVELOP AND HOLD STRATEGY

Property development and investment is a business fraught with risks, and the bigger the project, the higher the risk. However, there are ways to manage the risks. With a develop and hold strategy the risks can be broken into two categories namely, (a) development risk and (b) investment risk at a portfolio level. Listed below are the potential risk under each category and managing those risks through a mitigation strategy.

Management and evaluation of risk is a significant part of any successful real estate investment strategy. These risks come into play in many different ways at every stage of the investment process. Below is a list of some common risks and typical risk mitigation strategies used by real estate investors.

Risk management at the development phase

A good property developer has learned to be risk-conscious rather than risk-averse. If you never take a risk, you will never make a gain. The difference between successful and unsuccessful developers is that successful people take risks while always looking to minimise them.

Risk	Mitigation strategy
Risk of a bad purchase There is always a risk if you paid too much for a development site, buy in the wrong location or do not obtain the Development Approval (DA) for the type of building you had envisaged.	The risk of a bad purchase can be reduced by better-negotiating skills, more extensive market research or settling only after securing a DA.

Land valuation risk:	
The land you purchased has dropped in value more than your acquisition costs due to the changes to market circumstances.	Keep an eye on market movements by understanding the broader economic conditions in your area. Also, consider having an exit strategy.
Poor soil conditions risk:	
There may be bad elements or conditions in the soil which could not be seen when viewing a site — issues such as contamination, bad fill, poor water table, moving clay etc., which could be costly to remedy.	It is worthwhile getting a geotechnical report before purchasing and transferring the property into your name. If needed, obtain an environmental survey and test for contaminants (lead paint, asbestos, soil contaminants, etc.)
Planning approval risk:	
When a development approval is required, there could be unexpected delays which increase the holding costs while the planning application is being processed. There is also the potential that the approval will not be granted or will be granted on unfavourable terms. In getting your development approved, the approach is to hope for the best but expect the worst.	In mitigating this risk, allow for possible delays in your feasibility study and ensure you can cover your holding costs should the planning approval stage be drawn out indefinitely. By taking these precautionary steps, you will be less likely to find yourself in an uncomfortable position. Also, make sure you have the right professionals on board who can assist you in addressing any planning issues that may arise.
Revenue risk:	
There are plenty of factors that influence revenues. These include yields, rent levels, sales price levels, inflation and interest rate levels, demand and supply which will ultimately reflect on the return on the development.	You should thoroughly review the project's feasibility study prepared by experienced consultants. This study should be continuously updated during the development process. A sensitivity analysis should also be undertaken.

Regulation risk: Any changes to the laws relating to property development can affect your development. This includes changes to zoning and town planning regulations, restrictions on land use, environmental controls, landlord and tenancy controls, user restrictions, stamp duty, land tax, income taxes and capital gains tax.	Always check with council planners if there are any changes to the town planning scheme predicted in the near future before submitting for planning approval. Also, keep up with any industry changes or legislation by talking to people in the property industry.
Partner risk: With larger projects, most developers would like to take on a partner to share the risks or to provide additional equity. The risk is that a partner in the project cannot meet their obligations or disagrees on the way forward.	Carefully choose your partner by undertaking a due diligence. While both of you may have the same common goals, there is always the potential of personality and business ethics conflict.
Legal risk: This covers a broad area such as possible objections against zoning changes, liability risks or contracts that have not been drawn up correctly. It also concerns the risk of not obtaining the required approvals and the risks involved with buying existing companies to acquire land positions.	Having a good understanding of the laws relating to property development at the start can save you many problems with your project. It is wise to appoint a competent and experienced property lawyer who could advise you of any legal issues during the approval and development process.
Market Risk Any change in property market sentiment during the construction of a project may affect the price and the targeted return to be achieved. This could affect the profitability of the project or the developer's ability to repay the construction loan.	To mitigate this risk, you should undertake thorough market research and conduct a projected market analysis into the type of property, and the market needs in the area. Know your target market and what they are looking for before you start a project.

Borrowing risk Borrowings will magnify gains or losses and increase the volatility of your returns on a project. The instability will occur through fluctuations in interest rates and risks associated with refinancing loans once loan terms expire.	A way of mitigating this risk is not to leverage or to gear too highly. Depending upon the project's risk profile, it is recommended that you should aim not to exceed debt levels of 65% of the final asset value or 70% on total development cost.
Construction risk During the construction phase of a development, there are a number of potential risks, and these can include: • The risk that the construction costs may exceed the budget which will reduce the potential profit from the project. • The risk that the construction period could exceed projected building program and delay settlement of sales or leasing of the project. • The builder may run into financial problems and may not be able to complete the building requiring you to employ another builder which could ultimately cost more.	To lessen these potential construction risks, you should only appoint credible contractors who are reputable and experienced with adequate insurance cover and sufficient financial resources for the type of works for which they are engaged. A fixed price building contract is the best way for a developer to ensure that your development continues. Ask the building contractor to provide a fixed price contract and ensure you are familiar with the law under which you are signing the contract, and what this means when it comes to any possible dispute.
Interest rate risk: Upward movement in interest rates may affect the profitability of projects and therefore the profitability of your development.	Depending on the risk profile of the project, these risks may be mitigated by fixing interest rates.

Economic downturn risk: A downturn in the property market such as increases in interest rates, cyclical movement in the property market and depressed or unstable general economic conditions) resulting in lowered property values or increased holding costs until the properties are sold.	Remember that property markets move in cycles and you need to understand the fundamentals that drive booms and busts to time the start and finish of your project. It would help if you were looking at acquiring sites during quieter times and marketing your project when there is heightened buyer activity and demand.
Contractor dispute risk: This is a dilemma that poses obvious risks to any development. Such a conflict with your builder can result in lengthy delays, which means budget blowouts, as you must account for increased holding costs. Also, having tradespeople walk off the job halfway through necessitates finding an alternative builder. New builders brought into a project midstream will charge more to complete a task and as you will have very little bargaining power, they know you are caught in a difficult situation.	It would be best if you established good communication between you and the building contractor or tradespeople right from the beginning. Document all agreements formally to minimise the risk of such disputes occurring. Should any disagreements arise during the construction stage, be diplomatic in managing them and try to resolve them as quickly and cleanly as possible. This is an area where a good project manager can be of valuable assistance.
Management failure risk: The success of a business is reliant on good management, and property development is no different. Poor management or lack of experience in development can result in failure or loss of profit.	If you are a novice developer, it is wise to appoint a good and experienced development manager or project manager to ensure the smooth running of your project.

In addition to enacting these mitigation strategies, the aim of the developer is to minimise these risks as much as possible. Additional strategies as listed below can be applied:

- Allow for contingencies: To protect oneself against financial risk during the purchasing stage, you should add various contingencies to the contract.

- Diversify investments: Diversification of development and investment activity into different building types as well as other localities will assist in the mitigation of risk.
- Limit ownership liability: As a developer of a property, one should select a special purpose vehicle (SPV) for each project to protect yourself from personal liability. This will help to protect the developer from tenants, consultants, contractors and the general public.
- Limit financial liability: One should try to secure 'nonrecourse financing' for any loans applied for and use an SPV to shield one's personal assets. Another method would be to find financial equity partners who help to carry any financial losses.

Risk management at the portfolio level

At the portfolio level, there are still many risks involved but to a lesser degree when compared to the development stage. Below are possible risks and a number of risk-mitigating measures to put in place.

Risk	Mitigation Strategy
Liquidity risk: Property, unlike other commodities such as shares or bonds, cannot be traded on a daily basis. Property is generally sold with conditions, and this could delay the flow of funds to you when needed.	To mitigate this risk, it is advisable that you have a contingency cash reserve for this eventuality. It is advisable to have your property cash flow positive so that you can build up a cash reserve.
Low rental return risk: This can happen when there is an oversupply of rental properties in the area of your rental property. It often occurs after a boom period of heightened building activity bringing more properties into the marketplace.	Look for areas with evidence of future growth to ensure ongoing demand and with a diversity of employment and industries to reduce your risk. Also maintain a positively geared portfolio to give yourself a buffer if cash flow is reduced.

Vacancy risk: Having a rental property vacant is not good for your cash flow and repayments on your mortgage. If you fall behind with your payments, your bank could call up your loan and then sell your property for less than what it had cost you.	Engage only reputable rental managers who will ensure your property is actively marketed. Also be realistic about your expected rent. By keeping the rent high, you may experience longer vacancies that could ultimately cost you more than the extra rent you would have received.
Bad tenant risk: While a majority of tenants are reliable, some may not pay their rent and could mistreat your property. Unfortunately, sometimes good tenants can become bad ones, but more often through unforeseen circumstances to their personal situation, such as loss of employment, illness or divorce.	Once again, this comes down to hiring a great rental manager who will conduct thorough screenings of prospective tenants. Despite your best efforts, you may still end up with tenants who don't look after your property, so you should always maintain a landlord's insurance policy to compensate you.
Interest rate risk: During the life of your real estate portfolio, interest rates will change due to the economic conditions of the country. If you are highly geared, and rates increase it will put stress on your portfolio.	Don't leverage too highly and maintain a positively-geared portfolio and keeping a sufficient cash buffer making sure you can afford your repayments in the worst case. Also, consider the benefits of converting a portion of your loans to fixed rates.
Natural disaster risk: Various parts of Australia regularly experience a range of natural disasters, including floods, cyclones, and extreme weather. However, some areas are more prone to these disasters than others	Do your due diligence before investing in natural disaster areas. If you wish to invest in a cyclone area, ensure the property is built to cyclone codes and maintain an insurance policy that covers damage caused by natural disasters.

Change in lifestyle risk: Expect the unexpected to happen. You could be gainfully employed, but you could fall ill or lose your job. Alternatively, your marriage ends in disaster, and you end up in a messy divorce. These situations could change your financial circumstances to the point where you can no longer afford the mortgage repayments, or have difficulty meeting your loan obligations.	While you cannot predict the future, you can always be prepared. There are a number of actions you can put in place. Ensure that you have adequate insurance. Not just for your property, but you as well. It is equally important to maintain a financial buffer, such as a line of credit or offset account attached to your loan. This approach provides you with a cash reserve for unforeseen circumstances.
Maintenance risk: Regardless of how new a property is there will always be maintenance issues that arise now and then. Maintenance problems are unavoidable and can be a drain on your cash if you are not adequately prepared.	Never ignore maintenance issues as they will only get worse and can cause you to lose good tenants. Make sure you have put aside some cash reserves for maintenance which could even be paying for a new hot water system or replacing an appliance.

The risk-conscious approach

It is essential that you keep in potential risks in mind when developing or holding any property, and you should always look take a conservative approach when calculating potential returns or rentals. For example, do a sensitivity analysis and evaluate the property under the worst possible conditions. Assume that interest rates will increase substantially and that rental values will hold or even drop. If after these conservative calculations, you can still make a good return on property development, you can proceed knowing that even in a worst-case where the bottom falls out of the market, you will not lose money.

CONCLUSION

If you want to grow a real estate portfolio faster than the traditional format of buying existing buildings as an investment and waiting for the values to grow, then it is worth considering developing and holding your own properties. The theory behind this is that the development profit will accelerate your equity position. The developer's profit created when the building is completed becomes additional equity over and above the initial equity invested. The value of the equity created during the development will depend on many factors such as the location, quality, planning and finishes of the project and also in mitigating managing the risks such as council approval, builders' program and so on.

The typical develop and hold strategy can be further accelerated by either selling part of the development to increase your equity position and then to launch into another project where the process is repeated or (b) top-up cash equity to an SMSF. Alternatively, you can apply both and grow your portfolio a lot faster. Whichever strategy you intend to use it is strongly advised that you talk to your accountant or a superannuation expert, as each person's financial and work situation is different.

Table 4.2. Leveraging on initial equity

	Current	Year 1	Year 2	Year 3	Year 4	Year 5	Year 6	Year 7	Year 8	Year 9	Year 10
PROPERTY 1 (Duplex)											
TDC 2 Duplex Units	$ 800,000										
Equity @ 30%	$ 240,000										
Loan @ 70%	$ 560,000										
End Value	$ 960,000										
Sell 1 Unit		$ 424,320									
Value of holding unit		$ 480,000	$ 495,840	$ 512,203	$ 529,105	$ 546,566	$ 564,603	$ 583,234	$ 602,481	$ 622,363	$ 642,901
Loan after sale		$ 135,580	$ 381,925	$ 383,833	$ 385,268	$ 386,189	$ 386,551	$ 386,305	$ 385,402	$ 383,786	$ 381,400
Equity after sale		$ 288,640	$ 113,915	$ 128,370	$ 143,838	$ 160,377	$ 178,052	$ 196,929	$ 217,079	$ 238,577	$ 261,501
Gross Rent pa		$ 20,800	$ 21,486	$ 22,195	$ 22,928	$ 23,685	$ 24,466	$ 25,273	$ 26,108	$ 26,969	$ 27,859
Nett Rent		$ 16,640	$ 17,189	$ 17,756	$ 18,342	$ 18,948	$ 19,573	$ 20,219	$ 20,886	$ 21,575	$ 22,287
Repayment 5.5%pa		$ 6,784	$ 19,096	$ 19,192	$ 19,263	$ 19,309	$ 19,328	$ 19,315	$ 19,270	$ 19,189	$ 19,070
Shortfall/Surplus		$ 9,856	-$ 1,907	-$ 1,435	-$ 921	-$ 362	$ 245	$ 904	$ 1,816	$ 2,386	$ 3,217
LVR		28%	77%	75%	73%	71%	68%	66%	64%	62%	59%
PROPERTY 2 (Duplex)											
TDC 2 Duplex Units			$ 853,671								
Equity @ 30%			$ 256,101								
Loan @ 70%			$ 597,570								
End Value			$ 1,024,405								
Sell 1 Unit				$ 452,787							
Value of holding unit				$ 512,203	$ 529,105	$ 546,566	$ 564,603	$ 583,234	$ 602,481	$ 622,363	$ 642,901
Loan after sale				$ 144,783	$ 407,548	$ 409,583	$ 411,115	$ 412,098	$ 412,484	$ 412,222	$ 411,258
Equity after sale				$ 367,420	$ 121,557	$ 138,982	$ 153,488	$ 171,137	$ 189,997	$ 210,141	$ 231,643
Gross Rent pa				$ 22,195	$ 22,928	$ 23,685	$ 24,466	$ 25,273	$ 26,108	$ 26,969	$ 27,859
Nett Rent				$ 17,756	$ 18,342	$ 18,948	$ 19,573	$ 20,219	$ 20,886	$ 21,575	$ 22,287
Repayment 5.5%pa				$ 7,239	$ 20,377	$ 20,479	$ 20,556	$ 20,605	$ 20,624	$ 20,611	$ 20,563
Shortfall/Surplus				$ 10,517	-$ 2,035	-$ 1,532	-$ 983	-$ 386	$ 262	$ 964	$ 1,724
LVR				28%	77%	75%	73%	71%	68%	66%	64%
PROPERTY 3 (Duplex)											
TDC 2 Duplex Units					$ 910,943						
Equity @ 30%					$ 273,283						
Loan @ 70%					$ 637,660						
End Value					$ 1,093,132						
Sell 1 Unit						$ 483,164					
Value of holding unit						$ 546,566	$ 564,603	$ 583,234	$ 602,481	$ 622,363	$ 642,901
Loan after sale						$ 154,496	$ 435,663	$ 437,873	$ 439,548	$ 440,839	$ 441,096
Equity after sale						$ 392,070	$ 128,940	$ 145,361	$ 182,933	$ 181,724	$ 201,805
Gross Rent pa						$ 23,685	$ 24,466	$ 25,273	$ 26,108	$ 26,969	$ 27,859
Nett Rent						$ 18,948	$ 19,573	$ 20,219	$ 20,886	$ 21,575	$ 22,287
Repayment 5.5%pa						$ 8,497	$ 21,783	$ 21,894	$ 21,977	$ 22,032	$ 22,055
Shortfall/Surplus						$ 10,450	-$ 2,210	-$ 1,675	-$ 1,091	$ 457	$ 232.43
LVR						28%	77%	75%	73%	71%	69%
PROPERTY 4 (Duplex)											
TDC 2 Duplex Units							$ 972,057				
Equity @ 30%							$ 291,617				
Loan @ 70%							$ 680,440				
End Value							$ 1,166,469				
Sell 1 Unit								$ 515,579			
Value of holding unit								$ 583,234	$ 602,481	$ 622,363	$ 642,901
Loan after sale								$ 164,861	$ 464,067	$ 468,704	$ 470,564
Equity after sale								$ 418,374	$ 138,414	$ 153,659	$ 172,337
Gross Rent pa								$ 25,273	$ 26,108	$ 26,969	$ 27,859
Nett Rent								$ 20,219	$ 20,886	$ 21,575	$ 22,287
Repayment 5.5%pa								$ 8,243	$ 25,524	$ 23,435	$ 23,528
Shortfall/Surplus								$ 11,976	-$ 4,638	-$ 1,860	-$ 1,241
LVR								28%	77%	75%	73%
PROPERTY 5 (Duplex)											
TDC 2 Duplex Units									$ 1,037,272		
Equity @ 30%									$ 311,182		
Loan @ 70%									$ 726,090		
End Value									$ 1,244,726		
Sell 1 Unit										$ 550,169	
Value of holding unit										$ 622,363	$ 541,034
Loan after sale										$ 175,921	$ 164,022
Equity after sale										$ 448,442	$ 477,012
Gross Rent pa										$ 26,969	$ 27,778
Nett Rent										$ 21,575	$ 22,223
Repayment 5.5%pa										$ 9,676	$ 9,021
Shortfall/Surplus										$ 11,900	$ 13,201
LVR										28%	26%

Total Value @ Year 10	
Initial equity	$ 240,000
Property values	$ 3,212,638
Loans	$ 1,868,340
LVR	58%
Equity position	$ 1,344,298
Return on equity	560%
Nett Rent	$ 111,371
Loan repayments	$ 94,237
Surplus	$ 17,134

	Current	Year 1	Year 2	Year 3	Year 4	Year 5	Year 6	Year 7	Year 8	Year 9	Year 10
PROPERTY 1 (Duplex)											
TDC 2 Duplex Units	$ 800,000										
Equity @ 30%	$ 240,000										
Loan @ 70%	$ 560,000										
End Value	$ 960,000										
Sell 1 Unit		$ 424,320									
Value of holding unit		$ 480,000	$ 495,840	$ 512,203	$ 529,105	$ 546,566	$ 564,603	$ 583,234	$ 602,481	$ 622,363	$ 642,901
Loan after sale		$ 135,580	$ 381,925	$ 383,833	$ 385,268	$ 386,189	$ 386,551	$ 386,305	$ 385,402	$ 383,786	$ 381,400
Equity after sale		$ 288,640	$ 113,915	$ 128,370	$ 143,838	$ 160,377	$ 178,052	$ 196,929	$ 217,079	$ 238,577	$ 281,501
Gross Rent pa		$ 20,800	$ 21,486	$ 22,195	$ 22,928	$ 23,685	$ 24,466	$ 25,273	$ 26,108	$ 26,999	$ 27,859
Nett Rent		$ 18,640	$ 17,189	$ 17,756	$ 18,342	$ 18,948	$ 19,573	$ 20,219	$ 20,886	$ 21,575	$ 22,287

	C1	C2	C3	C4	C5	C6	C7	C8	C9	C10
Repayment 5.5%pa	$ 8,784	$ 10,096	$ 19,192	$ 19,263	$ 19,309	$ 19,328	$ 19,315	$ 19,270	$ 19,189	$ 19,070
Shortfall/Surplus	$ 9,856	-$ 1,907	-$ 1,435	-$ 921	-$ 362	$ 245	$ 904	$ 1,616	$ 2,386	$ 3,217
LVR	28%	77%	75%	73%	71%	68%	66%	64%	62%	59%
PROPERTY 2 (Duplex)										
TDC 2 Duplex Units		$ 853,671								
Equity @ 30%		$ 256,101								
Loan @ 70%		$ 597,570								
End Value		$ 1,024,405								
Sell 1 Unit			$ 452,787							
Value of holding unit			$ 512,203	$ 529,105	$ 546,566	$ 564,603	$ 583,234	$ 602,481	$ 622,363	$ 642,901
Loan after sale			$ 144,783	$ 407,548	$ 409,583	$ 411,115	$ 412,098	$ 412,484	$ 412,222	$ 411,258
Equity after sale			$ 367,420	$ 121,557	$ 136,982	$ 153,488	$ 171,137	$ 188,997	$ 210,141	$ 231,843
Gross Rent pa			$ 22,195	$ 22,928	$ 23,685	$ 24,466	$ 25,273	$ 26,108	$ 26,969	$ 27,859
Nett Rent			$ 17,756	$ 18,342	$ 18,948	$ 19,573	$ 20,219	$ 20,888	$ 21,575	$ 22,287
Repayment 5.5%pa			$ 7,239	$ 20,377	$ 20,479	$ 20,556	$ 20,605	$ 20,624	$ 20,611	$ 20,563
Shortfall/Surplus			$ 10,517	-$ 2,035	-$ 1,532	-$ 983	-$ 386	$ 262	$ 964	$ 1,724
LVR			28%	77%	75%	73%	71%	68%	66%	64%
PROPERTY 3 (Duplex)										
TDC 2 Duplex Units				$ 910,943						
Equity @ 30%				$ 273,283						
Loan @ 70%				$ 637,660						
End Value				$ 1,093,132						
Sell 1 Unit					$ 483,164					
Value of holding unit					$ 546,566	$ 564,603	$ 583,234	$ 602,481	$ 622,363	$ 642,901
Loan after sale					$ 154,496	$ 435,663	$ 437,873	$ 439,548	$ 440,639	$ 441,096
Equity after sale					$ 392,070	$ 128,940	$ 145,361	$ 162,933	$ 181,724	$ 201,805
Gross Rent pa					$ 23,685	$ 24,466	$ 25,273	$ 26,108	$ 26,969	$ 27,859
Nett Rent					$ 18,948	$ 19,573	$ 20,219	$ 20,888	$ 21,575	$ 22,287
Repayment 5.5%pa					$ 8,497	$ 21,783	$ 21,894	$ 21,977	$ 22,032	$ 22,055
Shortfall/Surplus					$ 10,450	-$ 2,210	-$ 1,675	-$ 1,091	-$ 457	$ 232.43
LVR					28%	77%	75%	73%	71%	69%
PROPERTY 4 (Duplex)										
TDC 2 Duplex Units						$ 972,057				
Equity @ 30%						$ 291,617				
Loan @ 70%						$ 680,440				
End Value						$ 1,166,469				
Sell 1 Unit							$ 515,579			
Value of holding unit							$ 583,234	$ 602,481	$ 622,363	$ 642,901
Loan after sale							$ 164,861	$ 464,067	$ 468,704	$ 470,564
Equity after sale							$ 418,374	$ 138,414	$ 153,659	$ 172,337
Gross Rent pa							$ 25,273	$ 26,108	$ 26,969	$ 27,859
Nett Rent							$ 20,219	$ 20,888	$ 21,575	$ 22,287
Repayment 5.5%pa							$ 8,243	$ 25,524	$ 23,435	$ 23,526
Shortfall/Surplus							$ 11,976	-$ 4,638	-$ 1,860	-$ 1,241
LVR							28%	77%	75%	73%
PROPERTY 5 (Duplex)										
TDC 2 Duplex Units								$ 1,037,272		
Equity @ 30%								$ 311,182		
Loan @ 70%								$ 726,090		
End Value								$ 1,244,726		
Sell 1 Unit									$ 550,169	
Value of holding unit									$ 622,363	$ 641,034
Loan after sale									$ 175,921	$ 184,022
Equity after sale									$ 446,442	$ 477,012
Gross Rent pa									$ 26,969	$ 27,778
Nett Rent									$ 21,575	$ 22,223
Repayment 5.5%pa									$ 9,676	$ 9,021
Shortfall/Surplus									$ 11,900	$ 13,201
LVR									28%	26%

Total Value @ Year 10

Initial equity	$ 240,000
Property values	$ 3,212,638
Loans	$ 1,868,340
LVR	58%
Equity position	$ 1,344,298
Return on equity	560%
Nett Rent	$ 111,371
Loan repayments	$ 94,237
Surplus	$ 17,134

CHAPTER 5

THE DISCOUNT INVESTMENT STRATEGY

INTRODUCTION

Chapter 4 focused on how to fast track a passive income through real estate development. While this strategy has significant benefits, there are risks to consider as part of the process. For those who are risk-averse or do not have the experience due to personal circumstances, there are strategies available through smart investment. For those who fit into this profile, the alternative is to source discounted or 'wholesale' investment real estate and add them to an income producing portfolio using the similar strategy as outlined in the previous chapter.

While the discounted investment strategy will not fast track your passive income portfolio as rapidly as the development strategy, the method is far better than purchasing real estate at retail prices. Purchasing retail property and waiting for its value to increase, at least with inflation, will take several years before you will be in the position to buy another, as it will take some time before your equity position increases.

The strategy of discounted real estate described in this chapter is not the North American version of 'Real Estate Wholesaling' where a house is purchased well below market value and then sold to another party at retail allowing the wholesaler to pocket the difference. What is being described is how to build a real estate portfolio through buying discounted property, holding onto the asset and speeding up the process of generating passive income. One method is to buy an existing property at a discount (that is if you can find them) or buy an existing building in a great location and add value to it through several strategies such as renovation or conversion. The alternative method is to purchase newly constructed buildings from developers, syndication or a property trust.

Finding discounted real estate in a good location with excellent rental potential is easier said than done. Finding genuinely discounted opportunities amongst the thousands of real estate properties on the market is never an easy task. Even when you find one, how can you be sure that the opportunity is a decent one? This chapter provides you with essential tips that you can use during your search for discounted investment properties.

THE PROCESS AND STRATEGY

Before embarking on a discount real estate buying spree, it is worthwhile sitting back and analysing your financial position and potential borrowings, and then working out a plan on how you are going to fast track your passive income portfolio through the discount buying method. Below are some steps that will guide you through the process.

1. **Evaluate your finances**
   This is a simple exercise where you can work out your expenses and liabilities and then offset them against your total income and assets. This will give you an indication of how much money you have available to invest.

2. **Get pre-approval from a lender**
   Pre-approval is an indication from a lender that they will grant you a loan for a certain amount based on your current financial position. While neither you nor the lender is obligated to follow through with the pre-approved loan, it does give you the confidence that you can negotiate a better discount on a property of interest.

3. **Select your preferred asset class**
   Decide upon which asset class that you would like to invest in, residential, commercial or industrial? This will depend on your knowledge and expertise in the selected asset class. Most investors would look at residential as it is easier to understand but it may be worthwhile to consider commercial, as there can be better returns to be made over residential.

4. **Establish a plan of action**
   To achieve a passive income, you should be planning your goals. In accomplishing these goals, you must first articulate what they are, and more importantly, you need to set yourself certain milestones and give yourself the time to achieve them.

5. **Research the market**
   It is essential to do your research in advance. Select an area in which you would to purchase a property and then look at properties that are under-priced relative to the market values in that area. Alternatively, investigate areas of potential growth and look for discounted opportunities from developers or properties where you can add value.

6. **Do your due diligence**
   Once you have found a property of interest, you should undertake due diligence to ensure that your purchase fits into your goals and direction that you have established. Your due diligence should include the motivation of the seller, the suburb profile, any valuations, potential rental income and the long term forecast growth.

TYPES OF DISCOUNTED REAL ESTATE

When looking at the various types of discount real estate opportunities, you need to assess your time and resources and whether you want to be actively or passively engaged in your investing. These roles are evaluated below:

- **Active investing**

  Active real estate investing needs a great deal of personal time and knowledge and hands-on management. You can work part-time or full-time, depending on the nature, type and number of properties in your portfolio. If this is the path you have chosen, then it is advisable to improve your real estate knowledge and negotiation skills to enhance the value of your portfolio. The type of discounted real estate which requires active participation include:

  – Distressed properties
  – Renovations
  – Conversions

- **Passive Real Estate Investing**

  For those investors who do not have the time but still want to build a real estate portfolio that does not require hands-on management, a passive approach can be undertaken. Under this form of investing, the passive partner typically provides only capital and allows professionals to take on the responsibilities of finding and managing discount opportunities. Types of opportunities that would fall under this category include:

  – Syndications
  – Developers
  – Joint ventures
  – Property Trust

  A breakdown of each type is described in more detail under its specific heading as each one has its unique approach and different involvement of the investor.

DISTRESSED REAL ESTATE

'Distressed real estate' describes existing residential or commercial properties that can no longer be maintained by the current owner, either physically or financially. Most distressed real estate are buildings in which an owner has been unable to keep up with mortgage obligations and are therefore at risk of falling into liquidation. In some cases, these properties are found to be in poor condition due to neglect, and the owner no longer has the interest to maintain it, or there is a dispute between the owners.

How to find distressed real estate

Finding distressed buildings whether residential or commercial it is not easy as there are many others searching for these opportunities as well. To improve your success, consider the following:

- *Find a knowledgeable agent*

  Distressed properties can have a wide range of unique conditions, so it's good to deal with a professional agent who is licensed to buy, sell and lease properties. As agents, they are bound to know about distressed properties as well.

- **Look for neglected properties**

  Driving around the location of interest, you will invariably find a property in neglect. Often a neglected property means that the owner has given up trying to maintain the property or is in some other problem. It may not necessarily be financial but may result from a family or partner dispute. Find out who owns the property and contact the decision makers. You may be surprised what you will find, as they could be a motivated seller willing to part ways with the home at a discount.

- **Online sources**

  With modern technology, it is no surprise that there are now websites dedicated to listing distressed properties. However, they do not always list all such properties and may be limited to their listings. Currently, the sources in Australia are Trovit, Mitula, Real Estate Investar, NMD Data, Select Property Invest and SQM Research. Some of them require you to subscribe as a member to access these listings.

- **Networking**

  Staying connected with a network of real estate industry professionals throughout your investment career will increase your odds of finding great investing opportunities. Also, work with brokers and lenders as part of a networking strategy.

- **Lenders and finance brokers**

  Many investors go through traditional financing to fund their investment real estate deals, while others may use finance brokers. Talk to them as they may know of some properties in distress. Besides, they could assist you in financing the property.

- **Direct mail campaigns**

  Whether you identify distressed properties for sale online or through your network contacts, you will still need a strategy for targeting the properties you have found. Direct mail or meeting the seller is an effective way to make a compelling offer directly to the seller.

Many distressed properties could be left empty for some time or have been left with damage, so be prepared to budget for repair work. It is wise to get some quotes from a builder before making an offer as there could be significant defects. These distressed properties are sold 'as-is,' and may need extensive repairs requiring a lot of your time to manage the works and then to find a tenant. However, the benefit of increased equity and rental opportunity can be worth it.

RENOVATIONS

Renovating an existing building is an active property strategy, and gives the possibility of creating immediate growth in a property rather than a passive approach that requires patience for capital growth. Renovating is a fast-track solution to achieving that goal by making value-adding cosmetic or structural changes to a property.

The aim of any renovation is to improve the functional space and its visual appeal within a property. The basic principle of renovation is to make a property look new again and in doing this, noticeably add value without adding too much cost. As a guide, the aim is to at least double or ideally triple for every dollar spent on a renovation.

Residential Renovations

The approach to renovating a residential property is a little different from that of a commercial property, which is described later in this chapter. Below are some pointers in renovating a residential building.

- ***Attend to the exterior of the building***

  The street front of the building has a substantial impact on people's impression and often governs whether they like or dislike the building. Simple aesthetic improvements such as painting the exterior, mowing the lawn, trimming the hedges or trees or replacing the mailbox can make an enormous difference.

- **Paint the interior**

  A new coat of paint goes a long way in adding value to a property. It is the most economical and one of the easiest, fastest and highest value drivers of a property.

- **Update the kitchen**

  The kitchen is the heart of any home, so it is worthwhile investing some money in this area to ensure a higher return on investment.

- **Update the wet areas**

  Bathrooms, laundry and toilets are the second most important areas in a home and if renovated well can significantly improve the value of a property.

- **Create an open-plan living**

  Older homes had a separate room for every function, but today people prefer open-plan living made up of the kitchen, dining and living rooms. Removing non-load bearing walls will make a significant difference at minimal cost.

- **Create an entertaining outdoor area**

  Australians love entertaining so adding an entertaining outdoor area with a roof cover that can be used all year round will add value to a property.

- **Improve the landscaping**

  Landscaping can make a significant difference to the value of a home. You can either do it yourself or get a landscaper to provide a quote to supply, install and clean up.

- **Add a granny flat**

  A stand-alone granny flat strategically positioned at the rear of a property can provide additional income. With modular technology, a new granny flat can be dropped into the back yard and connected to utilities within a short time frame.

- **Add a furniture package**

  This will depend on the location of the property and the type of tenants you would like to attract. Travelling executives, contract workers and students usually do not have their own furniture so adding a furniture package can improve your rental return.

Commercial Renovations

If you own commercial real estate, the best way to increase its value is through rent increases and decreasing operating expenses. Below are some tips in achieving this.

- **Make improvements**

  For office buildings, shopping centres and industrial buildings, cosmetic enhancements can make a big difference to their value and increase the amount of rent you can charge. Give the exterior a makeover, improve the entrance lobby, or repave the parking area to enhance the property.

- **Update the signage**

  With commercial buildings, signage plays an essential part in the marketing of your tenant's business. Good signage should attract traffic from the outside.

- **Improve security**

  With escalating crime rates, security of commercial premises plays an important part. Features such as alarm systems, gates, and shutters can increase property value by making the property more attractive to tenants and lowering your insurance premium.

- **Increase rents**

  With the changes recommended above, you should review the current market to determine the going market rent. You can check rental rates or by contacting a local property manager or leasing company in your area. If the rent is below the market for your type of property, increase the rent when you have the opportunity – especially when a lease expires.

- ### *Decrease operating expenses*

  You should review all your operating expenses carefully, analyse them and compare each expense with those of your other properties. Even though the commercial tenant pays most of these costs, it will help their bottom line and take longer leases.

- ### *Divide your tenancies*

  If you own a large building, consider breaking the spaces into smaller areas using lightweight partitions. This will allow you to find more tenants and increase the rent per square metre. It is better to have 50% of your building leased than it being 100% vacant.

CONVERSIONS

A real estate conversion means changing the current use of a property to another. For example, several older industrial or office buildings have been converted to residential apartments. However, this is a costly exercise and it involves development risks. The conversions described under this section are examples where the use of an existing building is changed with minor cost and therefore lower risk for an investor.

Residential to commercial office

With zoning regulations changing in many older suburbs, we see many homes along busy highways changed to mixed-use. This means that the house can be used either as a home or for some other commercial use. Purchasing a home on a busy highway which falls under mixed-use zoning and renting it out as a family home will attract low rent due to high traffic volume. However, by renting it out as an office, a higher rent can be charged with the additional advantage of the commercial tenants paying all outgoings.

For example, if you purchase a 250 sqm home on a busy road for $550,000 it may only attract $500 per week, plus outgoings such as rates and land taxes will be your responsibility. However, if you spend another $50,000 on cosmetic changes you could attract a commercial tenant that will pay an annual rent of $75,000 (250sqm x $300 per sqm). Based on a capitalisation rate of, say

7%, your new value would be estimated just over $1 million. This shows an increase in equity of $400,000 ($1 million less $550,000 less $50,000).

Convert a home for students

If you have a rented home within a certain radius of a university or college, it is worthwhile considering renting the house to students instead of a family. An average house near a university can yield 20 to 30% higher rents than the same house further away. These rental properties can hold their value for years while generating a higher rental income.

With millions of new students, including overseas students, entering universities across the country every year, this represents an opportunity for real estate investors. Renting to students offers immense benefits for investors looking to expand their investment portfolio, capitalise on passive income opportunities, and create a retirement strategy.

So which properties are more acceptable to students? A property with a minimum of three bedrooms and large open living lounge, kitchen and dining will appeal to students. More than one toilet or bathroom will also be a strong selling point, as will choosing a location within 30 minutes walking distance from the university campus. It's also worth noting that most students will expect properties to be fully furnished.

While the increased rental income is welcoming it does come with certain drawbacks. Properties rented to students tend to suffer more wear and tear, and as a result, you are likely to spend more money on maintenance at the end of a tenancy than you would with a traditional let. Also, you may only be receiving 11 months rental as there is the extended holiday period such as Christmas where the students return home to their families. However, this should be factored in your rental package.

Shared home

A shared home is different from a boarding house and can be defined as where two or more tenants rent a single property. The benefit of this model is that higher rent can be achieved, but there would be more time and paperwork involved. There are two types of share house leases, namely sub-letting and co-tenant.

- ***Sub-letting***

  With a sub-letting structure, one tenant who is called the head-tenant takes out the head-lease and then sub-leases the property to other tenants. In terms of the lease, the head-tenant must comply with the following:
  1. must live at the property
  2. must have the owner's approval
  3. is responsible to the owner for the rental bond and the rent payments.

  As a property owner, you cannot unreasonably deny permission for the head-tenant to sub-let. In terms of the Residential Tenancy Act 1997, the Residential Tenancy Commissioner cannot help a sub-tenant where there is a dispute. Instead, any conflicts between a head-tenant and a sub-tenant remain between the two parties.

- ***Co-tenant***

  Under this structure, two or more tenants rent the property with all names appearing on the lease and condition report. Only one bond is paid for the property which is shared between amongst each tenant. If anyone of the tenants leaves the house, they should contact the owner to make sure their name is removed from the lease. Any new tenant replacing the outgoing tenant needs to have the owner's permission to move in and should have their name added to the lease contract. The ingoing tenant is then jointly responsible for the property with the other tenants, to return it to the condition it was in at the beginning of the tenancy.

Airbnb

If you have a rented home near a tourist location or inner-city area, you may want to consider being an Airbnb host that allows you to rent out your home on a nightly basis in a similar way to a hotel. Airbnb is an online platform which offers holidaymakers or business guest to stay at your property on a short-term basis.

Unlike traditional rentals, Airbnb allows you to rent out a portion of your home, or your entire home. Property owners earn money by renting their property by night, which can provide regular or irregular cash flow, depending on the demand of the property within its specific market.

Property owners are responsible for furnishing and maintaining the home for renters but do not require the expertise and supervision needed to run a hotel. The Airbnb platform facilitates the booking of the property and creates the contract agreement between the property owner and renter. With Airbnb managing several components of the rental process, there is not a great deal of work to be done by the property owner except cleaning between guests and ensuring the needs of guests are catered for.

Being an Airbnb host means you can obtain a higher overall income compared to a standard residential rental income. By charging per night, the bookings may fluctuate, but hosts can still make more cash if they know how to manage and promote their home correctly.

While Airbnb rentals can be a lucrative proposition, you need to check with your local council if the zoning of your property allows short-term accommodation. In some parts of Australia, certain local council have the power to ban short-term rentals. Therefore, ensure that you have everything legally cleared before becoming an Airbnb host.

DEVELOPMENT SYNDICATES

If you are a passive investor who does not have the time, or if you are too busy in another business or profession to be actively engaged in any of the strategies outlined above, there are alternative investment avenues. One avenue is to become a member of a development syndicate where a professional development manager with a good track record has been appointed.

As a member investor, you do not have to be involved in the day-to-day management of the project as a professional manager will be responsible who is paid a fee for the services provided. In most property development syndications, investors pay for their share of development at cost and without a developer's profit margin. In other words, at the completion of the project you secure your investment property at a wholesale price.

Syndication Structure

There are several syndication structures available to investors with the more popular ones usually structured through a shareholding within a company. However, this structure does not give you total control or ownership of a specific property. The alternative structure that is available is through a Bare Trust structure.

A bare trust syndication structure (shown in Figure 5.1) may be used when development is initiated by a developer or by a group with a common interest in developing a property jointly. These apply mainly to residential developments. This structure could also apply to a commercial property if the project involves strata units such as offices, showrooms or small factory warehouses. The composition works as follows:

- **The Bare Trust**

  A bare trust is used where the trustee holds property of and on behalf of the beneficiary (syndicate members). In this case, the trustee has no discretion and no active duties other than to transfer the property to the beneficiary when requested by the beneficiary. In the case of a syndicated property development, the bare trust will purchase the land and with the help of an appointed manager will develop the strata units, whether residential or commercial.

- **The Trustee**

  The trustee is purely a nominee of the beneficiaries. Legally, a bare trust is a 'trust under which the trustee or trustees' hold property without any specific interest in the trust, other than having the legal title as trustee. The trustee does not have a duty or further duty to perform, except to convey it upon demand to the beneficiaries or as directed by them.

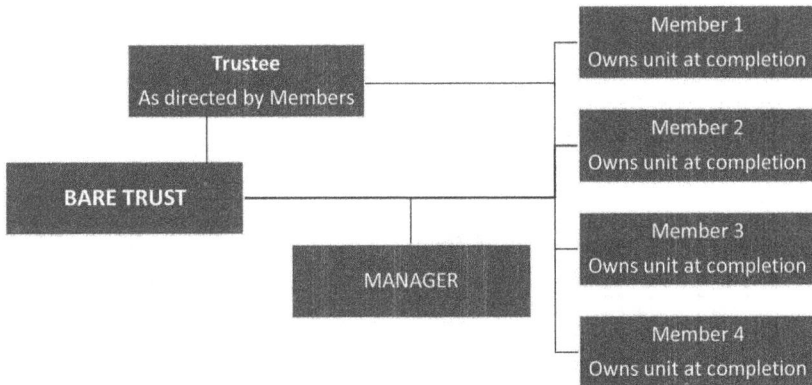

Figure 5.1 Structure of a typical syndicate using a bare trust

- **Members**

  The syndicate members are the beneficiaries who will direct the bare trust. These members will place the initial funds into the bare trust to purchase the land. The bare trust will borrow funds to construct the buildings. On completion, each member will pay for their strata unit and take transfer after paying out their portion of the construction debt within the bare trust.

- **Manager**

  The manager under a bare trust arrangement, an independent development manager, is appointed by the syndicate members and contracted to provide development services for a fee. Selecting an independent development manager for a bare trust structure avoids conflict between syndicate members as there could be some members who are more dominant than others which could lead to disagreements.

Benefits of Syndicated Property

- *Get into the market faster*

  The benefit of a property syndicate is the pooling together of investors' resources to develop an investment property that they probably could not do on their own. It allows investors to get into the real estate market quicker.

- **Build your portfolio faster**

  With a bare trust syndicate, you will own a newly built property at the wholesale price which creates instant equity which allows you invest in other syndicates which means that you can build your real estate portfolio much faster.

- **Freedom from management**

  Managing syndicated development takes considerable expertise and time. A syndicate run by a professional manager has the advantage that it frees investors from the task of day-to-day management. Investors also benefit from the manager's expertise in property matters.

- **Assurance**

  A syndicate develops or owns a specific property or a limited number of properties for a set period. There may also be restrictions on the sale of any existing properties by the syndicate. As such, the attributes of the investment are much more certain than a listed property trust where a portfolio can change significantly from year to year.

- **Security of Capital**

  Depending on the structure of each syndicate, your name or the name of an approved trustee will appear on the certificate of title and your interest will be held according to the proportion of capital invested by you against that of other investors in the property. You will, therefore, have the security of tenure with freehold title, as you would ordinarily hold with any other real estate investment.

- **Tax benefits**

  By owning a new building through a syndicate, there are significant tax benefits from stamp duty being applicable on the land only and not the built form to depreciation allowances on a new building rather than an older one.

The Risks with Syndicated Property

- *Less control over your investment*

  With the property syndicate, you are one small part of a larger pool, which means you have a lot less control over your investment during the development stage.

- *Liquidity*

  An investment in a syndicate is an investment in property, not units or shares. Accordingly, it suffers from the limitations of real estate investment. The main weakness is that it is not liquid.

- *Lack of management skills*

  While many syndicate managers are well schooled in the aspects of investment and development, property analysis and acquisition, not all may possess the necessary management skills. As opposed to a simple transaction, syndication is a medium- to long-term commitment.

- *Clarity of sponsor compensation*

  One of the primary reasons that developers sponsor syndications is the potential for profit. However, no law dictates the fee-splitting arrangement between the sponsor and the investors in private offerings, and there are as many different arrangements as there are syndications.

DEVELOPERS

This strategy is to buy a residential property off-plan at a discounted price during the initial stage of a developer's new project launch. Developers, especially during the capital raising or the pre-selling stage of residential development such as apartments, are either seeking equity investors or pre-selling some of their units with a substantial discount to cover the pre-condition of construction debt required by a lender.

Astute investors know when to take advantage of these opportunities. There are two stages where one can invest: (a) when the developer is looking for seed capital to initiate a project and would offer a heavily discounted unit to investors and (b) when the developer is looking to ramp up their pre-sales before the official launch of the project. The discount will be higher during the seed stage and less during the second stage. However, this will depend on the investor's negotiation at each stage.

This strategy carries a higher degree of risk, and it is imperative that you should undertake thorough due diligence before parting with any of your investment money. Bear in mind that the developer has several hurdles to jump before the project becomes bankable. These hurdles or risks include (a) securing development approval and (b) achieving 100% or more pre-sales over the loan before the lender would advance any construction funding. The construction loan is generally around 70% of the total development cost or 60% of the completion value.

As with any real estate investment, particularly if you are going to lease the property when completed, it is vital that you do your due diligence thoroughly. If you fail to research the development, surrounding area and the potential demand for a rental property before you invest, you could leave yourself in a very vulnerable position financially. So, what things should you consider before buying a property off-plan? The due diligence exercise includes the following:

- **Check the developer's capability**

  The developer's credentials are vitally important. What is their track record, have you seen the quality of their projects? Have you spoken to previous buyers or investors? Have you talked to other agents and asked what they thought of the project and the developer? There will always be both positive and negative comments, but if there are too many negatives then it's probably best to walk away.

- **Research the location**

  Location is a critical factor in evaluating the potential of the proposed development. Is the precinct or suburb being regenerated? How is the local economy performing? What are the current and projected rental values? Is the necessary infrastructure in place? How close is the development to transport links, retail shops, restaurants, parks and schools?

- **Know your rental market**

  If you are planning to lease the property on completion, you should establish the target market for the type of property you are planning to invest in. Talk to a local property manager operating in the area to get an understanding of the demand and where this demand is coming from. It is also wise to find out the rental competition close by as this could affect future rents in the area with new product coming into the market.

- **Find out the retail price in the area**

  It would help if you also researched what similar properties in the area are being sold for, including the sale price of new developments by other developers. This will give you an indication of the possible increase in equity you could expect when the developer's new project is completed. However, note that the market could change when the new building is ready for occupation as there could be an oversupply for the area which will bring the prices down.

- **The property**

  Carefully study the plans of the unit you intend investing in plus the communal facilities within the new development. Study the details, floor area and specifications of the units on offer. If you are leasing upon completion, will the property be suitable for the target market? Also, find out what extra charges there will be such as levies and strata management fees as these costs cannot be recouped from your tenants.

- **Evaluate the developer's team**

  The developer is only as good as the team that is employed on the new development. This ranges from professional consultants to the contracted building company. The design of the building must be both functional and aesthetically pleasing so ensure that the developer is employing well-qualified architects. Also, find out the type of builder that will be employed on the project and check their capability and track record.

Benefits of buying directly from the developer

- *Discounted Price*

  The discount price has been described earlier but remember the properties generally take a few years to construct so the price could appreciate with inflation as well.

- *Customisation*

  You may be a position to select different colours, finishes and layouts which the developer may be able to incorporate. However, when it comes to making any custom changes, bear the future tenant in mind and not yourself unless you intend moving in at some future date.

- *Tax benefits*

  As the property is being purchased for investment purposes, you will be able to claim depreciation on your tax for items including fixtures and fittings. It is recommended that you consult your accountant to find out whether you are eligible.

- *Stamp Duty Concessions*

  Several states offer stamp duty concessions to purchasers of new properties. It will be worthwhile investing these concessions in your state.

Risks of buying directly from a developer

- *Lack of certainty*

  Investing in a property 'on paper' carries significant risk compared to viewing and making a choice on a completed product. The finished product may not live up to your expectations in terms of the visual representations, and the final quality may not be up to your expectations.

- *Delays*

  The proposed completion date for a building is generally an estimate, and there can be delays. Delays could the lack or tradespeople or supply of material, union strikes or inclement weather. Therefore, the contractor that the developer will be using is essential. Efficient builders normally complete projects on time.

- *Developer risk* on some significant developments, cash-flow can be an issue, and there is a risk of developers going bankrupt making them unable to complete the project. As an early investor you could potentially lose your money should the developer declare bankruptcy.

JOINT VENTURES

As a passive investor looking for an opportunity to build your asset portfolio, another strategy is to find a joint venture partner such as a developer or a builder. These parties are always looking for investors to get their projects off the ground.

Joint ventures come in various shapes and forms. In real estate, a joint venture can be defined as a temporary or short-term partnership for a specific project. The term joint venture is used to describe several different legal relationships, although there is no statutory definition of the term. Joint ventures are not separate legal entities. Hence, the relationship between joint venture parties is governed by the terms of the agreement between them, as well as by the general law. There are three common types of joint ventures:

1. *Incorporated joint venture.*
   A company is established to conduct the business, with the joint venture partners being shareholders in the company.
2. *Unit Trust*
   The joint venture partners are the unit-holders. Again, the tax treatment is the same as for any unit trust.
3. *Unincorporated joint venture*
   The joint venture partners enter into a contract to establish their legal rights and obligations concerning the business venture.

Under this strategy, if you aim to have a property or a few in your portfolio, you may consider structuring either an incorporated or unincorporated joint venture with the developer or builder. A joint venture agreement must be structured the roles and responsibilities of each party and sharing of the profits or the take out of specific properties within the development. Most real estate developments undertaken are generally 'one-off' projects, so a joint venture structure is ideal as it does not create a long-term business relationship which comes with other obligations.

Partnership vs Joint Venture

Under the current law in Australia, the arrangement of a joint venture, as opposed to a partnership, is where:

- The purpose is to do no more than producing a product to be shared by the parties;
- There is no power under the arrangement for any of the parties to legally bind the others; and
- All parties have power under the agreement to assign their interest in the joint venture.

For tax purposes, it is essential that the joint venture is not seen to be carrying on a business. Therefore, a management company should be contracted who will operate the business for and on behalf of each of the joint venture parties. It is also vital that each party enter a separate agreement with the management company. Under a joint venture, the parties derive a share of the output which they will handle themselves.

The tax and legal rights and obligations of a joint venture are different from those of a partnership. It is these differences that produce advantages in using a joint venture business structure. Joint ventures that are not partnerships are not required to lodge income tax returns. Each joint venture party lodges a separate tax return and claim their deductions. This provides flexibility not available under a partnership.

Lastly, the parties under a joint venture arrangement can assign their interests to another party subject to the approval of that other party. Under a partnership any third-party assignment is considered as effectively dissolving or changing the partnership.

To ensure that a joint venture is not be construed as a partnership, you should establish a structure, prepare documentation and execute agreements ensuring that:

a. Each joint venture party is responsible for managing with their share of the joint venture development;

b. Each joint venture party is a tenant in common of the

property in the same proportion as the legal interest of each party;

c. The project is not a partnership arrangement and that it is intended to be a joint venture;

d. Statements are made that each party is liable for their actions and liabilities and that the other party is not responsible;

e. Each joint venture party enters into a separate agreement with the management company; and

f. That the management company enters into separate contracts with third parties as agents for each of the joint venturers separately.

If these guidelines are followed, joint ventures can prove to be a flexible, clean and straightforward tax option. It is worthwhile seeking professional advice from an accountant before an agreement is formally executed.

Joint Venture Development Structures

Below are some samples of joint venture structures where you are the passive investor and the other party is a developer. It could also apply where the other party is a builder but with slight variations.

- ### *Traditional Joint Venture*

  The traditional joint ventures are similarly used in the '70s and '80s. The limited partnership agreement is still the most popular ownership structure today. However, limited liability companies are also standard. Before entering into a contract, all legal arrangements should be investigated and analysed for liability management and tax issues.

  Advantages
  – Each party earns development profit pro rata based on equity contributed;
  – Each party shares in any cost savings on a pro rata basis;
  – As an owner you have rights and can participate in any decision making;

– Any losses are shared on a pro rata basis, and the developer has 'skin in the game' as well;

– The responsibly of any debt required for the project is shared between the parties;

– There is more equity in the project which makes the chances of securing funding easier.

Disadvantages

– Potential for disagreements between parties during the development and construction phases;

– The provision of personal guarantees may be required. If so ensure that the personal guarantees are not defined jointly and severally but on a pro rata basis;

– The developer party may run into financial difficulty, and it will be your responsibility to finish off the project;

– Partnership documentation is complicated and usually more expensive and more time-consuming.

- **Fee Development structure**

 Under this structure, the developer is paid a development management fee for providing his development expertise. In a fee development transaction, the philosophy is for you to own the property during the entire construction period and for the developer to manage the project from initiation to completion. You may also consider providing the developer with a performance fee which means that if he or she achieves minimum targeted return, the surplus profit is shared between the parties.

Advantages

– It frees you from day to day running and managing the development;

– You have a contracted a developer with experience managing the project and any profit made is all yours;

– You can sell some of the units and hold the balance, therefore, reducing the residual debt;

– The land is under your name, so any units you hold after completion do not attract additional stamp duty.

Disadvantages

– You are relying on the development management expertise to a developer, and if he or she mismanages the project you could lose money;

– You are liable for any debt such as a construction loan and may have to provide personal guarantees;

– You carry the development risk, and any failure on the builder's part or delays will be at your cost.

- **Agreement to purchase upon completion**

This structure carries the least risk as an investor. You provide an undertaking with certain pre-agreed-upon conditions to acquire a unit of more of a development form the developer with an agreed price which is discounted to the market value. Of course, you may not get the same discount as per the previous two structures as the developer is carrying the development and financial risks of the project.

Advantages

– You are purchasing a property or properties at a discounted price;

– You are not carrying and development or financial risk;

– It will assist the developer to secure development funding;

– You do not have to provide any personal guarantees for any debt during the development stage.

Disadvantages

– The discount on the properties will be less;

– You may have to pay a deposit, and this could be at-risk should the developer run into financial difficulties;

– You are committed to purchasing the property and should there be a delay in completion, you may miss out on other investment opportunities.

CONCLUSION

In addition to the strategies described in this chapter, there are other strategies by which you can invest in property at a discount or below-market value. These are property trust, either unlisted or listed – also known as a REIT. However, under this structure you are a unitholder or hold shares in property or multiple properties with other investors, which defeats the purpose of holding a real estate portfolio which is totally in your control.

As pointed out earlier, the discounted investment strategy will not fast track your passive income portfolio when compared to the development strategy. However, if you are cashed up and depending on your negotiation skills, you could speed up the process in achieving your passive income goals. While most of the strategies explained under this chapter are based on residential development, the same approach could be applied to commercial investment opportunities.

CHAPTER 6

FINANCING YOUR PORTFOLIO

INTRODUCTION

When financing a 'develop and hold' real estate portfolio you require will require different levels of funding for the various stages of a project, to cover (a) the purchase and acquisition of land, development application and pre-construction costs; (b) a construction loan to cover the building of a project; and (c) an investment loan to retain your project as a long-term investment. From a broad perspective, this financing can be split into three areas of funding: (1) equity, (2) property development finance and (3) long-term investment finance. If you decide to follow the 'develop and hold' strategy, you will need to have a good understanding of finance and what the banks look for when seeking finance for your developments.

All banks and financers look after their interest and safety first, so they will assess the level of risk involved, starting with you as an individual and your capacity to repay the loan, and then on the viability of the project itself. This means that lenders will not provide a loan based on the security of the project alone, they also want to know your experience as a developer. If you do not have the development experience, then it is crucial that you surround yourself with an experienced development team. It is essential to submit your loan application professionally, listing your professional team and a detailed feasibility study prepared by the team.

In this chapter, the three levels of funding are explained. This includes what equity is and how to raise further equity if you do not have the amount required by a bank; how you should present your project when raising property development or construction finance; and how to structure your long-term loans within your real estate portfolio?

EQUITY

For property development, most lenders would lend around 70% to 80% of total development cost, which means that you must make up the balance of 30% to 20% in the form of equity. This is generally required in cash or other types of security like your own home. With bigger projects such a four-unit residential site, the funding needed is more than a single dwelling, which requires a larger amount of equity. Unless they have plenty of cash, most developers do not always have the equity for larger developments and will look for other equity sources. Additional equity can be raised by way of (1) extra cash from other parties (2) through sweaty equity or (3) mezzanine finance. Outlined below are the three avenues to raising the required equity.

1. Additional cash equity

* ***Bring in an investor partner.***

  If you need additional money that you cannot secure on your own, you may want to consider finding a partner with cash to cover the shortfall. You will in all probability have to share up to half the profits or more, but remember that half profits are better than none at all. If you are serious about developing property, you should begin to cultivate partner relationships, as there will always be an opportunity where you find yourself to be financially stretched. Many people have substantial amounts of money in savings accounts earning low interest. Your accountant or attorney could be approached, as they will know of people or clients who have such savings and are looking for a better return on their money. If you can prove to them that your development will bring higher yields, you will have a number of interested people.

  While it is easy to convince people to become partners these friendships can always lead to problems if some basic rules are not adhered to. Stick to the following principles, and you will have fewer problems down the track.

  – Choose partners very carefully;
  – Form partnerships only if you have to;
  – Define the role of each partner early;

– Define early how the profits are to be split;

– Reduce the fear of your partner;

– Maintain control of the partnership;

– Retain a partnership with one property at a time; and

– Work resolutions if the partnership has to dissolve.

- **Negotiate a joint venture**

Another source of funding a project can be through a joint venture. Joint ventures are usually seen as short-term arrangements set up for specific projects. Basically, it is a short-term partnership when parties agree to pool their skills and financial resources and share the agreed profits at the end of a specific project. Joint ventures are not uncommon in larger scale projects or where an out of town developer forms a temporary partnership with a local developer who knows the local property market.

In some instances, joint ventures are created where a specialist developer provides his expertise, and other provides the land. The joint parties approach a lending institution and borrow funds for the construction of the buildings using the land as equity. Therefore if you are a specialist who has expert knowledge in a specific type of development, you can approach a landowner and form a joint venture without using your cash, but still, share in the profits of the project.

Form a private syndicate

A property syndicate is a way for smaller investors to pool their funds to buy into a larger project. Syndicates can either be public or private. In raising additional equity through a syndicate, a private syndicate is the better option where a small group of individuals, perhaps friends or business associates, band together to buy and develop a property. Larger syndicates such as a unit trust structure must comply with the Managed Investments Act.

When setting up a syndicate, it is crucial that you and your co-investors agree on specific key terms. These terms can then be used to prepare the formal legal documents. Below is a list of the basic terms you will need to agree on.

1. The type of development: Specify the property to be developed or define the generic type such as residential or commercial including location, price, projected return and so on.

2. Investment strategy: Outline your strategy, for example, develop and sell, long-term hold, change of use conversion.

3. Individual roles of the syndicate members: Define the roles of the syndicate member and establish who will manage the development.

4. Capital required: Calculate early the total funds needed, the minimum contribution from each party and the shareholding according to each party's equity contribution.

5. Debt borrowing: Outline the policy on the amount of bank debt that can be leveraged that all syndicate members are comfortable with and on what terms.

6. Consultants and conflicts: Specify which consultants and advisers are to be appointed (e.g. surveyors, lettings agents, lawyers, accountants and tax advisers), and ensure that members disclose any conflicts of interest.

7. Profit sharing: Establish early in the agreement the profit sharing which is usually according to the pro rata to the amount initially invested, but weighting may be given to the party who initiated the opportunity or is managing the development.

8. Methods in dealing with defaulters: A policy should be established for parties that are not doing their job according to the terms or fulfilling their obligations. For example, if an investor fails actually to contribute their funds on time, the other investors may have the right to buy out the defaulting investor.

- **Vendor Finance**

This is a simple concept used when you are buying a development property and where the seller provides part of the total finance (deposit amount). The borrowed equity is secured by a second mortgage on the property purchased, and the terms and conditions are negotiated between the seller and purchaser. The balance of the purchase price is financed through a bank who secures a first mortgage on the property.

Not every seller will look at this type of proposal as they may require the equity to purchase another property, but for those who can finance the buyer they will benefit by:

– Obtaining a potentially higher sales price

– Obtaining a better interest rate on their money than that offered by the bank

– Getting a quicker sale

As far as the developer is concerned, he or she will benefit by:
– Obtaining a loan that does not require standard qualification

– The interest rate and terms usually are better than those offered by the bank

– The approval time is quicker than the bank

– 100% financing if the bank approves the balance of the loan

- ### Development rights

In this situation, the developer negotiates a deal with a land-owner to develop on his land. The developer provides his expertise, erects the buildings, markets the building, and the landowner is paid for the portion of the land with accrued interest when parts of the building are sold. These deals are generally not available to a novice developer as a landowner would be sceptical of the developer's experience whereas experienced developers with a track record will be looked at more favourably.

There are many advantages to the developer, namely:

– They do not have to outlay capital or borrow funds to purchase the land

– Their cash is not at risk

– There is a saving on settlement fees, stamp duty etc., that will help to reduce the development cost and increase the profit, and

– There is no pressure to build immediately, ensuring the correct planning can take place compared with borrowed funds where there is the pressure of the landholding cost.

The advantages to the landowner are:

– They do not have to wait for a buyer and pay a sales commission on the sale

– They receive a higher interest rate on their money compared to bank interest on savings

– If the developer defaults they retain the land as they still hold the title.

In formalising a development rights agreement, both parties should consider the following aspects of preventing any misunderstanding during the period of the agreement:

– The value of the land: An agreement should be reached as to the real market value of the land, and a sworn appraisal by a property valuer will help in this regard.

– The terms and conditions: A time should be set for the development to be completed, which will depend on the scale of the development, the area of the proposed project and the prevailing market conditions. The developer should aim towards a more extended period, as there may be unknown factors that may delay the project.

– The interest rate: Try and negotiate an interest rate with the landowner below standard bank rates with interest only, but more importantly try and set the start date of the interest after all approvals and outstanding conditions have been met and better still from the start of the first drawdown from the construction development loan.

– The development finance: The development finance will be for the construction of the development. These funds can be either supplied by the landowner or by another financial institution. If external funds are used there will be a mortgage over the property and the developer will be the guarantor of the loan.

– The distribution of funds after the sale: After the development has been completed and when a successful sale has been concluded, the distribution of funds should be established. The process would be paying out any money owing to the bank first, then the landowner plus their interest. The balance would be the developer's profit.

2. Creating sweat equity

Equity is defined as hard-earned cash you put towards a property, whereas 'free equity' is money that is created or built up over the period. It is this free equity that all property developers are aiming for and the more free equity you create in the early part of a project the less risk you will encounter, therefore requiring less cash for the deposit of the property. Here are some ideas in creating additional, or 'free' equity.

If you have a career in the building industry, you certainly have an advantage when it comes to property development. As an architect, builder, building estimator, engineer, bricklayer, plumber or carpenter you will be able to provide the cost of your job on your own development project for free, thus providing free equity. However, as a non-member of the building fraternity you can still generate sweat equity through the following concepts:

* *Development and project management*

    This role is generally required on larger scale projects. The role of the manager is to find the development site, negotiate the deal, coordinate the development team, strategise the marketing and so on. This takes many hours of work on the manager's part and depending on the scale of the residential project, a fee of 2 to 5% can be charged. If the project is your own, you could include the management cost as sweat equity as long as the project meets the projected investment return.

* *Skilled negotiations*

    As a good negotiator, you could generate a reasonable amount of sweat equity. Financial institutions and the building industry have guidelines, which will constitute a fair market value of goods and services. Whatever you negotiate below the fair market value can be viewed as your sweat equity. For example, if the standard total professional fees are 10% and you negotiate a total fee of 7% you have generated a 3% saving on your part. The same applies if the site you negotiate with the vendor says $1million and the actual bank valuation is $1.2million you have created equity of $200,000.

3. **Mezzanine finance**

Mezzanine finance can be defined as finance that is subordinated to debt provided by private lenders. This finance can be used when there is a shortfall of full equity required by a senior lender. For example, if the required equity of your project is $2million and your equity is $1.2million, then the $800,000 shortfall can be made up of a mezzanine loan. However, not all banks like to have a mezzanine loan as part of your financial structure, so it is essential to check with your bank if you intend using mezzanine as a shortfall of your equity. Mezzanine finance can also give rights to convert to equity or ownership in the company if the loan is not paid back in time and in full.

Mezzanine loans are often a more expensive financing source for a developer than secured debt or senior debt. The higher cost of capital associated with mezzanine financing is the result of it being an unsecured, subordinated (or junior) debt in a project's capital structure which means that in the event of default, the mezzanine finance is only repaid after all senior obligations have been satisfied. In compensation for the increased risk, mezzanine debt holders require a higher rate of return for their investment than secured or more senior lenders. This type of financing is aggressively priced with the lender seeking a return in the 15-30% range.

PROPERTY DEVELOPMENT FINANCE

Property development finance or construction finance is short-term finance which funds a development project until the buildings are completed and occupied. It predominantly finances the construction element of the project. As this is short-term funding, the approval of this finance is not based on your income but more on the viability of the project and your experience in property development. Where you have little or no experience, your lack of experience should be supported by employing qualified and experienced professionals such as an architect, development manager or project manager.

Another difference between development finance and ordinary permanent investment finance is that the interest can be capitalised. This means you do not pay interest during the construction phase of your project. However, the interest is added to the loan. Once the project reaches practical completion and occupation takes place, the settlement of sales occurs to pay out the loan. If you intend to retain an interest in your finished project, you can pay out the development loan by refinancing the property and securing a long-term investment loan. Construction loans typically come in two options with some variations:

Option 1 - Construction Permanent Loan

This loan provides construction as well as permanent financing. This eliminates the need to pay two sets of cost. If you are developing and holding your project as an investment, this loan is worth considering.

Option 2 - Construction Only Loan

This loan is only good for the construction period of the project. With this product, you can either work with the same bank or take out a permanent loan from another. Either way, you will have two sets of cost, one for the construction loan and a second one for the permanent mortgage.

Below is an outline of the process of finding the best construction loan available for your project. It also outlines the various options and items to be aware of.

1. **Research the various sources of development finance**

Banks are still the primary source of funding property developments. Unless you have a strong relationship with a specific bank and know that they will give you the best financial package, it may be worthwhile to do a bit of research on other sources of finance before committing to a specific lender. Terms and conditions can vary between lenders. Besides the major banks and since the global financial crisis, there are a number of private lenders offering finance for developers. This has given developers a wider range of choice, and they can select a lender who provides the best terms.

If you have limited knowledge on development finance and need an expert to shop around for the best offer, it is worthwhile to speak to a credible mortgage broker. As this is their daily task, they would know which lender will best suit your project and which of these would offer the best financial package. An additional advantage is that the lender generally pays their fees. Some brokers will ask for a nominal or small upfront fee together with a mandate to act your behalf. Be careful of brokers asking for a hefty upfront fee and before committing ask for references so that you know that they can deliver.

2. Prepare for your loan application.

With most application for finance, the approving party is not the person that you meet. With most banks, there is a credit committee that will evaluate the merits and risks of the project and will then decide to grant approval or not. So to ensure you have the best possible chance of securing finance for your project, you need to compile a professional document outlining the feasibility of your project. The document should demonstrate to the lender that you have researched the development site including the market the and that the numbers provided show a viable return on investment and that you have the team with experience to ensure that the project will be developed successfully.

A good finance document is one that outlines the project's objectives. The layout and content of the study will depend on the scale of your project. The bigger the project, the more information will be required. The document should cover important factors such as land cost, building costs and finance cost and the return on the development. Below is a guide of the information that can be included:

a. *Executive summary*
- Outline the broad scope of the proposal
- The amount of money required for your project

b. *The description of the property to be developed*
- The location of the property (a locality map will help)
- Property dimensions and site area (a survey plan will help)

- Lot number and title references
- Legal tenure of land (Torrens Title, Crown Tenure, Native Title etc.)
- Encumbrances such as easements and mortgages
- Existing improvements if any
- Description of adjacent properties
- Soil conditions (a report from a geotechnical engineer)
- Availability of essential services (water, sewerage, gas, electricity etc.)
- Town Planning Zoning and Regulations

c. *The description of the proposed development*
- Description of the overall project
- Description of important details of the proposal
- The site plan
- Plans (can be reduced to a scale, but must be readable)
- Elevations of the building(s)
- Sections (depends on the size and complexity of the project)
- Perspective (not necessary but sometimes helps)
- Specification of materials to be used (this can be brief and not too technical)

d. *A market research report*
- Customer profile
- Population demographics
- Competition
- Type of product
- Pricing structure – existing and future
- Promotional material required

e. *Program from inception to completion*
- A program showing the development process together with the various stages from the inception of the idea to the completion of the construction

- A graphic illustration such as a critical path analysis will help

f. The complete financial analysis

The purpose of this analysis also known as a pre-feasibility study is to establish the expected return on the development. On the income side, the following should be taken into account:

- Sales, less GST (if applicable) and sales commissions
- Rental income – which can be capitalised to show its value if sold
- On the development cost, the following should be taken into consideration:
- Land price including stamp duty and conveyancing fees
- Construction cost (allow for contingencies)
- Professional fees (all consultants used on the project)
- All government and application fees
- Rates and taxes
- Management and administration fees
- Marketing fees
- Legal and accounting
- Finance cost and bank fees
- Development interest /holding cost

The income should be higher than the development cost otherwise the development is not worth pursuing. The return is usually shown as a percentage.

g. Sensitivity analysis

As part of the above analysis, a sensitivity analysis should be brought into play giving worst and best case scenarios of the project. The main variables that should be considered are:

- Projected sales
- Projected income/rent
- Land price
- Construction cost
- Holding cost/interest

A method that can be used to assume the sensitivity of the development is to adjust the above variables by a percentage, usually 10per cent, and then recalculate the profitability.

h. A marketing strategy

- The marketing team
- Budget estimates
- Analysis of the current market situation
- A clear definition of the marketing objectives
- The position and differentiation of the development with competitors
- The market selection ensuring that there is a demand for such a development
- Setting out the plan of your marketing mix
- Identification of critical success factors

i. Outline of the developer and development company

The information required would be to prove the developer's credibility and capacity to undertake the development.

- History of the developer's previous experience
- List of directors and their curriculum vitaes
- Business and career references

j. Development team

If you are a novice developer, it will be helpful to include your development team especially your development manager who has a good track record. Other team members include:

- Project manager
- Town planner (depending on the size and complexity of the project)
- Architect / Designer
- Quantity surveyor (depending on the size and complexity of the project)
- Engineers (structural, civil, hydraulics etc.)
- Lawyers

- Accountant
- Sales and marketing team
- Building contractor if appointed

As this document may be viewed by a number of people including the management of the lending authority, your document has to look impressive and professional. Enclose all the above research and information in a bound folder, preferably an A3 format. Add colour graphics, and colour photographs as this always creates a lasting impression. If your document is quite comprehensive, a numbered table of contents at the beginning will assist the reader to find specific information.

3. The lender's approval process

In addition to the above document and depending on the lender, a formal document of the lender may be required to be completed and signed. They may also request your personal assets and liabilities and those of any of the other directors if you have a development company. In assessing your loan, the lender will look carefully and critically at the quality of the security you are offering which is the development when completed. As lenders are conservative by nature, they will be assessing the following:

- The fire sale price of the development. Should you as the developer or the development run into difficulties, this refers to the lowest price they would achieve if they had to take possession as the mortgagee and to sell it to the market.

- The location of your development. Lenders have a preference to lend against properties in areas that have a good history of strong capital growth with larger population numbers.

- The end value of the buildings you are developing. If the values are higher than the median price in your area, they see these as lower quality security as they may be more difficult to sell.

- The zoning of your security. Residentially zoned land is preferred as it is easier to sell compared with commercially zoned land.
- For larger projects, most lenders require a certain level of pre-sales or pre-leasing to minimise their risk. The percentage of the pre-sold varies but can be around 60% or the total debt cover which is generally the amount they are lending you.
- Your track record as a developer. Your experience and that of your development team will add weight to getting the approval.

Once the lender is satisfied that the project stacks up, they will instruct a valuer to undertake a valuation of the property and the completed development. Unlike the valuation for a regular property purchase, the development valuation process can be quite extensive. A professional valuer from the bank's panel of independent companies will be appointed. Their role is to assess your project thoroughly and determine whether the development will work in today's market. The valuer will go through your development proposal in detail and ensure that you have included all of your development costs. Even if you are not planning on selling the project, they will consist of selling and agents' fees in case you default and the lender needs to liquidate. Before formally approving your loan, a lender may request all or some of the following:

- A fixed priced building contract from a credible builder
- Detailed construction costings from your builder or a quantity surveyor's report
- Detailed drawdown schedule or progress payments
- Proof of pre-sales in the form of deposits that are held in trust. These deposits are generally cash to the value of 10% of the purchase price.

4. Progress payments

As the project progresses during the construction phase of your project, you or your project manager will need to keep your lender updated with the following:

- Progressive claims made by the builder
- Documented reports from your project manager
- Cash flows and any revised financial projections
- Any delays in the project
- Any amendments to the feasibility study
- Any sales that may have taken place

Before making progressive payments to the builder, the bank will require assurance that the particular stage of construction they are paying for is completed. Sometimes they even need proof that the builder has paid all of his suppliers and trades so no claim can come back to the lender. To ensure that the building stage has been completed the bank may send out its valuer or request certification from a project manager or quantity surveyor.

Before the final payment is made, the lender would want a certificate of occupancy by the council and verification from your architect or project managers that the building(s) is practically completed. Any retention money will also be held back until all maintenance items have been attended to.

LONG TERM PORTFOLIO FINANCE

When your building has been completed, and if you intend to hold part of the building as a long-term investment, you would have arranged with your development lender or another lender for your long-term finance. With a long-term investment portfolio, there are many options to consider, so it is wise to get sound advice as it could make a difference to your financial well-being. Structuring your long-term loan correctly is critical, and this should be done with the help of a trusted financial advisor such as your accountant or your financial planner. For example, it is not wise to mix your real estate investment loans with your home loan; they need to be separate so you can maximise your ongoing taxation benefits and reduce your accounting costs.

Things to consider with a permanent loan

1. *Cash flow*

    If you already have a loan on your home, a second loan on an investment property is going to have an impact on your monthly cash flow. Ensure that you are a position to service both of them by having a steady income. From the lender's perspective, the key to minimising risk as a borrower lies in your ability to earn enough income to service both loans on top of the cost of living. This not only ensures you are ready to take on a second mortgage, but it also satisfies your lender's requirements for approving the additional finances.

2. *Rental income valuation*

    With the investment properties that you are holding, it is vital to get rental valuation letters from a property manager who operates in the same area or suburb of your investment property. The lender will require this letter with the loan application. Most lenders are unlikely to take into account 100% of the rental income as part of your serviceability. They generally factor in around 50–75%, depending on the property type and its location.

3. *Contingency plan*

    If you have two loans or more, it is crucial that you have a contingency plan in case something goes wrong, and you cannot meet you're your repayments. For example, you could lose your job or have a bad tenant that delays their rental payment. Depending on your ability to save, a safety buffer could come in the form of three to six months' worth of repayments and living expenses. Also, if you are planning to have a family, there will be additional expenses which could, in turn, affect your monthly cash flow.

4. *Loan type*

   Whether you choose a fixed rate, or a variable rate loan will depend on your personal circumstances. Carefully consider both options before you decide. It has been proven that over time variable rates have been cheaper, but selecting a fixed rate loan at the right time can pay off. With a fixed rate, it makes budgeting easier as you know exactly what you will be repaying. Whereas a variable rate loan, your repayments can 'vary' as rates change. If interest rates rise above your fixed rate, you will be happy knowing you are paying less than the variable rate, but if the rate drops below your fixed rate you will be repaying more than the variable rate. If there is a chance that you might sell a building in the near future it is best to avoid a fixed rate on that particular loan, as the exit fees or break fees charged to get out of the loan will more than cancel out any savings you would have made.

5. *Assessing your borrowing capacity*

   Similar to a home loan application, your investment loan is assessed on your overall position in relation to your income against expenses, and assets against liabilities. This means that if you have a mortgage or other credit already, such as personal loans and credit cards, your borrowing limit is less than it would be if you were debt-free. Your lender will factor in both your equity and your potential rental income to determine what loan to value ratio (LVR) they are comfortable with. With most investor loans, lenders are likely to cap this LVR at 80per cent or more as they consider investment properties a bigger risk. Unlike your own home, if you have tenants and should something go wrong, borrowers can more easily walk away from an investment property than they would their owner-occupied ones. If you have a high income but low equity in the family home, your borrowing limit is reduced. So having a right combination of equity and income is essential.

6. Staying with your current lender

   Before finalising your investment loan and if you have an existing mortgage on another property such as your home, take some time to reconsider your loan needs and ask yourself how well your current lender is performing for you. If you are satisfied with the service being provided and you have ascertained that the interest rate and fees you are paying are competitive, there is little reason for you to spend time and money financing with a new lender. However, with an investment loan, it is wise to speak to a mortgage broker as rates and terms may vary compared to your home loan. A mortgage broker can suggest specific mortgage products from a variety of lenders and will help you organise your loan application free of charge. Their payment comes from upfront and ongoing commissions paid by the lender you choose.

7. *Watch out for fees*

   Fees can vary with lenders, so always check the latest information. When comparing different loans, check the fees, so you know exactly how much the loan is costing you. Different credit providers charge various fees. The same fee might also be called different names by different providers. Below are some common fees you will come across.

   - *Establishment fees*: Also known as 'application', 'upfront', 'start-up' or 'set-up' fees. An establishment fee is a one-off payment when you start your loan. If you are not charged an establishment fee, you may pay higher ongoing fees.
   - *Mortgage insurance*: Lenders' mortgage insurance (LMI) is a type of insurance that lenders take out to protect them from borrowers not being able to repay the loan. The fee the lender charges you for LMI can be substantial and is usually added to your home loan amount. Lenders normally charge you a one-off payment to cover this insurance if you borrow more than 80per cent of the value of your loan.
   - *Ongoing fees*: Also known as 'service' or 'administration' fees. These fees are charged monthly or yearly for administering your loan. Some ongoing fees may only be payable in certain circumstances, such as you may be charged a fee to redraw any additional repayments you might have made.
   - *Break fees on a fixed rate mortgage*: A 'break' fee may be applicable if you break your fixed rate mortgage. This fee

may be very high. The more interest rates have come down since you took on the fixed rate loan, the higher the break fee will be.

- *Early exit fees*: This fee can be described as 'early termination', 'deferred establishment', 'deferred application' or 'early discharge' fees. These fees may be charged if you pay out your home loan in full, within a specified time (for example, in the first five years). Exit fees on new loans were banned on 1 July 2011. Competitive lenders providers will pay your exit fees for you when you move your loan across to them.

- *Discharge fees*: Also known as 'termination' or 'settlement' fees. These fees may be charged when you pay out your mortgage in full.

- *Refinancing fees*: When you refinance your loan, you can be charged a range of fees by a lender. It should be remembered that different lenders charge different fees, and some may be negotiable.

Financial tips for building a real estate portfolio

Finance, whether for development or investment, is equally or more important than finding the right investment property. The size of your real estate portfolio is determined by the amount of finance you can borrow. Therefore, if you cannot get your finance adequately structured, then you may be restricting your capacity to acquire further loans for your growing real estate portfolio. It is a well-known fact that wealthy people have a good understanding of the mechanisms of finance which allows them to borrow when an opportunity arises. Below are some finance tips for building an investment real estate portfolio.

- *Control and consolidate loans*

  It is wise to take control and consolidate your loans no matter how large or small. This includes personal loans and credit cards as they usually attract a higher interest rate. Even if the cost and rate are not costing you more interest, it may still affect your borrowing capacity when looking for a loan for your new property to add to your portfolio.

- *Set up a correct loan structure*

  By setting up a well-organised loan structure with proper record keeping will hold you in good stead when looking at any additional loans for your portfolio. A spreadsheet outlining all your current loans, borrower, repayments and so on will give you a good overview of your loan position and what actions to take if required. Also, a poorly structured loan portfolio reduces your flexibility, increases your risk profile and can create reporting and tax nightmares.

- *Have access to other lenders*

  Most borrowers tend to use the same lender when taking out a new loan. This is mainly due to loyalty and convenience. Unfortunately, this reduces the amount that you can borrow as the lender is exposed to funding the whole of your portfolio. They consider this as a risk as should something go wrong with one property it may affect other properties in your portfolio. It is advisable that you use different lenders so that you can always find the best deal, increase your borrowing ability and stay in control of your assets.

- *Set up separate entities for different loans*

  As your portfolio grows – and taking note of the two points above – it is wise to set up separate entities such as companies or trusts for properties within your portfolio. With property, there is the potential that something could go wrong such a drop in value or a bad tenant. By setting up a separate entity, it quarantines other properties within your portfolio from the property that has been adversely affected. It also allows you to use different lenders for each property.

- *Avoid cross-collateralising securities*

  It is advisable not to provide more than one property as additional security to a lender. This can potentially cause problems when the properties increase in value, and you would like to release some of the newly created equity. The lender has your properties tied up so if you want to go to another lender that is offering a better deal, the current lender may not partially discharge their mortgage to allow you to refinance the property.

Also, if you are experiencing financial difficulties and you need to sell part of the portfolio, the lender may call in their loans which may mean selling all the properties that have been collateralised.

- *Review your security on a regular basis*

  With all lenders, the more security offered, the better, and they would grab what is on offer. By giving too much security to a lender, it can significantly restrict your investment and additional borrowing capacity. Take the time to review your property values on an annual basis by having them re-valued with the bank that has the loan or getting a valuer to appraise their current value. Doing this may allow you to remove the security from one of the investment properties.

- *Have access to a line of credit*

  As mentioned earlier, with property there is the potential of something going awry which may affect your rental income and your repayments on your loan. It is therefore advisable to be prepared for these eventualities. Having a cash reserve set up correctly from the start will help your cash-flow. This can be done by structuring a line of credit or redraw facility on your loan.

- *Don't sign personal guarantees*

  Banks and lenders will dislike this advice been given to you, but it is imperative that you do not sign any personal guarantees. Most lenders will have this prerequisite to a loan they are providing to you, but there are ways to negotiate out of this condition. If you are providing enough security concerning their covenants, it can be argued that there is no need for personal guarantees. Also, some lenders may waiver personal guarantees by offering a higher interest rate.

- *Have an experienced mortgage broker*

  With the banking industry, there are constant changes. This can include interest rates and charges for various types of loans, especially with investment loans. If you do not have the time to research and keep up with these changes, it is wise to have an experienced and a well-connected mortgage broker who specialises in investment property loans. They would know which lender would best suit your investment needs. Generally, their fees are typically paid by the lender, but in some cases, fees will be paid the borrower. It is advisable to know this upfront.

CONCLUSION

Sourcing funding and finance for the projects that end up being in your real estate portfolio are one of the most critical aspects of achieving your financial independence. Borrowing money for your project if you are an established property developer is relatively easy. Unfortunately, the failure rate for property developers is high, and many first-time property developers have many hurdles to jump before they can secure funding for their project.

By learning the basics of the development process, what funding is required at various stages and how lenders assess their loans, will assist in getting your loans across the line. If you are thinking of submitting a loan application yourself for your project, you definitely must know the process in advance and prepare your documents in a professional manner that outlines the critical factors of your project. However, if you do not have full knowledge of funding your project you can contract a professional property development fund broker who will be able to advise you and assist in locating the best funding sources.

CHAPTER 7

STARTING A PROPERTY PORTFOLIO

INTRODUCTION

Your success in whatever you want to achieve in life is guided primarily by your conviction and the discipline you have in working towards your goals. This is especially applicable to real estate investment and more so with property development where a strong focus is required to ensure your success. The critical factor is to eliminate your emotions and stay focused on buying and developing property with the intent of building a wealthy real estate portfolio that will provide you with an income in your retirement.

If you do not have experience, the first thing to do is to educate yourself continually by reading, watching, listening, learning, attending seminars, and ideally finding a mentor. It is advisable to read up-to-date books, magazines and reports on property, property development and finance. Also place yourself in the company of successful property investors, developers and mentors to absorb their knowledge and learn from their mistakes. With this knowledge, the right attitude, a sound strategy and meticulous research will come the confidence you need to develop property and build a lucrative real estate portfolio.

The level of success you achieve as a property investor is dependent on the level of planning and preparation you carry out before purchasing and developing the property. The key to achieving high levels success is by implementing a calculated and action-oriented real estate investment strategy that will suit your goals as a property investor. This strategy is described as a step-by-step process in the section below.

STEPS IN CREATING A REAL ESTATE PORTFOLIO

Step 1: Review your financial position

Before going out to purchase and develop property, it is wise to undertake a complete analysis of your current financial position and your current and potential future income. This will help to establish how much you can afford to spend with your first project. You need to write down all your assets, including incomes and work out your expenses and liabilities. This will give you an idea of how much cash you have available to invest. As long as you have a stable and reasonably well-paying job with a solid employment history, you should not have a problem obtaining a loan. If you need assistance, speak to your accountant. Also, consider the following:

- Do you have a steady and stable job?
- Do you have any savings as an emergency account?
- What is the level of loans in the current real estate portfolio?
- If you intend purchasing additional investment properties, where will the deposit come from?

Step 2: Set your goals

After establishing your financial position, set out your goals specifying how you would like to improve your financial situation in the next 5 to 10 years. Firstly, you must first articulate what your goals are over the next 5 to 10 years in writing and more importantly, you need to set a deadline as to when you want to achieve these. For example, if you are looking to replace your income and retire on your investments within 10 years, you can start by creating a 10-year plan, broken down further to 5-yearly, yearly, bi-annual all the way down to a monthly timeline. By doing this, you will not get overwhelmed by the enormity of the task and the timeline will help to shape your financial goals for the next ten years.

If your goal is to own four or more properties in 10 years, you may need around $50,000 in savings or accessible equity to purchase and develop your first property, to cover a small deposit and acquisition costs. That means you need to save around $30,000 to $50,000 each year, or your current real estate portfolio needs to grow in value by that amount. After you have worked out your financial goals, you can then work out how to achieve it.

Step 3: Study property development

If you like property development as a faster way of achieving your financial goals in a shorter period of time, it is essential to have a good understanding of the development industry. Property development is the act of purchasing property, constructing new buildings on it or making improvements to the buildings and selling the property again at a higher price. To succeed as a property developer, you must recognise potentially lucrative opportunities and predict market trends. The following is a broad outline of how to become a property developer.

- **Education**

  Obtain an education related to property development. Undertake a course in finance, business management, construction or building design. Take the necessary classes to get a real estate license in your state. If you cannot afford tuition fees or no have the time to work in the property environment, read as much as you can on the subject and speak to people who are involved in the industry.

- **Gain experience**

  Work for an employer in the property business. Alternatively, find a job that gives you the opportunity to deal in the buying, developing or selling of property. While working in this capacity absorb as much information about the industry as you can. During this period, build your savings and improve your credit rating to help you finance your own property development business in the future.

- **Understand finance**

  Read as much as you can on finance so that you fully understand how borrowed money works in property development and in your strategy in building an investment real estate portfolio. Build relationships with local and independent lenders or finance brokers to finance your investment activities. As they come to trust you, these lenders can give you swift, personalised service at competitive rates.

- ***Understand building construction***

  Visit construction sites or work with a building company so that you have a better understanding of how a building is constructed. Also, undertake a small building project yourself, watch television shows or read construction books and magazines. Talk to and build relationships with construction professionals or consultants such as architects and engineers.

- ***Establish a company***

  As property development carries a number of financial risks, it is wise to establish a business entity that protects you from liability, such as a limited liability company. Setting up such an entity attracts higher fees and more accounting tasks when compared to a sole proprietorship, but these matters are minor when compared to the personal cost you could face as a result of a sudden downturn in the property market.

- ***Research***

  Research market trends to understand or project rises and falls in property prices so that you can buy when prices are low and sell when prices are high. The Internet today provides a vast array of up-to-date information regarding property prices and trends.

- ***Understand commercial property***

  Many developers find it easier to break into property development by working only in residential property. It is also wise to understand commercial property as this sector tends to deal in larger cash values and is subject to less government regulation. This is where highly successful property developers make their money.

Step 4: Set out a 10-year strategy plan

If you want to build a lucrative real estate portfolio, it is essential to make sure that your actions match your goals and having a 10-year strategic plan will assist you in achieving it. Generally, most property investors have a broad idea of their goals for the future. You may want to own three investment properties within five years, or you may wish to retire on your real estate portfolio in 10 years. In reality, you need more than broad goals and ideas. You also need to know the steps you should take to turn these goals into reality. Essentially you need to write down your plan which covers the short-term goals to be achieved as part of the 10-year plan.

In creating your 10-year plan, you need to consider all of these things from the perspective of where you want to be in ten years. Once you have established your goals, you need to work backwards and break these into smaller goals over shorter time frames. For instance, say you currently own one investment property, and in ten years, you want to own an additional five investment properties. This means you need to acquire one additional property every two years. Many other factors will influence your 10-year plan, and they can loosely be grouped under three headings: finance, family and lifestyle.

Similar to a business plan, your 10-year plan should be a flexible working document. It should be a document that can be changed and updated to reflect changes in your lifestyle and financial situation, and it should be reviewed every six months to ensure you're still on the right path. Most importantly, it should be tailored to your financial position, so that you can be sure you are making every last dollar work for you.

Step 5: Start small, learn and grow

Developing investment property is not an overnight get-rich-quick scheme. Smart investors minimise risk by starting with a small project, learn from it before venturing into a larger one. Great things almost always start small, so you have to walk before you can run. As Albert Einstein said, 'Anyone who has never made a mistake has never tried anything new.' We rather need to learn from our mistakes so that we do not run the risk of repeating them. We must gain the wisdom and sense to make sound investment decisions. Prudent judgment will only develop if you truly learn from your mistakes. Experiences will help us learn lessons and fine-tune our sense of judgment and knowledge can be gained by making mistakes. Before starting with your first project consider the following aspects:

- **Understand your attitude to risk**

  Having a good understanding of your risk profile will help in your investment strategy. What level of risk are you able to handle? The level of risk that you are comfortable with will depend on your experience and confidence in the project you intend to undertake.

- **Research and ask**

  To build confidence, take time to research and ask people in the industry the risk involved in your intended project. The more information and knowledge you have of the project the more comfortable you will feel in making decisions.

- **Create an investment criterion**

  Once you have a good idea of what type and size of a project relating to your risk profile and information you have gathered, you can set out your investment criteria. For example, you may conclude that your first project will be a duplex, within a specific suburb or suburbs, with a return of 20% on development cost and so on.

- **Research your finance product**

  Take time to discuss your objectives, investment strategies and risk profile with your bank or a finance specialist to find an appropriate finance product and strategy for your purchase. A finance specialist could be a mortgage broker or a financial consultant, but with the ability to identify and understand the financial requirements of investors.

- **Form a partnership**

  Starting your first project can be daunting, so it may be wise to find a mentor with development experience or you may also decide to take on an experienced partner so that you can learn from them. However, if you choose to go it alone then ensure that you have a professional team with the relevant experience.

Step 6: Start with a first project

The next step is where you commit. Before you make the final decision here are some items to consider and act upon.

- ### *Select the location*

  Do your research on the suburbs you are interested in, physically go out and see what the market is doing in the area where you are looking at buying, and check the demographics of the area, who lives there. This information will help you determine what type of development you will need to create. Understand who your target market is before you design your development. Always go with your instinct. If it does not feel right, move on to the next one.

- ### *Choose the right ownership structure*

  The ownership structure can vary from being held under your own name, tenants-in-common, to a company with limited liability. Choose ahead of time so when it comes to purchasing, you know which structure will help better your situation now and into the future. If you are uncertain of the ownership structure, seek the advice from a good real estate investment accountant.

- ### *Have suitable property development finance in place*

  As the project will be a development, you need to ensure that you will have funding for both the land and construction. You also need to understand that until you sell your first property, your money will be tied up leaving you unable to grow or expand financially. It is essential to ensure that you will be able to raise the necessary development finance. Most banks have dedicated property finance experts who can advise you on available and suitable funds.

- ### *Undertake a due diligence*

  When sourcing a property to develop, pay particular attention to the title documents and town planning regulations. It is in this document where you will find if there are any restrictions on the property and its zoning. Also, from the title document, you will identify if the property has any easements. If you don't explicitly check these two essential elements, it may affect the viability of your development.

- ***Pay the right price***

  Market research and comparable properties are essential to ensure you buy at a sensible price. With property development, it is a known fact that you make more money when you buy the land than when you sell. Therefore, negotiate hard when it comes to the asking price and ensure that the terms of the contract suit your development.

- ***Timing is important***

  It is crucial that you don't rush into buying a property. Don't be pressured by estate agents who insist you will be missing out if you don't buy now. You should spend time getting to know your market and the area, however, once you have found a suitable property in the right location, it helps to move fast. The quicker you can turn a property around the better, as the sooner it is finished, the sooner you can realise a return on your investment.

- ***Consider the rental yield and return***

  If you intend to develop and rent then rental yield is essential, but also analyse the return-on-investment in case you have to sell due to unforeseen circumstances. The rental yield is calculated by measuring annual rental income against the value of the property. For residential properties, target at least 5% as a gross yield, and when selling properties, you need to aim for a minimum of a 20% return on development cost.

Step 7: Find a good development team

The success of your development is dependent on having a good development team that can provide you with correct and professional advice. A development should only start after assessing your current financial position, after examining how the development would fit into your overall strategy and after you have received expert advice from professionals.

- **Selecting the right consultants**

  Property covers a broad and diversified range of buildings, which has created specialist consultants operating in specified areas. Before appointing a consultant, ask for a profile of the person or company to ensure that they have the knowledge, expertise and experience of the type of project you will be building. For example, it is pointless to hire a small architectural practice that has only designed residential buildings to design a multi-million-dollar shopping centre.

- **Number of consultants**

  The number of consultants required will depend on the type and scale of the project. Most consultants offer the complete range of services from inception to completion, however, depending on the size of the project to be tackled; the scope and brief to the consultant may be limited to the section where their expertise is required.

- **Consulting fees**

  Most professional consultants have a standard guide for fees as set out by their association or institute but, depending on the level of service, these fees are negotiable. Fees are generally charged as an agreed lump sum or as a percentage of the development construction cost. It is understandable that most developers aim to reduce the cost to improve profit margins, but you should be fair when negotiating a fee for your projects.

- **Professional indemnity insurance**

  Mistakes can happen on any building project, and even the best professional consultants can be responsible for negligence. It is therefore important that the consultants you employ have current professional indemnity insurance in place. Professional indemnity cover provides protection against the risk of substantial financial losses, but if a consultant does not have a policy in place and is found negligent, you may have to sue the consultant in his or her personal capacity.

- **Build a team of professional advisors**

  After you have selected the consultants you are comfortable

with, it is vital to ensure that the group works as a team. As these professionals have to work together, any personality conflicts will be detrimental to the project. As a developer, you should be aware of any problems that may arise and resolve them as soon as possible. As well as building the right team, you as the developer must feel comfortable that the consultants are serving you to the best of their ability and that you can call on them at any time when a problem or concern arises.

Step 8: Find a good marketing agent

If your strategy is to sell part of your development to reduce the debt on the units you will be holding in your portfolio, then one of the first tasks will be to find the right project marketing real estate agent who can sell off plan. The following are a few of the important factors to consider before you choose the agent to sell your project:

- *Professional experience in your market*

  Most real estate agents will focus on a particular neighbourhood or region. Selecting an estate agent who knows your suburb will make a world of difference, as they know exactly what buyers are looking for in a specific area. This could include the location, public transport, schools, businesses and local amenities.

- **Credentials and references are important**

  When checking the credentials of the real estate agent you need to find out how long they have been working in the field and their sale success rate in project marketing. Asking for references will help as well.

- **Comparative market analysis**

  Another factor to research is the history of sale prices for comparable units in your area. Good real estate agents will be able to give you a Comparative Market Analysis or CMA, which outlines the sales of comparable homes in a specific suburb for the past six months. A local agent would also be able to give you an understanding behind these numbers and demonstrate how this would impact your sale.

- **A solid marketing strategy**

  You will also need to find out how the real estate agent intends to market your project. There are many ways to advertise property in today's multimedia market, and you do not want to choose an agent who limits your buyer pool with a singular approach. Ask the agent for a written marketing plan.

- **Negotiation skills**

  A way to get a sense of how a good real estate agent will handle negotiation is how well prepared they are in the first meeting. They should have a list of comparable properties, which will help them provide you with an accurate price range for your project. Another is to look at their marketing material by asking them to see print-based and online marketing samples.

- **Agent fees, commissions, fees and contracts**

  Commission, fees and contracts should be discussed early with a potential real estate agent. It is essential to remember that the lowest commission does not provide the best and efficient service from an agent. If the agent is willing to lower their fees or commission from the offset, this could indicate that they are desperate. Similarly, they may tend to reduce the sales price of your project during contract negotiations. The best agents are those that know their business and their worth, making them comfortable in sticking to their commission and their contract terms.

It is always best to interview several real estate agents to find the right agent to work on your project. Take time to find and interview candidates who have a reputation for hard work, are experienced and the necessary sales skills to close a deal.

Step 9: Find a good property manager

Managing a property is not as simple as it sounds. If you are considering self-managing your investment property, there are some things to think of such as do you have the time? There is a lot involved in the process, from finding suitable and reliable tenants, collecting rent, holding property inspections and being on call at any time for emergencies and repairs.

In the early stage of your portfolio building where you have one or two properties, it may be worth the effort to self-manage to save cost. However, when you consider the cost of employing a professional property manager, it is undoubtedly good value. The additional rent an experienced manager can get you, can offset their fees, in addition they can also save you money by getting better prices on repairs, for example. They will save you time, allowing you to concentrate on your project.

A property manager is usually a licensed real estate agent and their role is to manage your property, keeping both you and the tenant happy. As professionals, they can provide you with ongoing advice, manage your tenants and get you to get the best possible rental value from your property. A good property manager will advise you when you should review rents. Also, they should be able to provide you advice on property law, your rights and responsibilities as a landlord. They will also deal with any maintenance or repairs and get your approval for these costs before they proceed.

The responsibility of the property manager is to find the right tenant, conduct reference checks and make sure they pay their rent on time. It is important that you don't interfere with your tenants because there are laws that give them certain rights. The property manager should make regular independent inspections of your property to make sure that the tenant is looking after your investment.

Selecting the right property manager for your investment is an important task. With more Australians investing in property every year, there is a growing demand for top industry professionals to handle the day-to-day management of these investments. Before contracting a property manager to take care of your investment, be sure to undertake the following:

- ***Obtain referrals***

It is advisable to talk to real estate agents and other property owners in your area by asking which property managers they use or have used. However, bear in mind that some referrals can be biased.

- ***Do an online search***

  Before spending too much time interviewing a property manager, you can check out the company's reviews on sites like Facebook. The Better Business Bureau can also provide the rating of the company and indicate if any complaints have been made against them.

- ***Check on their advertisements***

  Look at some of the property manager's current rental advertisements to see if they professional, compelling and free of discriminatory statements? Do they advertise in a variety of places, or are their ads limited?

- ***Check out properties they manage***

  Review the properties that a property manager is managing and check if they are clean and well cared for. Speaking to the tenants of properties they currently manage will give you a good insight into their management skills. Property management is to keep you and your tenants happy, and it is essential to get a tenant's opinion as well.

- ***Interview several managers***

  Similar to any person you employ; you should interview several property managers or management companies so you can find the one you are most comfortable with looking after your property.

- ***Check their license***

  All Australian states have a law stipulating that a property manager should have a real estate broker's license or a property management license. Check with your state's Real Estate Commission to see if they have an active brokerage license.

- ***Examine their management agreement***

  A typical property management agreement should clearly define the roles and responsibilities of the property manager with respect to the landlord. Examine the sections on services provided, additional charges, responsibilities of the owner, compliance with fair housing laws, hold harmless clause and reasons for cancellation.

Step 10: Enjoy the process and stay focused

Starting a real estate portfolio through property development is an exciting experience. A lot more thought and creativity are needed compared with buying established property. The great thing about this strategy is that your profit margin is your manufactured equity, which means that should values drop in the short term you have a buffer. It is also a great way to increase your portfolio a faster. Below are a few areas to think about when building your portfolio:

- *Stay focused*

  Ensure that you stay focused on the goals that you have set out. Investing in property is a business decision, not an emotional reaction.
  - Be clear about what you want to achieve
  - Set target dates as to when you want to achieve specific goals
  - Identify the milestones you need to do to get to your goals.

- *Take a long-term view and manage your finances*

  Remember that property is a long-term investment. The longer you can afford to commit to property the better, and as you build up more equity, then you can consider purchasing and developing your next property. Be careful with each move you make and try not to get too greedy by stretching your finances for your next project. It would be best if you had the right balance between financial stability and still being able to enjoy life.

- *Budget for emergencies*

  Unlike shares or managed funds, you cannot just sell part of your investment property if you need money in an emergency. You need to budget for the bad times and possible emergencies, but also your livelihood. While negative gearing is right for taxation reasons, it is wiser have a strong equity position and positive cash flow. You can always borrow against your equity.

- **Don't give up**

  There will undoubtedly be challenges along the way in building your portfolio but don't give up. Imagine in 10 years; if you buy the right properties to develop, you could be sitting back, feeling happy and secure. You will be proud that you have done the hard work and built a million-dollar real estate portfolio that your friends will envy.

MISTAKES TO AVOID WHEN BUILDING A PORTFOLIO

Before you go rushing out to start your real estate portfolio, you should understand there are potential mistakes you could make as a new developer investor. Investment property should be about increasing your wealth and securing your financial future. You need to bear in mind that how effectively you manage your investment will determine whether or not the investment will reach your financial goals. Listed below are some of the common mistakes made by new property investors.

1. **Not purchasing the right property**

   This is the most common mistake made by novice developers and investors. When you look at a potential property, you need to view it as a developer with the intent of making a profit and as a long-term rental property. An excellent development investment property will be in a good location with transport facilities and social infrastructure such as schools and retail precincts. The property should also have good potential capital growth in the long term.

2. **Not doing your research**

   Buying a property without doing your research is a potential financial disaster. Don't have an attitude 'build it and they will come'. You need to look at the local buying and rental market. Is the buying market made up of owner buyers or mainly investors? Find out who is renting property, how much they're paying for it and whether there is good demand. Study the demographic profile of people in the area. If the area full of students and young professionals who might prefer a large apartment, or is it an area with growing families? Without looking into these facts and figures, you could buy a property which is of no interest to the buyers or tenants.

3. Not buying at the right the right price

Developing and investing in property is about making sure that the project is profitable from both a selling and rent aspect. So buying at the right price is critical. Research what current properties are selling for in the area. Soon you will become very good at working out what a property is worth. Never consider buying property in an area that you are unfamiliar with. As you will be developing it is essential that you have a 'due diligence' clause inserted in the sales contract. This allows you to check if the site can be developed in a project you intend building. You will need to consider planning approvals, engineering and finances before you go ahead. Also, ensure that the agent inserts a 'subject to finance' clause in the contract, as your lender will want to undertake a valuation of the property before they provide you with finance.

4. Not understanding the market dynamics

If you are developing a property, it is vital that as a developer and investor you should follow the market dynamics. Targeting a market where there is an oversupply of a product will delay your project and will be less profitable. Reading articles on property and talking to experts will give you a good understanding of the market and where your product would sit. Also, find out what changes may be happening in your suburb; local council can often help with this. Accessing independent information from a source such as RP Data can give you information on average rents, property values, demographics and suburb reports.

5. Not doing your sums

Property development is about making a profit against the risks undertaken. One can easily make a mistake by underestimating or not allowing for a specific cost in developing the property. This will reduce your profit and your manufactured equity, and therefore slow the growth of your portfolio. Also, you may have to raise more cash because of the shortfall. Work with industry experts that can provide you with the actual cost of a project. Prepare a feasibility study and ask an expert to review it in case you have omitted or underestimated any items. Also, allow a contingency in your feasibility study to cover any excluded cost items.

6. **Not having any spare funds**

It is essential to have extra or emergency funds set aside for both your development project and investment portfolio. During the development process, there may be some funds required that you have not accounted for. When the property is leased it may be that some expensive repair is needed, and you will need access to cash. A smart way to build your emergency fund is to take some of your rental profit each month and have it paid into a separate account. This account should be held separately from your regular bank accounts so that you will not be tempted to dip into it.

7. **Believing you know everything**

Believing you know everything and not taking advice and trying to do things on your own thinking that you are saving money and increasing your profits could be a huge mistake. It takes years to gain the knowledge and experience to guarantee development profits. Developing an investment property requires more work than you may think, and some new developers try to save money by doing everything themselves. It is almost impossible to do everything on your own and stretching yourself too thin leads to costly mistakes. Therefore, build a team of reliable experts to outsource the work to, so you can spend your time on your building your real estate portfolio. In many cases, professionals know how to save you money.

8. **Rushing into decisions**

Entering the property development investment market is very exciting and can be very lucrative but making rash decisions without thinking them through can cost you a lot of money. Be informed and analyse your options before making a decision. Take the time to research potential properties, get to know the local market and be sure to interview a number of professionals before choosing whom you want to work with.

9. Not having a strategy

If your strategy is that development investment is to 'build and they will come' then you are on the route to lose money. Before you contemplate developing a property as an investment need to have a short- and long-term strategy. The short-term strategy would be for the development stage. Consider where do you intend to develop, what type of build will it be and what are your contingency plans if something goes wrong. The long-term strategy would be holding property as an investment in your portfolio. Give thought to your plans after the project is completed. Consider how what portion of the development you will be selling and what you will be renting and the tax implications of both.

10. Developing and investing from a distance

No matter how lucrative a property deal may be, don't be tempted to buy and develop a property a long distance away in another state or even country unless you're prepared to travel to the site yourself. Starting a development investment without seeing to the day-to-day operations is a recipe for disaster. If you do decide to buy and develop a property from a distance make sure you have a good reliable project manager or form a joint venture with a local partner whom you can trust, and find a competent property manager to manage the property for you. Meeting them in person is also a must, regardless of where they are based.

11. Ignoring your competitors

Wherever you decide to undertake a development investment ensure that you know who your potential competition is or will be. Remember that your product should be better in cost and quality to attract both buyers and tenants. Don't overlook what other developers are doing in your area. Find out how much they are selling their completed properties for and what they are offering regarding space and finishes. Also, make a point to research the advertisements for properties that are selling and renting in the area of your project. You can get some handy tips from studying the competition.

12. Failing to plan ahead

We have all heard about property developers and property investors going broke and being forced to sell some or all of their properties. The reasons can vary from being financially overextended or too highly leveraged, to losing their jobs or income sources due to a slowdown in the economy. These situations can occur at any time, and the biggest mistake a developer and investor can make is failing to plan. With the right preparation and risk mitigation strategies, you can protect your investments and ensure that you keep moving forward, irrespective of what the market is doing. It is, therefore, best not to leverage or gear your portfolio too high and make sure that your cash flow is positive even if you have to pay more tax.

Without a doubt, real estate investment and development can yield extremely lucrative rewards. Many novice developers and investors are attracted by stories of self-made millionaires who have come by their wealth through property development and investment. Less talked about are the many failed projects and losses taken by the less experienced. Things can go wrong such as builders going bankrupt halfway through construction, planning approvals denied, loans called in before they are due, and new regulations causing increasing costs. However, with a little careful planning and being aware of the potential mistakes such events can be avoided.

CONCLUSION

Building a lucrative real estate portfolio is easier said than done. It requires discipline and a methodical approach. Most importantly, eliminate your emotions and stay focused on your goals which should be set out with both your long-term target and mini targets along the way. If you are a novice in both property development and investing, be prepared to spend some time and money educating yourself in this field. This game is not purely investing cash into a property but also investing in improving your skills and knowledge.

Never be over-confident and believe that you know everything as this can lead to making incorrect or bad decisions which ultimately ends up in business failure. Surround yourself with smart people especially those who are smarter than you or build a team who have the discipline and knowledge, especially those who have the experience and know the pitfalls in both the development and investment arena.

CHAPTER 8

OWNERSHIP STRUCTURES

INTRODUCTION

Starting a real estate portfolio can be daunting as there are many challenges you must get through. Besides having the capacity and financial resources, you need to understand the best investment structure or ownership entity to set up in order to protect your investment while benefitting from tax deductions. There are a number of entities which you can choose from but before doing this carefully analyse your position together with your accountant so that you can determine the type of entity that will best suit your investment strategies. In reviewing the type of entity, consider some of these pertinent questions:

- What are your long-term goals as a developer and investor?
- What control do you want over your investment?
- Who will run the daily management activities?
- Which ownership entity has the best tax advantages?
- Can the ownership entity be transferred to another party?
- Who will be responsible for any losses?

The selection of an investment structure or vehicle depends on certain factors such as asset protection, personal protection, income tax, financing requirements, capital gain tax and cost of compliance. Also, if you are developing you need to select an entity that can provide you with self-protection in the future, should your development or investment fail or if you are sued for other reasons. By buying a property in the wrong tax structure and you may find that:

- You will not be able to transfer the property to a super fund;
- You will incur stamp duty if you change the ownership of the property;
- You lose the ability to refinance and pay down non-deductible debt; and
- You may incur land tax and other charges.

An individual can easily purchase smaller investment projects such as a renovation project or a duplex with lower capital cost and risk, but larger projects, such as an apartment block, will require partners to help finance it and to spread the risk. An individual can still tackle the latter, but it would be wise to register the development under a company in case future partners may be invited to participate in the project.

SELECTING THE RIGHT OWNERSHIP ENTITY

When it comes to structuring an ownership entity for property development and investment, there is no one-size-fits-all structure as each party's circumstances are different. In assessing these differences, you can set up a structure that is specific to the needs of the ownership entity. Below are some key areas to consider before establishing a structure.

a. Legal liability

With property, there are a number of risks involved especially during the development phase and to a lesser degree when a project is completed. With the development and investment process you will be dealing with various parties and institutions, and there is always the potential of legal disputes if these dealings are not managed correctly. Sometimes these could be unforeseen circumstances that you have no control over and are not your fault and that place your hard-earned assets at risk. It would be best if you structured your investment so that it is quarantined from these potential liabilities. You would want to put your assets in an entity that makes it difficult for creditors or the trustee in bankruptcy to make a claim against you if you get sued.

b. Tax implications

Property investment offers one of the best tax benefits, and failure to take advantage of this would be foolhardy. It would be best if you evaluated which is the best and most efficient tax structure, which ensures that you optimise all the benefits offered by the ATO. For example, if one of the investment properties within your portfolio is returning net taxable income each year and you have a tax loss in another property, then you should set up a structure in a way that allows the income to be offset against those tax losses to minimise your overall tax liability.

c. Exit strategy and succession

Each person's personal circumstances change over time, so it is wise to consider what would happen if you had to sell a property, or how you would pass on the asset when you are no longer on this earth. You need to plan an exit strategy and the structure you establish will need to take this into account. At the same time, you have to take into account future succession and the implications it will have on your estate and who will inherit your assets in the future.

d. Additional parties

With most larger projects it could be necessary to have additional partners or investors to spread the risks or to add additional equity into a project. You will have to consider what is the best structure that is flexible and that has a mechanism to accommodate other parties, as the introduction of new parties adds another layer of complexity in terms of shareholding, taxation, roles, management, debt finance, guarantees and so on.

e. Development and investment strategy

If your strategy is to develop a project where you sell part and retain the balance as an investment, the structure may be to have two entities. The first entity develops the project protecting you from development risk and the second entity that will hold the completed development when most of the risk has been taken care of. Unfortunately, this will create double stamp duty however, you may consider using a single structure if the project is small with low risk, but for larger projects, it may be worthwhile with two structures especially where a joint venture or syndicate is formed.

Finding a structure that suits all of these criteria is easier said than done. For example, while one structure may be the best for asset protection, it may not be the most cost-effective. It is essential that you keep your ownership entities within your real estate portfolio simple by using less complex structures. Your accountant and a property lawyer would be best to consult, but you would have to present the short-term and long-term goals of your portfolio so that they can advise on the most cost-efficient structure.

THE RANGE OF OWNERSHIP STRUCTURES

There are many different entities available for an owner of the assets used in property development and property ownership. Some entities are more complex than others. Listed below some typical ownership entities, all of which are explained in more detail later in this chapter:

1. Individual Ownership – controlled by a single individual
2. Joint Tenants – jointly controlled by two or more individuals
3. Tenants-in-Common – controlled by two or more individuals as tenants-in-common in equal or unequal shares
4. General Partnership – controlled by two or more partners
5. Limited Company – controlled by directors and shareholders
6. Discretionary Trust – controlled by trustees on behalf of beneficiaries
7. Family Trusts – controlled by trustees on behalf of family beneficiaries.
8. Unit Trust – controlled by trustees on behalf of unitholders
9. Hybrid Discretionary Trust - a cross between a discretionary and a unit trust
10. Bare Trust – controlled by the beneficiaries

11. Self-Managed Super Fund (SMSF) – controlled by people managing their superannuation

1. INDIVIDUAL OWNERSHIP

Registering a property under one's personal name is the simplest and easiest investment structure of all the structures mentioned here. As a sole proprietor, you have the power to dispose of or leave a property in a testament to another individual, such as your spouse or children. You will be investing by yourself and in your name. You have no partners, and you are personally responsible for all decisions made during the course of the development and investment. While you may have total control of your decision-making, you can be held liable for any failures and can be sued personally. This vehicle is fine for your first and smaller projects, but it is wise to use an alternative ownership entity as your projects increase both in size and scale.

Having a property in your name has many tax benefits such as tax depreciation and tax losses. Negative gearing losses can be used to offset salaries, other investment income or business income of the individual taxpayers. Negative gearing is the most effective for high-income earners as 46.5% of the losses are effectively paid by a reduction in tax payable. On the other hand, when the investment property is sold, you will be taxed on the capital gain and most likely at the top marginal rate. One exception is when the property is passed directly from a deceased estate to the next of kin.

Advantages of Individual Ownership
- As a sole owner, you have complete control and decision-making power over the property
- Minimal legal costs in forming a sole proprietorship
- Few formal business requirements
- Negative gearing against personal income tax.

Disadvantages of Individual Ownership
- As a sole owner, you can be held personally liable for the debts and obligations

- All responsibilities and decisions fall on your shoulders
- Investors won't usually invest in sole proprietorships.
- Sole owners often have more difficulty in raising finance.

2. JOINT TENANTS

Joint tenants simply mean whether you are married or in a de facto relationship with the person you are buying the property with. The registration of a property in joint names is straightforward and inexpensive. There are no special legal documents required compared to trust deeds or formal partnership agreements. The income from the investment held in joint names is always taxed in equal proportions as having been earned by each party in equal shares. Therefore, as far as net income is concerned, the effective tax rate for a couple is higher compared to that of an individual. This structure does not have the flexibility of sharing the tax implications of one tenant who has a lower income with the other who has a higher salary.

On the death of either of the joint owners, title to the assets automatically passes to the surviving owner. The estate of the deceased party has no bearing on the joint arrangement. This type of ownership vehicle should be used only when family members are partners because ownership passes to the surviving partner upon death. If the other partner is not a family member, the vehicle works only when the 'key man' insurance is used to buy out the deceased partner's family.

Advantages of Joint Tenants
- It allows the owners to obtain various tax benefits
- It entitles the owners to their proportional share of rents paid by third parties
- The owners are entitled to a proportional share of any profits
- You have the right to a share of the property proportionally if one of the joint tenants becomes deceased.

Disadvantages of Joint Tenants
- Owners must pay their proportionate share of taxes, mortgage payments, and any other assessments related to the property

- Owners are liable for their proportional share of costs
- If one owner dies, the property title is transferred to the surviving owner.

3. TENANTS-IN-COMMON

Tenants-in-common structure is a bit more complicated as there are different types of ownership structures that fall under this umbrella. Unlike Joint Tenants where it's 50/50, one person can own 40% of the property, and the other person can own 60%. Each owner receives income and allocation of expenses according to the proportion held and retrieves their share in their respective tax returns. Each person can leave their share to anyone in their will.

Under this vehicle, each owner receives his or her income or loss directly without regard for the others, which means that each owner is liable for their tax. There is no limit to the number of members, and the vehicle is only viable for passive investors who want little or no management in the daily activities in an investment property. This type of ownership structure can cause problems should one of the owners pass away. Disputes can be made over the share and how the property is to be disposed of. There is a great deal of legal input required into this type of structure, and all parties must be aware of the details and the ramifications involved if one party dies or decides to get out before the property is sold.

Advantages of Tenants-In-Common

- Ability to avoid probate which means if a co-owner dies the right of survivorship may allow an individual's estate to avoid probate which means the process does not have to go through a court process such as a will.
- The tenants are entitled to a proportional share of the rent that the property receives.
- The tenants allow the other tenant to receive the decedent's share at the time of death.

Disadvantages of Tenants-In-Common
- One of the tenant's creditors can force a sale of the property, leaving the other tenants exposed to such risks.
- Tenants generally have greater responsibilities related to the property than owners in severalty. They must pay their share of taxes, mortgage payments and assessments.
- You must get permission from the other tenants to make specific arrangements regarding the property.

4. GENERAL PARTNERSHIP

A general partnership is a contractual arrangement under which two or more parties carry on a business in common with a view to making a profit. A legal partnership will always be considered a partnership for tax purposes. However, an arrangement that is not defined under common law is that a partnership is still a partnership for taxation purposes as the tax law defines a partnership to include an association of persons who jointly receive an income without necessarily jointly carrying on a business. Therefore, two people who together own an investment property will effectively be a tax law partnership for income tax purposes.

Partners need not all make equal contributions to the development, and different partners can, if desired, have different proportionate claims to the income and the capital. The ratios for income and capital do not have to be identical either. Unlike a company, a partnership is not a legal entity. A significant disadvantage of a partnership is that all the partners have joint and several liabilities for obligations affecting the partnership. A fair amount of trust in the integrity and competence of all partners is therefore necessary. A partnership does not pay any income tax itself, but it is required to lodge a partnership tax return each financial year, which sets out, among other things, the amount of profit or loss attributable to each partner. The relevant amounts are then are returned in each partner's tax return. Unlike trusts and companies, partnerships are able, for tax purposes, to distribute losses as well as gains.

Advantages of a Partnership
- The formation of a partnership is easy under an agreement in oral or written words.
- A partnership brings added financial strength making it easier to raise finance.
- The partner provides additional skills and expertise.
- The partners share the losses and other associated risk in property.
- Since the partners meet quite frequently, they can arrive at decisions promptly.
- Partners take an active part in the management which leads to greater efficiency.
- All important decisions are taken unanimously by the partners protecting the interest of a minority group of partners.
- The partnership can bring changes in its operation easily and quickly review changing circumstances.

Disadvantages of a Partnership:
- Similarly to individual ownership, unlimited liability is a drawback of partnership.
- There is instability in existence because a successful firm can be dissolved on the death, insolvency or insanity of a partner.
- A dishonest or incompetent partner can lead to difficulties because the other partner will have to pay for their dishonesty or inefficiency.
- A difference of opinion is the natural cause in the split of a partnership.
- No partner can transfer their interest to a third party without the other partner's consent.

5. LIMITED COMPANY

If a more substantial property is to be developed where some strata units are sold and the balance held as an investment, a company structure is attractive for a number of reasons as the developer can only lose what they have invested. Most companies have 'limited liability' which means that the members of the company (the shareholders) are not liable for the obligations of the enterprise beyond a particular stated amount unless personal guarantees are provided to a lender.

Holding development assets through a company structure also protects the assets of the company from seizure by creditors of the individual shareholders, as long as the control of the company itself does not change hands. In contrast, shares in the company are assets of their shareholders and the shares could thus be taken away from their owners in bankruptcy proceedings. The assets owned by the company are not safe from seizure by creditors of the company itself, who can, in some circumstances, force the winding up of the enterprise.

The personal assets of shareholders, directors and other company associates can also be at risk if these people have given personal guarantees, regarding the obligations of the company. Lenders have a different perspective and will seek to overcome the protection afforded by limited liability. They will look for suitable personal guarantees from those behind the company and a charge over the company's assets, in addition to registered first mortgages over its properties.

Other variations of this are also possible. The company could raise a loan from some or all of its shareholders or their associates, paying a commercial rate of interest. Shareholders could fund the loan by borrowing from an outside lending institution, using, with the consent of the company, the company's assets or investments as security. The company could simultaneously use the money raised to develop property without borrowing debt.

If an investment property is held under a company, any negative gearing losses will be contained within the company, and they cannot be distributed to shareholders. However, the company can deduct carried forward tax losses if it satisfies the continuity of ownership test. The company tax rate is capped at 30% (at the time of writing), and both the investment income and capital gain on the sale of property are taxed at 30% only. However, companies are not eligible for the 50% general CGT discount, which could result in a much higher capital gain tax compared to holding investments through a trust.

Advantages of a Limited Company

- The shareholders are not liable for the company's debts and can only lose the value of their shares.
- The tax rate for companies is less than the highest rate for individuals.
- Legal arrangements are in the company and not in the name of its directors and managers.
- This structure ensures continuity of management and ownership in the event of the death or disability of key people.

Disadvantages of a Limited Company

- Companies are more regulated by the Australian Securities and Investment Commission (ASIC) than other business structures.
- The rules for running a company are more complex and costly to manage than those of other structures.
- Profits distributed by companies to shareholders are taxable.
- Banks and lenders are reluctant to lend money or enter into contracts with a limited company unless directors or shareholders provide personal guarantees.
- Should any of the directors fail to meet their legal obligations, they may be held personally liable for the company's debts.

6. DISCRETIONARY TRUST

Trusts are treated quite differently from companies. A trust is a relationship, based on confidence, where property is held by one party, the trustee, on behalf of other parties who are entitled to the fruits of that ownership, the beneficiaries of the trust. Under a discretionary trust structure, the trustee has the 'discretion' to select among a number of 'potential beneficiaries', who may receive a distribution of profits, capital gains or the original 'settled capital'. The trustee of a discretionary trust can hold the assets of a property on behalf of its beneficiaries, and their rights are set out in a legal document called a trust deed. In some trusts, certain beneficiaries are entitled to a defined share of the assets or the income. These are known as nondiscretionary trusts.

In exercising their discretionary powers, all trustees must act in accordance with the relevant trust deed. This means taking into account all pertinent aspects, not just tax. A trust deed can specifically authorise the trustee to borrow funds for a development property. Any lenders to trusts will look for appropriate joint and several guarantees from persons associated with the trust as trustees or as directors of the company acting as trustees or as principal beneficiaries.

Advantages of a Discretionary Trust
- Estate planning for the benefit of family members in the event of an unexpected death
- Any property held in a trust is legally protected from creditors
- Distribution of trust income and capital is flexible and easy

Disadvantages of a Discretionary Trust
- Complexity in establishing and maintaining a trust structure
- Only profits (not losses) are distributed
- Investors are more likely to invest in a company structure than a trust structure

7. FAMILY TRUST

A family trust has similarities to a discretionary trust, but in this case the beneficiaries are related. Under a family trust, the trustee company buys the property and borrows finance in the trust name. Should the family trust be caught up in litigation concerning the property, it is the trustee company who is sued and not the family members. A creditor pursuing a family member within the family trust for a debt cannot lay claim to any of the trust's assets. The family trust assets are protected from creditors for the legal reason that none of the family members has any ownership rights in the trust assets.

A family trust is a tax-effective investment vehicle because profits can be split in different ways each year. The trustee can decide how the profits are distributed at the end of each year. Taxable profits can be allocated to a low-income family member, instead of a family member with a higher income, therefore taking advantage of a lower income tax bracket.

A family trust can also be set up under a will. This is called a testamentary trust. In a family trust, the control of the trust assets can be passed onto the next generation in line with the trust deed, outside of the will. The trust assets do not have to be sold or transferred on death, and no death duties or taxes are payable. The trust deed will describe the individual family beneficiaries who may benefit, and the trustee has the freedom to distribute profits to each family member.

A family trusts are best suited for positively geared investment property. There is no benefit to the members when losses occur unless there is cash flow from other sources in the trust to offset the losses. If there are losses in the trust, these can be carried forward to future years.

Advantages of a Family Trust
- The assets held in trust are usually protected from creditors of the trustees or beneficiaries personally.
- Your children continue to benefit from the trust's assets and therefore cannot be subject to claims by your children's partners.
- If any assets are transferred into a family trust before establishing a relationship with a new partner, these assets in the trust are not likely to be subject to a relationship property claim.
- If you pass your assets to a family trust, then the trust can provide a vulnerable child with income or capital to meet their cash requirements for their future.
- Modern trust deeds allow limited rights of variations to deal with changes in the law.
- A typical family trust is not publicly registered keeping the dealings of the trust confidential.

Disadvantages of a Family Trust
- There are costs involved with setting up a trust, and this depends on the complexity of the trust and the type of assets to be transferred.

- You need to allow for the cost involved with meeting the trust's annual accounting and administrative requirements.
- Possible changes to the legislation of trust law may remove or affect some of the original objectives for the trust formation.

8. UNIT TRUST

A unit trust functions similarly to a company with its shareholders where unrelated investors contribute capital to the investment purchase and would like a share of capital and income. The trustee divides the trust funds between unitholders, according to the number of units that they have. Unit trusts can be an open-ended investment which means that unlike other investment trusts there is no finite number of units in issue. These can increase or decrease depending on the net sales and re-purchase by existing unitholders.

The underlying value of the assets in a unit trust is directly represented by the total number of units issued multiplied by the unit price less the transaction or management fee charged and any other associated costs. Each trust has a specified investment objective to determine the management aims and limitations. In a unit trust, a unitholder is entitled to the income and capital of the trust in proportion to the number of units held. Similar to a company, it is possible for a unit trust to have different types of units with different rights.

When compared to a beneficiary of a discretionary trust, where the beneficiary has no proprietary interest in the property, a unitholder in a unit trust has a proprietary interest in all the property of the unit trust. Below are the advantages and disadvantages of unit trusts:

Advantages of a Unit Trust
- It is easier to introduce new equity partners – no value shifting rules
- Fewer regulations than a company
- 50% discount method for Capital Gains Tax (CGT) is available
- There is asset protection available through a correctly drafted trust deed

- They are simple to wind up

Disadvantages of a Unit Trust
- If a trust is financed by debt instead of equity, the disposal of units can lead to capital gains
- A change in unit holding can make pre-CGT assets to post-CGT assets
- Losses are trapped in the structure
- Losses cannot be transferred to other controlled entities like a company
- Unitholders can be subject to complex PAYG calculations
- Varying the terms or objects of the trust can amount to resettlement and have CGT and stamp duty consequences

9. HYBRID TRUST

A hybrid trust is a cross between a discretionary and a unit trust. The beneficiaries still hold units, but the trustee has the discretion to distribute funds to any unitholder they wish to. This type of structure can be appealing as it includes the benefits of both. You can split the trust up into units while also having beneficiaries to distribute to at your discretion.

Hybrid trusts take advantage of the better features of both a discretionary trust and a unit trust and blend them in the one entity to create a flexible and powerful tax planning solution. They allow the rights and entitlements of unrelated third parties to be respected, while still allowing flexible income and capital distributions between those parties.

The income tax, capital gains tax and asset protection related to hybrid trusts means that they are often the preferred method of structuring a business or investment. This is particularly useful where more than one unrelated party is involved such as two separate family groups buying a property together.

Advantages of a Hybrid Trust
- With a corporate trustee – limited liability
- Flexible tax planning with the ability to issue income units and discretionary distributions of capital gains to different people depending on their financial situation

- Ability to issue and redeem units without triggering capital gains tax.
- Capital gains tax only in the hands of beneficiaries
- Income can be passed to beneficiaries without a change in the ownership of the investments
- Control of investments can be retained by the appointer of the trustee who normally places the asset in the trust
- Confidential information is not public as there are no statutory disclosure requirements
- asy entry and exit of owners
- Trusts are relatively simple to wind-up.

Disadvantages of a Hybrid Trust

- The cost of creation and administration of the trust is higher
- Potential changes to legislation such as taxation of hybrid trusts
- Careful structuring is required for negatively geared investments as capital and revenue losses could get quarantined in the trust

10. BARE TRUST

A bare trust is used where the trustee holds property of and on behalf of the beneficiary. In this case, the trustee has no discretion and no active duties other than to transfer the property to the beneficiary when requested by the beneficiary. The trustee is purely a nominee of the beneficiaries. Legally, a bare trust is a trust under which the trustee or trustees hold property without any specific interest in the trust, other than having the legal title as trustee. The trustee does not have a duty or further duty to perform, except to convey it upon demand to the beneficiaries or as directed by them, for example, on sale to a third party.

When it comes to CGT, any disposal of an asset of the trust by a bare trustee will be treated as a disposal by the beneficiary. The GST position for bare trusts, like all other trusts, is determined by the general rules in the legislation. However, a bare trust can raise specific GST issues that need to be addressed – in particular, regarding who the relevant supplier is, who the relevant recipient is and whether a taxable supply or creditable acquisition can arise in such an arrangement.

Advantages of a Bare Trust

- The beneficial ownership does not change as the bare trustee holds the asset on behalf of the beneficiary
- The trustee does not have any power to deal with the asset
- The trustee does not have any power to make any decisions regarding the asset
- The trustee must adhere to all instructions given by the beneficiary.

Disadvantages of a Bare Trust

- Bare trusts do not prevent creditors from accessing the property
- The bare trust without a mortgage does not provide any significant asset protection
- The trustee holds the asset for the beneficiary
- As a bare trustee, you must follow the instructions of the beneficiary

11. SELF-MANAGED SUPER FUND

A Self-Managed Super Fund (SMSF) is a trust that is established by people who want to manage their own superannuation. A member of an SMSF has a retirement fund in their name, which they cannot access until they retire. SMSFs provide complete asset protection because a member's fund is not available to their creditors by law if the member becomes insolvent. SMSF ownership is a tax structure in which you can pay less tax on your investments if you purchase an investment via your SMSF. Below are some critical elements to an SMSF:

- An SMSF is set up with a deed of settlement. This deed is similar to a family trust deed, but with a single purpose of providing for the member's retirement.
- SMSF members must wait until they retire before they can

access their funds. Upon retirement, members must draw a minimum income stream of 4% of their retirement fund annually, and only four members are allowed.

- When it comes to investing a SMSF has certain restrictions. A SMDF is not allowed to run a business, cannot buy family or holiday homes, and cannot provide a loan of more than 5% of their assets to the members. Buying and selling investment property occasionally does not constitute running a business.

- A SMSF utilises a custodian trust when it borrows to buy property. The SMSF custodian trust deed permits the nominee to own, borrow and mortgage the property. When the loan is paid out, the nominee transfers the property to the SMSF, without stamp duty. Generally, lenders often finance 65% and no more than 80% of the price to SMSFs.

According to ASIC, you can only buy property through your SMSF if you comply with the rules below:

- Address the 'sole purpose test' of solely providing retirement benefits to fund members
- The property is not acquired from a related party of a member
- The property is not lived in by a fund member or any fund members' related parties
- The property is not rented by a fund member or any fund members' related parties.

When investing in property, a limited recourse borrowing arrangement can only be applied to purchase a single asset such as a residential or commercial property. Before committing to a geared property investment, you should assess whether the investment is consistent with the investment strategy and risk profile of the fund. Geared SMSF property risks include:

- Higher costs: SMSF property loans tend to be more expensive than other property loans which must be factored into your investment decision.

- Cash flow: Repayments on a loan must be made from your SMSF which means the fund should always have sufficient cash flow to meet the loan repayments.
- Hard to cancel: If your SMSF property loan documentation and contract are not set up correctly, the unwinding may not be allowed, and you may be required to sell the property, potentially resulting in losses to the SMSF.
- Possible tax losses: Any tax losses from the property cannot be offset against your taxable income outside the fund.
- No alterations to the property: Until an SMSF loan is paid off, no alterations to a property are allowed.

Advantages of a SMSF

- As a member, you have complete control over the fund's investments, but you must maintain an appropriate investment objective and strategy.
- By controlling your fund, it allows you to invest in a range of assets including bank deposits, direct property, shares, managed funds and pooled investment trusts.
- As a member, you are a trustee and have a degree of control over the rules of the fund and how it operates.
- The SMSF can continue after your death, which benefits you, your spouse and even your children.
- The cost of managing a SMSF does not increase as your super investment grows.
- The SMSF can provide tax concessions such as the deferral of lump sum tax in the pension phase.
- Your SMSF could potentially purchase your business premises, which allows you to pay rent directly to your SMSF at the market rate.

Disadvantages of a SMSF

- All decisions and responsibilities in managing the fund rest with you as trustee and must comply with specific rules and certain deadlines.
- Although you can invest in a greater range of assets, you may not have sufficient money in the fund to invest in these assets.

- It could be costly to maintain the fund such as the administration and consulting assistance you receive.
- As a member of a SMSF, you are not able to bring complaints or disputes to the Superannuation Complaints Tribunal.
- Any borrowing into property must be done under stringent conditions called a 'limited recourse borrowing arrangement.'

CONCLUSION

As explained, there are numerous ownership structures that you can take advantage of when developing and investing in property. With the majority of my developments which are larger in scale, I set up a special purpose vehicle (SPV) under a limited liability company for each development site. This structure provides me with flexibility and allows me to partner with other shareholders. In addition to setting up a SPV for each project, it protects and isolates one project from the other should the other run into difficulty. However, the financial position, knowledge and experience of each individual is different. For those of my property investments which are completed buildings, I hold these in a trust structure that will benefit my children.

It is recommended that for whichever ownership structure you decide to use, ensure you do undertake the necessary research into the ramifications, limitations and legalities surrounding it. It is also helpful to ensure that you consult a trusted tax accountant and property lawyer before making your final decision regarding the type of structure you set up for your real estate portfolio. When you do consult an expert, ensure that the advice they give you is unbiased and in your best interest.

CHAPTER 9

SYNDICATES & JOINT VENTURES

INTRODUCTION

When it comes to development projects that are not within your reach due to their size and complexity an alternative strategy needs to be considered. The increasing cost of viable land and escalating construction cost, along with the high cost of raising finance, not to mention the high risk involved, if you decide not to go it alone it would be wise to share resources and knowledge. The solution to sharing such risk can be achieved through the structures known as syndicates and joint ventures.

In general, the process of syndication is when a group of investors pool their resources to achieve a financial goal that cannot be accomplished by an individual investor acting alone. A joint venture, on the other hand, is a partnership between two or more parties with each contributing their skills or finance together to develop a project that is financially beneficial to the partners. These strategies allow you to grow your portfolio with properties in better locations and with lower risks by spreading the financial obligations.

However not all developer or investors will be comfortable with such associations as they prefer to go it alone or they lack the skills to manage a group of people having an equal say in a project that he or she conceived or found. Unless these parties have deep pockets, they will have to focus on smaller scale projects.

SYNDICATES

A property syndicate is a group of investors who pool their funds to purchase or develop one or more properties jointly. Syndicated property can vary significantly from small residential projects to larger commercial projects. The investment can be made through a number of legal structures such as partnerships, incorporated joint ventures or a unit trust structure. Depending on the size of the syndicate, some schemes have to comply with the Managed Investments Act 1998 which is offered through a trust structure.

There are two categories of syndicate: private and public. In a private syndication a small group of individuals, perhaps friends or business associates, buy and develop a property. Most syndicate offers to the public require the promoter or manager to prepare and lodge a product disclosure statement (PDS) or information memorandum (IM) with the Australian Securities and Investments Commission (ASIC). The PDS sets out detailed information about the syndicate and the risks and expected returns relating to the investment. The syndicate may be promoted to the general public through licensed securities dealers, property managers, financial planners and accountants.

Under this chapter, we will focus on private syndicates, where a syndication structure can be set up allowing a group of interested parties to develop their property and to secure their individual property to be placed into their real estate portfolio.

The advantages of a syndicate

Syndicates have many advantages:

- ### *Affordable*

  The price tag attached to larger development projects is generally well beyond most individual investors. The formation of a syndicate provides investors with affordable access to the returns of such properties in proportion to the amount they can afford.

- ### *Assurance*

  In general, a syndicate develops or owns a specific property or a limited number of properties for a set period. There may also be restrictions on the sale of any existing properties by the syndicate. As such, the attributes of the investment are much more certain than those of a listed property trust where a portfolio can change significantly from year to year.

- **Lower capital outlay**

  A development syndicate member generally does not require as large a capital outlay. As an example, purchasing an investment property or even a development site would typically cost hundreds-of-thousands-of-dollars or more. A development syndicate member generally requires a minimum investment of between $50,000-$100,000 per member, making your capital outlay significantly lower.

- **Portfolio diversity**

  With a lower capital outlay, investors can spread their funds across multiple investments. This could incorporate a spread of residential syndicates and commercial property syndicates in various locations. By holding a diversified real estate portfolio, investors are effectively mitigating their risks.

- **Freedom from management**

  Managing a more substantial development or investment property takes considerable expertise and time. A syndicate run by a professional manager has the advantage that it frees investors from the task of day-to-day management of the property (such as managing the development team or negotiating and signing leases.) Investors also benefit from the manager's expertise in property matters (including financial, taxation and legal issues) and from the economies of scale a manager can achieve by overseeing a number of properties.

- **Security of Capital**

  Depending on the structure of each syndicate, your name or the name of an approved trustee will appear on the Certificate of Title and your interest will be held according to the proportion of capital invested by you against that of other investors in the property. You will, therefore, have the security of tenure with freehold title, as you would ordinarily hold with any additional real estate investment.

The disadvantages of a syndicate

Some of the disadvantages of syndicates include:

- *Liquidity*

  An investment in a syndicate is an investment in property, not units or shares. Accordingly, it suffers from the limitations of real estate investment. The main limitation is that it is not liquid. There is a minimal secondary market for interests in syndicates, so it can be difficult to exit the syndicate before the end of its term. This illiquidity means that syndicates should only be viewed as a long-term investment.

- *Lack of management skills*

  While many syndicate managers are well schooled in the aspects of investment and development, property analysis and acquisition, not all may possess the necessary management skills. As opposed to a simple transaction, syndication is a long-term commitment. The amount of continuing communication between managers and investors, such as quarterly and annual reports, can be overwhelming. Very few developers are trained in this type of group communication and management.

- *Clarity of sponsor compensation*

  One of the primary reasons developers sponsor syndications is the potential for more considerable profit. However, no law dictates the fee-splitting arrangement between the sponsor and the investors in a private offering, and there are as many different arrangements as there are syndications.

- *Too much risk for too few rewards*

  There is often more risk in property development than anticipated. This problem is even higher for a syndicate's manager, who may take on the risks of ownership for all the group members. The mistake most often mentioned is that the managers assumed too much personal liability in return for the amount they expected to receive in profits. Whatever the cause, managers should examine their expected profits carefully before taking on a syndication. In specific projects, the best decision may be to collect a development fee and leave the syndication to someone else.

- **Too many investors**

  Managers have found that the care and maintenance of investors is something they are not prepared to handle. Managers can deal with this problem in two ways. First, they can limit the number of investors in each syndicate group. As a result of these smaller groups, each investor is required to make a more considerable minimum investment, and sophisticated investors who can contribute more money are better able to absorb the risks associated with a real estate investment. Second, the use of the Limited Liability Company always demands a smaller group of investors so that each investor can have an active role in management. Too many investors make the decision process cumbersome.

Developer Syndicate

A developer initiates a developer syndicate. Listed below is the process of creating a public syndicate registered under the Managed Investments Act, although many of concepts apply equally to private syndicates.

1. The manager (developer) finds a suitable development site.
2. The manager obtains an option over the property or exchanges a contract of sale, which is conditional upon the manager obtaining finance through the syndicate.
3. The manager and development team prepare a feasibility study of the project to be developed.
4. The manager then makes an offer of interest in the syndicate to the public according to a prospectus registered with the ASIC.
5. Investors then subscribe for an interest in the syndicate, using their funds plus money borrowed from a lender organised by the manager. This loan from the lender is secured by a mortgage over the property and a fixed and floating charge over the assets of the trust.
6. The trust then acquires the property for and on behalf of

each syndicate member and proceeds with the development.

7. On the completion of the project, and if the project is being sold, the manager will ensure all sales contracts have been computed and profits distributed pro-rata to the syndicate members.

8. If the project is being held as a long-term investment, the manager will arrange for regular maintenance and repairs of the property and will ensure the property is fully tenanted.

9. On a regular basis, the manager will distribute, to the investors any net income and will provide audited financial statements and tax statements.

10. At the end of the syndicate's term, the manager will arrange for the property to be sold, the syndicated loan to be repaid and all syndicate expenses to be paid out. The balance of the proceeds is then distributed pro-rata to investors.

Cooperative Syndicate

A cooperative syndicate is initiated by a group of friends or a group with a common interest in developing a property jointly. These apply mainly to residential developments and there are various models applicable to this concept, namely (a) co-housing or (b) cooperative housing.

Cohousing is an intentional community of individual private homes clustered around shared space. Each attached or single family home has traditional amenities, including a private kitchen. Shared spaces typically feature a common house, which may include a large kitchen and dining area, laundry, and recreational spaces. Shared outdoor space may consist of parking, walkways, open space, and gardens.

A housing cooperative (or 'co-op') is a housing development initiated by a developer where the homes are owned and controlled jointly by a group of individuals who have shares, membership, and occupancy rights to the housing in a complex. A co-op is essentially a company, complete with a board of directors. All the members of this cooperative purchase shares in the corporation and are labelled as shareholders.

Managing a Development Syndicate

One of the major problems in the operations and roll-out of a syndicate is the level of trust between syndicate members and members having their own opinion or say. It is often the initiator or key person of the syndicate who is targeted.

To overcome this problem, the syndicate members can appoint an independent development manager who has experience in property development and in handling syndicates. The development manager can help resolve any disputes or provide independent answers asked by syndicate members.

The development manager can also complete the necessary research, negotiation and acquisition of a development site, as well as manage planning approvals, project designs and construction of the project. For their services, the development manager charges a percentage fee on the cost of the project.

JOINT VENTURES

Joint ventures are usually seen as short-term arrangements set up for specific projects. Generally, each person or entity contributes assets and shares risks. A joint venture can be structured in a number of different legal relationships, and the relationship between joint venture parties is governed by the terms of the agreement between them, as well as the general law. There are two common types of joint ventures:

- **The incorporated joint venture:** A company is established to conduct the business, and the parties are shareholders in the company.
- **The unit trust (usually with a corporate trustee):** The parties are the unitholders.
- **The unincorporated joint venture:** The parties enter into a contract to establish their legal rights and obligations in relation to the business venture. Depending on terms of the agreement, the parties may constitute a partnership for general law purposes.

In order to minimise the chance of the joint venture being interpreted as a partnership, you should establish a structure, prepare documentation and an execute agreements that cover the major areas that should be agreed by the joint venture parties. Listed below are some key items:

- **Purpose of joint venture:** This should define the reasons why the joint venture is created and the business goals of the parties concerned.
- **The roles of each party:** The role and scope of work for each party or individual should be clearly defined so that there is no overlap of responsibility.
- **Capital contributions:** The capital contributions made by each party should be made clear. In addition the parties should consider how future capital contributions will be made – specifically, whether the funds will come from each party or as loans from a lender.
- **Share of ownership:** The parties should agree what percentage of the deal each partner will receive. In most circumstances, these deals are structured on a 50/50 basis but can be varied by mutual consent.
- **Management:** It should be made clear, which partner of the venture will be responsible for the daily management and decision-making.
- **Fees and compensation:** Other than profit sharing it should be documented as to who will be paid for the daily services contributed.
- **Duration:** Joint venture developments are typically created for a specific project and in most circumstances will end when the development is completed or sold.
- **Record keeping:** It should be made clear who will be responsible for the daily accounting and record keeping for tax purposes.
- **Liabilities:** The parties should agree that each party is liable for their actions and liabilities, and not jointly accountable for any actions by the other party.
- **Disputes:** If there is a dispute between the parties, it should be clarified under what circumstances the venture can and will be terminated.
- **Sale of shareholding:** The partners should agree what

action should be taken if one of the parties to the venture wants to buy the other party's shareholding.

In addition to the above and depending on the scope of the development, the other areas to be considered are loan guarantees, responsibility of loan defaults, the timing of distributions, tax allocations and so forth.

Advantages of a joint venture

- As two or more parties join together to form a joint venture, there is the availability of increased capital and other resources.
- The joint venture partners can share both costs and risks in a project.
- One partner can provide a complementary skill that the other does not have.
- Joint ventures can be flexible, e.g. a joint venture can have a limited lifespan and only cover part of what you do, thus limiting both your commitment and exposure.
- The partnership can provide increased productivity and the potential of higher profits.

Disadvantages of a joint venture

- It takes time and effort to form the right relationship.
- The objectives of each partner may differ; therefore objectives need to be clearly defined and communicated to everyone involved.
- Imbalance in the share of capital, expertise, investment etc., may cause problems between the partners.
- A difference in the culture and style of business may lead to poor co-operation between parties.
- Lack of assuming responsibility by the partners may lead to the collapse of the project.
- Lack of communication between the partners may affect the project.

Joint Venture Development Structures

Despite many different joint venture structures in property development, these transactions generally fall into one of five general categories.

1. Joint Venture / Partnerships

Joint ventures or partnerships are the most common ownership structure. The two parties set up a SPV (special purpose vehicle) under a limited liability company. The roles and responsibilities of each party are defined, and a shareholder's agreement established. Before entering into an agreement, all legal structures should be investigated and analysed for liability management and tax issues.

The advantages of this structure are that the parties earn development profit pro rata based on equity contributed. It also makes it easier to attract investment partners, as they prefer pro rata structures with the developer putting in real equity. Interim financing is more easily attainable, as the additional capital of the two partners will allow for a better loan-to-value ratio for interim lenders.

The disadvantages of this structure are that the joint venture agreement can be complicated and usually more expensive with delays. If the partner is a cash investor, they may insist on a buy/sell provision with an agreement that generally benefits the investor.

2. Fee Development

This is the simplest of a joint venture structure where the developer charges a development fee for undertaking the project. Many developers prefer this structure, especially with a high-risk development. In this structure, the concept is for the capital or investment partner to own the property during the entire construction period. The developer's risks are for cost overruns and can be limited to a portion of the total development fee.

The benefits to the developer are that he or she has minimal capital risk as the finance partner provides funding for the project. Also, the developer has a certainty of income for the duration of the project.

On the flip side, the developer does get any share of the

profits derived from the project as he has no capital at risk. Generally, these arrangements are difficult to negotiate, and there is the potential of being sued by the finance partner if he does not perform or if the project fails.

3. Performance Development Fee

This joint venture structure is a hybrid between a development fee structure together with the opportunity to earn additional profits through a performance incentive fee. Under this structure, the investor owns the property from the outset, and the developer earns an agreed development fee plus a potential for additional fees, based on the financial performance of the development. The performance fee is based on an expected return of cash equity invested called the 'hurdle rate', and an excess above this rate is shared between the investor and the developer.

For the developer, he or she is being incentivised to ensure that the project is viable, cost-effective and making returns above the norm. For the investor, he or she is guaranteed their targeted return before any profit is split with the developer.

There is more to be gained by the investor who entertains the majority of the profit while utilising the expertise of the developer. This is nevertheless a proven model used by the majority of fund managers who are in charge of investor funds.

4. Joint Venture / Partnerships with Landowners

This structure is a partnership between a developer and a landowner. The landowner's property is valued which forms part of the equity required for the development project. The developer has to raise the additional equity that is needed, which forms his or her share of the structure. For example, if a project is $10 million and $3 million (30%) is required, and if the land value is $1.5 million and the developer raises the $1.5 million balance, then the share of the profits will be 50:50.

The major benefit to the developer is that he or she does not have to find the funds to purchase the land and cover the holding cost. Also, the developer controls the project and shares development profit pro rata. Furthermore, the project is easier to finance as the land value is considered as equity by lenders.

The risk falls mainly on the landowner who could lose their

land should the project not succeed, as the land is generally subordinate to the construction loan. However, there are mechanisms to protect the landowner such as ensuring the developer guaranteeing the any loans undertaken for the development.

5. **Agreement to purchase upon completion**
Also known as a 'take out' this is most rewarding for the developer where an agreement is signed with an investor or an institution to purchase the project on completion. Generally, the developer prearranges to sell the property to an end purchaser when it is complete but subject to being fully leased and with other pre-agreed-upon conditions and specifications.

By having a development sold before construction, it starts to eliminate the risk to the developer who knows of their profit over the prearranged price. Depending on the credit credentials of the end purchaser, funding from lending institutions is a lot easier with better terms and fewer conditions.

With this joint venture, the agreement between the parties could contain conditions that are numerous and could become onerous. The potential risk to the developer is that the end-purchaser fails to settle on completion. During the development stage, the developer assumes the risk of guaranteeing the interim loan, construction delays and all leasing and tenant improvement.

The above joint venture structures are relatively broad. It is up to the joint venture to negotiating a 'win-win' for the mutual benefit of the parties. If a structure is too lop-sided and leaning mainly to the benefit of one party, these joint ventures can become unstuck over the course of the venture.

SOME BASIC RULES REGARDING PARTNERS

Most of the structures explained in this chapter involve some form of partnering or working together with other people. Successful developments do not only depend on the location, finance, market forces and expertise, but also the business relationship between the people involved. Here are some good basic rules concerning partnerships:

1. **Choose partners very carefully**
   Whether you are choosing relatives, friends or business associates as partners, be very selective and make sure that your
   personalities do not clash. Find partners who understand the
   property industry. There is nothing worse if the development
   does not reach the expected returns and a partner, not understanding the issues involved, accuses you of indiscretion.
   Make sure all of the terms of the partnership are in writing
   and that there is a signed agreement if a joint development is
   undertaken together.

2. **Form partnerships only if you have to**
   Do not form a partnership unless you have to. Only find
   partners to cover a shortfall on your part such as a lack of funds.
   A partnership functions a lot better when people complement
   each other and work as a one driving body. Do not form a partnership unless you need to, as it can be expensive if you have
   adequate funds, adequate experience, sufficient time, and fair
   determination to do it yourself. Only form a partnership if you
   are weak in any of these areas.

3. **Define the role of each partner early**
   At the beginning of the association, define precisely what each
   person will contribute to the partnership. For example, your
   partner's responsibility may be to provide the money, and your
   responsibility may be to negotiate and complete the development. Obvious contributions that a partner would make
   include cash, equity in other property, the ability to borrow
   money, stable credit history, and good business associations.
   Obvious contributions you could make include your time, your
   knowledge, and your determination. Whatever you decide on,
   get it down in writing and make it specific and clear so that
   there will be no misunderstandings.

4. **Maintain maximum control of the association**
   If you find a partner, who is not compatible with your thinking
   and is limiting the progress of the development, it is best to
   dissolve the partnership as soon as possible. Do not waste
   time with a partner who does not understand the development

process and does not show trust in your actions. A good relationship sometimes takes time to establish, and the best thing you can have on your side is a good track record of making a profit for both yourself and your partners. If partners have made money with you before, they will find a way to say yes to another venture.

5. **Reduce the fear of your partner**
   If a partner is putting up the money, you may have to reduce his or her fear of losing their money. You can resolve the situation by placing the property in their name but have a written agreement on how the development should run, how the profits should be split, and the understanding that they won't have total control when it comes to the selling of the development. Transparency, regular updates and good communication are essential in allaying a partner's fears.

6. **Retain a partnership with one property at a time**
   Keep each partnership on a property-by-property basis. Each project should be evaluated on its own merits, the profits should be split when the property is sold, and the partnership should then be dissolved. This practice allows you to be more flexible should other opportunities arise. For example, if you have an agreement to develop a property with a partner and he runs out of money, you should be free to look elsewhere for another partner if you run across a good deal. It should be clear from the very beginning that your partnership is temporary.

7. **Establish dispute resolutions procedures early**
   Decide from the outset what procedure you will follow if one of the partners decides to sell out to the other or if there is disagreement. Establishing a resolution early will help to prevent any misunderstandings as the longer it takes to find a resolution the more the delay will increase tensions with your partner. A written document should spell out the rights and obligations of each partner as well as a procedure for both parties to follow to find a resolution.

8. **Decide early how profits will be shared.**
   Try to negotiate the best arrangement you can for yourself while still making it attractive enough for the partner who is putting up the money. Here are some ideas to incorporate:

   - If you are sure that your project is going to be a winner, do not give a large percentage of the profit to your partner. Instead, offer to pay your partner 25% return on his money or 25% of the profits. Most people are very satisfied with 12 to 18% yields on their investment.

   - If your partner is financially established, he or she may wish to forgo your offer of a guaranteed percentage return and will opt instead for a less-guaranteed program of a percentage of the profit. The harder the bargain you drive with your partner, the better off you will be when it comes time to divide the profits. If possible, never give away more than 50% of the profit to anyone in a partnership, and try to retain as much control as possible.

   - Agree to pay the partner their share of the profit and invested capital first after the sale of the development. Your partner will thus know that your profit is secondary to his or hers and that you will probably work harder to see that things happen as you say they will.

   - Remember, when you find yourself in a bad partnership, get out as soon as possible. Learn your lesson and don't make the same mistake again.

CONCLUSION

Both syndicates and joint ventures are helpful structures in a develop and hold strategy, especially when it comes to larger scale projects – especially if you do not have either the finances or skill set to complete the project on your own. With the increased cost of buying well-located land, the cost of financing and the high risk involved of going it alone, the formation of a syndicate or joint venture will ease the risk of entering larger and better projects. This strategy allows you to grow your portfolio with properties in better locations and with lower risks by spreading financial obligations.

If you are a first-time developer, these structures are an avenue to see how a typical development process occurs and to gain knowledge and experience by participating in one of these structures. Finding an opportunity to participate in one of these structures is not always easy. However, over the last decade, there are more of these offerings coming from developers, especially those looking for cash equity partners.

CHAPTER 10

RESIDENTIAL PROPERTY AS AN INVESTMENT

INTRODUCTION

History has proven that many ordinary people have made significant profits from residential developments and investments providing them with ongoing income and capital growth. However, the market in this sector is constantly changing due to a number of factors. This includes affordability, practicality, the changing demographic distribution of our population and the changing structures in household formations. These changes have created a demand for more diversified types of housing, which have included moves towards a range of medium to higher density housing options. This surge in demand has occurred in both fringe and inner-city areas, and in older suburbs near educational and transport nodes. New government policy and legislation has facilitated this demand and councils have rezoned and revised their structure plans in various cities where the need has occurred.

Many smart developers have taken advantage of these new trends and changes in the marketplace. Some have been very successful and have specialised in a specific market niche. Unfortunately, there are also many amateur developers who have failed. The latter, having heard how much money is being made believe that this is a get-rich-quick-scheme, have been short-sighted and unprofessional in their approach to their developments.

Applying the develop and hold strategy, residential is probably the easiest of the asset classes in which to be successful, compared to commercial properties. The entry level in starting a residential development is low as one can start with a small duplex and later branch out into four units or a larger project. Also, the market is larger, and financing is more accessible as lenders fight for market share.

THE DEMAND FOR HOUSING

Shelter especially housing is a significant need in every modern economy. In most countries around the world, there are a number of factors that contribute to the demand for housing. These factors affect the supply and demand for housing in all regions of the world. The demand, it seems, is ever increasing due to factors such as:

- **Population growth**

  Continued strong population growth will drive demand for housing. According to the Australian Bureau of Statistics, Australia's population growth rate averages 1.5%. If population growth continues this trajectory, it will likely be a factor that underpins national housing demand.

- **International immigration**

  Increasing immigration rates have added to demand for housing, especially as the age of immigrants tend to be disproportionately in the young adults' bracket. Most immigrants tend to head for areas where housing is already short, such as Sydney, rather than to country regions. This partly reflects a perception of where the best job opportunities are located.

- **Interstate immigration**

  Besides overseas immigration, there is also interstate migration within Australia that also fuels the demand for housing. With 86% of its population living in urban areas and 64% residing in capital cities, Australia is one of the most urbanised countries in the world. The reason for interstate migration is due mainly to the level of economic activity in other states and the improved quality of life together with more affordable housing.

- **Speculative investment**

  There is also the speculative element to the demand for housing which has led many households to borrow to purchase a second investment property. Also, there has been a strong demand for housing investment from China. Investors now account for about a third of new home loans in Australia.

- **Aging population**

  In Australia, the birth rate is decreasing as a result of career aspirations, a delay in first births, a decrease in family size, contraception, divorce and increased cost of raising and educating children. In addition, there is a decline in mortality rates due to improved advances in medical technology and increased awareness towards fitness and health. This has led to an increase in the aging population and a demand for retirement homes, aged care facilities and smaller homes for empty nesters. It is expected for this group to dominate the market for the next decade.

- **Housing affordability**

  Housing affordability in Australia has declined since the early 1980s. Demand for affordable housing far exceeds the current supply. This continues to put pressure on rents and house prices leading to a decline in the number of available, affordable properties. It is therefore not surprising to find that young aspiring first-time buyers are finding it increasingly difficult to purchase a home.

- **Healthy economy**

  Australia's proven economic resilience, adaptability and record of steady growth provide a safe, low-risk environment in which to invest. With its 26th year of consecutive annual economic growth, the Australian economy is underpinned by strong institutions, an exceptional services sector and an ability to respond to global changes. Australia's economy is the world's 13th largest with a AAA rating by all three global rating agencies and is forecast to realise average annual real GDP growth of 2.9% over the next five years which is the highest among major advanced economies.

- **Government housing programs**

  Government at all levels in Australia is involved in housing with a specific aim to encourage home ownership and investment. These schemes vary from state to state and could change at short notice. Some of the government programs include:

– *First Home Owner's Scheme (FHOS)* – FHOS has been established since 1 July 2000. Eligible applicants are entitled to a one-off $7,000 payment for purchasing established and newly built homes.

– *Deposit Assistance Scheme (DAS)* – DAS is used to offset the effective sale price and is not a cash payment useable for any purpose. Should the property be resold within three years of purchase, the purchaser is liable to refund the amount on a pro-rata basis.

– *Private Rental Assistance* – Rent Assistance gives extra help to eligible people who pay rent in the private rental market. Assistance is also provided to people who are homeless due to eviction, family disputes or who are unable to afford to rent a home.

– *Community Housing Program* – Community housing is similar to public housing except that it is managed by a community organisation and can also be initiated, planned, partly funded, developed and owned by community organisations including local government.

– *Defence Force Loans* – The Defence Service Homes (DSH) Scheme provides housing benefits to eligible veterans and their dependents of Australia's defence force by offering benefits such as housing loans at reduced rates.

- **Favourable Tax Laws**

  There are many tax incentives for the private sector to invest in residential property. These laws have been covered in detail in Chapter 2 but it is worth highlighting them again.

  – *Negative Gearing* – under the current Australian income tax law, negative gearing refers to the situation where the interest and other costs incurred to acquire an investment property are more than the rental income received. This cash loss is offset against other sources of income, reducing the amount of income tax payable by the owner.

  – *Depreciation Allowance* – Under the Income Tax Assessment Act, property investors are entitled to capital works taxation deductions. This is a proportion of the cost, which can be deducted annually as a legitimate expense. A depreciation of 2.5% per annum is allowed on a newly built rental home or improvement, over a period of 40 years. The allowance is also transferable to another investor who may buy the building.

– *Capital Gains Tax (CGT)* – CGT is a tax charged on capital gains that arise as the result of the sale or disposal of assets acquired after 19 September 1985. The tax is levied on the real or inflation-adjusted profit realised from the sale. In the housing market, a family home is exempt from such taxes. The tax is calculated on the difference between the asset cost base indexed to the Consumer Price Index (CPI) and the resale price. Any gains determined are added to the investor's other taxable income and taxed at the marginal rate.

- **Foreign Investment**

   The Australian foreign investment guidelines allow foreign investors to purchase up to 50% of new residential developments 'off plan' or residential conversion properties. The majority of investors are from the Asian region, and capital cities have been targeted.

TYPES OF RESIDENTIAL DEVELOPMENTS

The residential housing sector covers a range of property types that vary in scale and market profile. Adopting the 'develop and hold' strategy, smaller projects such as renovations or speculative homes can be considered. However, when it comes to larger projects such as five units or more, the strategy would be to develop, sell some of them, and hold the remainder such that the units held as an investment are geared positively. The following is a list of all the types of residential projects that are available for development and investment:

- **Renovation**

   Some older suburbs in capital cities offer some exceptional opportunities to renovate older homes providing some good returns. These renovations may require some alterations or additional rooms or by just adding some paint to bring the building to the present market standards.

- **Speculative homes**

  The speculative new home, which is usually built on a single lot in a new land subdivision or on an older block that has been subdivided into a smaller lot generally found in older suburbs.

- **Small units**

  These smaller unit developments are commonly found in suburban areas of both new and old subdivisions and can be defined as duplexes, triplexes and so on. They can be developed as strata type units or small green title lots.

- **Group dwellings**

  Under this category, one would find group dwellings such as townhouses, villas, and retirement villages. Each development will have their architectural theme defined by the use of similar materials, scale and building style.

- **Apartments, flats**

  These buildings can be found mainly in the inner city areas of most capital cities. This building form is defined as those dwellings in a group of more than one where any part of a dwelling is built vertically above the part of any other.

- **Government housing**

  Also known as public housing and provided by the State Government. Each state has their housing program, and in some states, these bodies get involved in joint venture housing developments with private sector developers or offer these developers to tender on certain housing development.

- **Niche residential developments**

  In addition to the above residential developments, there are a number of developments, which we can consider as niche markets. These include: holiday homes, timeshare apartments, cooperative housing, student accommodation, transportable homes and caravan parks.

The quality of the development property can be further categorised by class as well as by type. The following are the four classes of property.

- **Class A**. These properties are trophy properties. They have the best locations and attract AAA tenants. These types of properties command the highest prices.
- **Class B**. These properties are a cut below Class A. Although they still are in good locations, they are typically older than Class A properties.
- **Class C**. These properties are sometimes called 'fixer-uppers.' They still occupy good locations but have been neglected because of the poor management or limited financial staying power of the previous owners.
- **Class D**. These properties are the 'dogs.' They are poorly located and would and are surrounded by Industrial areas or have a history of crime.

The size of your bank balance will usually dictate the size of your development. If you have limited equity resources, the size of your development will be relatively small. Mortgage financing allows you to use leverage to finance larger projects. In most residential developments, developers are usually required to put in from 10 to 25% equity. In some cases that will be discussed in later chapters, you can reduce this equity contribution by using creative negotiating and financing techniques.

In deciding the class of property to develop, determine the range as well as the type of construction with which you are comfortable. Many developers will want to build in urban areas only while others focus on suburban areas.

LOW-DENSITY RESIDENTIAL PROJECTS

Under this category, renovations, single homes and small units such as a duplex or triplex are considered as low-density residential projects. These developments, whether they are homes built for speculative reasons or renovating an older house for resale, is an ideal start for a novice developer who would like to learn about property development without risking a great deal financially.

The two more popular developments are the speculative new home, which is usually built on a single lot in a new land subdivision or on an older block that has been subdivided into a smaller lot generally found in older suburbs; and a renovation of an older character home in an older suburb. Depending on financial resources and the time available, the novice developer can also tackle a duplex, triplex or quadruplex. Anything larger in size or cost would require more expertise, additional financial backing and could increase the risk to the beginner.

Benefits and risks

When compared with larger development projects, low-density residential projects can provide the following benefits:

- *Low initial investment*

  Most homes require a smaller amount of capital to get started. Depending on your financial position some lending institutions may not require a deposit, and at times only 10 to 25% deposit is required to start. This allows the developer to leverage his or her financial position.

- *Ease of financing*

  Most lending institutions have the infrastructure and systems to make home loans easier for the consumer to apply for. With more banks and new mortgage companies entering the market, finance for a home is a lot easier than other forms of development.

- *Favourable tax laws*

  If you build a home, live in it for 12 months and sell it after that, the profit made will be free of capital gains tax. However, this will not always be possible if the process is done on a frequent basis. If you retain the home as an investment and rent it out, you will be able to negative gear the property. This means that the shortfall in interest payable on the mortgage loan is tax deductible.

- ### *Superior liquidity*
  With finance more readily available, housing developments are a lot easier to sell than other forms of development. Also, there are generally not as many conditions attached, making settlement and sales procedures a lot quicker.

- ### *Market not as sophisticated*
  Purchasers entering this market are not as sophisticated compared with seasoned investors who will generally negotiate actively on many issues and in doing so, delay the settlement that in turns affects the developer's profit.

- ### *Good capital growth*
  Housing prices fluctuate according to supply and demand. Quite often during a boom period, housing prices peak and set the benchmark for future prices. The capital growth in this instance can be quite significant. Prices on commercial buildings, on the other hand, are governed by the leases they have in hand.

While low-density residential projects have been traditionally considered as safe developments, there are still certain risks involved such as:

- ### *Volatile market*
  Within the housing market, the phenomenon called 'herd mentality' occurs where people follow others rather than taking a rational approach and time their project according to the economic cycle. Whenever there is a boom, building resources are pushed to the limits causing a shortage of material and labour, and the opposite occurs in recessive periods.

- ### *Strong Competition*
  Single housing is a less complicated form of development with many players are entering this field. However, there is still money to be made by the astute developer who is one step ahead of the competitors.

- ### *Inefficient use of land*
  Plot ratios and densities set out by the local authorities on the traditional quarter acre lot makes the cost of land more expensive when compared to a higher density residential development.

- ### *Inept contractors*
  You could be caught out by unscrupulous building contractors or subcontractors if you are new the market and not familiar with the building industry. Poor workmanship could devalue the property or delays in the renovation program could increase the holding cost.

- ### *Cost overruns*
  You can get carried away with the emotional experience of upgrading a character home or underestimate the actual final cost of a new building. Therefore ensure that your cost estimation is as accurate as possible.

Recommendation

If you are a novice and want to gain some experience in property development, buy a block of land, get a home designed, contract a builder and then hold it as a start of your portfolio or sell it at a profit so that you can start another. Only by taking the initiative and starting with a small development will you be able to get an insight into this industry. Whether you make a significant or minor profit on your first single home development, the important issue is that you gain invaluable experience so that your next development is a better success.

MEDIUM DENSITY RESIDENTIAL PROJECTS

This category falls under 'grouped dwellings' which is made up of townhouses and villa units. In terms of housing form, a group dwelling usually is one of a group of two or more homes constructed at the same time, with each dwelling having its private garden area attached. These developments are quite common in Australian cities and towns. In many respects, they are contemporary versions of the 19th-century terrace house. Driving through the suburbs, especially those closer to the city, one will invariably come across some form of unit development, consisting of two to ten homes on a single site.

These developments have occurred due to a number of factors which include affordability, practicality, the changing demographic distribution of our population and the changing structures in household formations. These changes have created a demand for more diversified types of housing, which have included moves towards a range of medium to higher density housing. This surge in demand has occurred in older suburbs, and near educational facilities such as universities and technical colleges. New government policy and legislation has facilitated this demand and has rezoned, and revised structure plans in various cities where the need has occurred.

Definitions

The definition of these developments varies between states and territories and even from city to city. Listed below are further definitions of grouped dwellings:

- ### Units

  A unit is a broadly used word to define higher density residential type developments, be they townhouses or apartment buildings. Smaller scale unit developments can be referred to as a duplex, triplex or quadruplex depending on the number of dwellings. These smaller developments appeal to apprentice developers, who do not want to invest a great deal of capital in their early developments.

- ### Villas

  Villas are units in a development consisting of five or more dwellings, built with a specific visual theme, and generally given a collective name for identity. Villas tend to be smaller than suburban houses and are usually single storey, independent of each other (i.e. without a common shared wall) and have front and rear gardens. This form of development usually arises from the developer's desire to take maximum advantage of the number of units the Council's planning codes allow on the site. Council codes often set minimum sizes for one, two- and three-bedroom units, and developers try to keep the size down to the code limits to increase the number of units on the site.

- ## *Townhouses*

  Similar to villas, townhouses are dwellings that are typically found close to city centres and are built on sites at a higher density. They are generally two storey units, with or without common shared walls. Each usually has a parking garage with direct access to their unit and a private garden area on the ground level. Townhouses can fall either under a strata title with a body corporate or under a vacant strata title where they have their definite site area but share a common driveway.

- ## *Terrace housing*

  Similar to townhouses, terrace housing is built on two levels, has common walls and may have a communal parking garage and fall under a strata title tenure. Each unit will have access to a private garden on the ground floor. A typical example would be the Paddington style developments.

Benefits and risks

If you are thinking of undertaking one of these types of develop- ments, you should evaluate the benefits and risks relative to your expertise and financial resources. The following benefits can be considered.

- ## *Competent use of land*

  With the increase in coverage and plot ratio, land in higher density residential areas frequently utilises the developable land to its best extent. Generally, land with a higher density zoning is at a premium in terms of real estate prices and is located in prime locations, therefore forcing developers to build to the maximum allowable number of units on the site to capitalise on their investment. Concern can arise from a design aspect, as increased densities tend to have a negative impact on privacy and solar orientation.

- **The range of sizes and prices**

  Experienced developers do not build and sell only one typical floor plan. They try to incorporate as many flexible designs as possible to cater to the broader taste of the market. They offer choices such as two- to three-bedroom units and single or double garages. By using a standard format, they can vary the room combinations and floor areas.

- **Less sophistication required**

  As the units are standardised and at times the elevations are not seen from all sides, less elaborate detailing is required for both the internal and external parts of the buildings. Depending on the market niche, standard finishes can be used for all the units unless the buyer's request changes. This increases the developer's profit, as he or she can negotiate better prices for a higher volume and repetitive finishes. Any variation requested by prospective purchasers will have a surcharge and therefore lead to a higher mark-up by the developer.

- **Broader market**

  Depending on their location, higher density residential developments can cater to a broader market. This includes singles, young couples without children, young families or empty nesters, and even retirees. Not only can they provide for most people looking for a home with convenient facilities nearby, but they can also attract investors looking for a long-term investment in a good location and a building with very little maintenance required.

- **Better control**

  Unlike the simultaneous development of several single homes or renovations where the developer is building in different locations, villa and townhouse developments, being on one site, can be better controlled. Preliminary costs (such as set-up cost) are reduced, and there can be a continuity and flow of work for tradespeople, thus allowing management to control the flow of materials on site. Materials and finishes are repetitive, meaning there is less wastage.

The following risk should be taken into account.

- ### *Volatile market*

  The 'herd mentality' in the housing market is very relevant. Whenever there is a boom, building resources are pushed to the limits causing a shortage of material and labour, and the opposite occurs in recessive periods.

- ### *Exposure to overbuilding*

  As these developments are higher in number and therefore take longer to build, you may be midway through the project and be caught at the tail end of the boom cycle, thus leaving you with some unsold units. This could have a severe effect on the developer's profit and cash flow especially if he or she has borrowed money to finance the buildings. In addition, at the tail end of a building boom interest rates tend to rise, forcing the developer to look for alternative forms of financing or to cut their losses and sell the units at cost.

- ### *Higher demands for management*
-

  The greater amount of building activity together with a larger number of clients to deal with will require more staff and therefore more management expertise. A developer's failure to manage the development and the people involved at its various stages will cause delays, poor construction and therefore a loss in sales.

- ### *Higher demands for finance*

  These projects require larger budgets and therefore more personal equity into the development. By using debt finance, the developer is exposed to fluctuations in interest rates. To give you peace of mind you should sell as many units off-plan before you start building. Regrettably, this is easier said than done, as buyers are becoming more astute when buying through this method.

- *Shifts in consumer taste*

  With the aim of attracting buyers and renters, developers and their designers are always creating new concepts, which invariably set new trends. Other developers have to keep in touch with these new ideas so that their own proposed development is in line with the latest consumer tastes.

Recommendation

With medium density residential developments, most developers tend to sell their product to the public, but this is not the way to build wealth, especially after tax issues have been taken into account. Astute developers who have accumulated great wealth often rent out their units instead, therefore giving them an excellent cash flow in their retirement years. So instead of waiting for a government pension or for your superannuation to pay out (which will eventually dry up), start building a portfolio of housing units. If you are concerned about over gearing, sell one part of the development but retain the other portion for rental, or get an equity partner involved with your project.

HIGH-DENSITY RESIDENTIAL PROJECTS

Over the last decade, we have seen a surge in new apartments blocks erected in most capital cities of Australia. One of the motivating factors is the drive by town planners to bring more life to the city after regular business hours. Also, with increasing workload and the demand for convenience, older style inner-city apartments have grown in popularity. Land values close to the central business district are increasing and property prices are becoming more and more expensive. These high land values, in turn, have forced densities to increase so that developers can use this expensive land more efficiently by constructing well-planned apartments.

Types of apartments

The accommodation and size of these apartments will to a greater degree depend on the target market but are similar in planning concepts. Apartment developments are defined as a building that incorporates five or more housing units on different floor levels and is categorised in the following manner:

- Low-rise: Two to three stories without elevators
- Mid-rise: Three to six storeys with elevators
- High-rise: Over six stories with elevators

Types of apartment units

Depending on locality and market requirements, apartment units can be categorised or designed into the following segments:

- Penthouses: Usually located on the top floor and generally occupying the whole floor
- Luxury: Spacious and lavishly decorated to appeal to the executive
- Family: Two- and three-bedroom apartments
- Singles: Studio apartments and one-bedroom units

Benefits, risk and challenges

The development of apartments has the following advantages over other types of developments:

- Efficient use of land due to higher plot ratios
- Responsiveness to entrepreneurial efforts
- Less sophistication required due to repetitiveness
- Variety of sizes and prices from 1 to 3 bedrooms
- Higher loan-to-value loans available to prospective buyers
- Broad rental market
- Good resale market
- Relatively stable cash flows as a long-term investment
- Rapid depreciation write-off and high tax-shelter potential

The developments of larger apartment complexes may have even additional advantages over developments in smaller apartment units because of lower per-unit operating costs (due to scale economics) and ease of renting due to the additional amenities (pools, tennis courts) which large apartments may provide. The development in an apartment block may involve some or all of the following disadvantages:

- Incomplete market assessment of consumers' needs
- Consumers' ability to pay projected sales price or rents
- Competition from other projects, either existing or in development
- Inappropriate site or location
- Insufficient working capital
- Politics of community opposition
- Inexperience – lack of capacity to manage a complex business line involving a significant development and operations team
- Higher demands for management time, skill and money
- Greater exposure to government regulations
- Transient tenants
- No key tenants
- Exposure to overbuilding and swings in residential construction cycles

One of the biggest challenges of apartment developments is to get the timing of the economic cycle correct. You would not like to be selling or building an apartment project in the downward cycle. Unlike villas or townhouses which can be built in phases, an apartment block once started cannot stop its construction. Invariably, developers caught in the downward cycle are often stuck in a situation where they cannot cash their profit as the profit is held in the last few unsold apartment units. In addition to this risk, apartment developers have to overcome additional challenges:

- Securing sufficient operating capital
- Planning for long-term responsibilities
- Building or contracting for specialised skills in finance and asset management
- Understanding the broader housing market, both short and long-term
- Managing a large development team of both staff and contractors
- Expanding political and community support
- The availability of suitable and affordable sites

- Understanding and handling complex laws and regulations
- Humility to know your limitations and get proper help

Selecting the project type and the site

The selection of an apartment development project involves consideration of both size and location. The optimal size will be dependent upon the available capital, market demand, lender attitudes, site limitations and the developer's own willingness to accept the risk and handle operations at various project sizes.

The location may be a question of opportunity or comparative judgment. Quite often experienced developers will seize upon an available option if the terms are correct and the location appears viable. Where there is an opportunity to choose it would pay to consider the alternatives before selecting a site.

The preferred site should be large enough to accommodate a project of the preferred size, located in an area or neighbourhood that will be attractive to potential buyers who are able to pay the price. Also, the site should have:

- High visibility
- Adequate soil conditions
- Good drainage
- Availability of all services
- Pleasant environment and surroundings
- Appropriate access and egress
- Distinguishing amenities such as a good view
- Desirable microclimate.
- Access to restaurants and entertainment facilities
- Access to public parks and other communal facilities

The required zoning should be in place or available within a reasonable period. Environmental or other constraints limiting development must not be unduly restrictive, and the site should be available on terms which gives the developer maximum freedom to investigate the site before committing large amounts of money and, if possible, under an option agreement which can be extended if necessary.

Some renowned developers with deep pockets can operate in many market areas and select their sites in terms of long-range marketing objectives rather than the immediate attractiveness of the site itself. For most developers, though, a key question is operating convenience, which usually dictates a site in or near the developer's primary area of operations

Recommendation

Apartment development is demanding and challenging, but when the timing and market variables are in place, it also can be gratifying. Applying a 'develop and hold' strategy in this asset class is more complicated due to the increased project size and financial commitment. If the decision is to follow this asset class, it would be best to tackle a low-rise project with no more than 18 apartments which you can syndicate to spread your risk. These syndicate investors are also seeking to build a real estate portfolio. Alternatively, you can negotiate with an experienced apartment developer to purchase a unit or two at a wholesale price. These developers need to secure a number of off-plan pre-sales to secure their construction finance.

CONCLUSION

When starting out, most novice developers choose to tackle a residential project as it is simpler to understand and learn from, compared to a commercial project. They have probably bought or built their own home, so upskilling to understand the fundamentals of development is relatively easy. In addition, most banks and professionals allied to the residential industry have systems and resources in place to provide funding and services to residential development. With these systems in place, a smaller residential project would be quicker to start and finish and provide you with a wealth of experience along the way.

If you are too conservative or cautious to tackle your first residential project on your own, then it may be worthwhile forming a partnership or employing a development manager who has the experience. As each development is a standalone project, you can always start your next project on your own without your partner of development manager if things do not work out on the first development.

CHAPTER 11

COMMERCIAL PROPERTY AS AN INVESTMENT

INTRODUCTION

Investing in commercial real estate requires an understanding of the complex market forces at work, alternative funding require- ments, property management options, leasing arrangements and a good appreciation of the potential risks. In this chapter, we explore commercial properties specifically under the asset classes of office, retail and industrial properties. By developing or adding a commercial property to an investment portfolio, offers the private investor a good hedge against inflation as commercial leases are linked to the consumer price index (CPI). Historically, commercial property has equalled or exceeded the inflation rate. The primary driver for commercial property growth is similar to that of the residential market, and that is 'market demand'. However, the commercial demand is driven by economic factors as well as population growth. A strong economy is fundamental for any suc- cessful commercial real estate investment. Booming commercial markets are supported by strong international, national and local economies.

If you are thinking of adding a commercial property to your real estate portfolio, remember that the commercial property industry is one of opportunity for people who are prepared to take the time to acquire the knowledge that most buyers and sellers do not have. It is a business that will reward those who act quickly and spontaneously and those who operate on gut feeling honed by experience in commercial property. Some profits are made by luck, but those who depend on luck alone to bring success often find themselves failing in their endeavours. It is a risky business with the stakes placed fairly compared to other ventures. However, with high risks come higher returns. The successful commercial property developers I know use strategies to lessen the risks associated with their projects and minimise their personal financial exposure.

RESIDENTIAL VERSUS COMMERCIAL

So what are the differences between residential and commercial properties? Should you invest your time exclusively in one type or have a mix of both in your development portfolio? Although the principles of developing and investing are similar, you should be aware that these categories have their own merits and demerits. These variables determine the differences between residential and commercial real estate which are evaluated under the following headings:

- **Financing**

  – Most residential developments require a smaller amount of capital to get started. Depending on one's financial position most lending institutions would require a deposit of 10% to 25% to start. With residential development, lending institutions have the infrastructure and systems to make home loans more accessible for the consumer to apply for.

  – Commercial developments require more capital and the application for funding is more complex and generally takes longer for approval to be obtained. When banks evaluate a commercial loan, they generally will look at a loan of 60% or less.

- **Market forces**

  – Residential developments can cater to a broader market. The market covers singles, married couples, families, retirees and smaller investors. It is easier to market a residential development as it can be broken down into smaller sections. For example, an apartment block can be divided into strata sections and sold to a number of purchasers.

  – With a commercial development, there are two markets. Firstly, tenants are mainly large businesses and small business owners. When selling the completed development, the market is relatively small, e.g. a small office block or shopping centre would look to a single purchaser.

- **Buy-in land prices**

  – Residential land for new development tends to be more available in greenfield and brownfield locations. Depending on the demand in the property cycle at that time, land prices can generally be more competitive.

  – Commercial development sites in the right location, such as a well-established inner-suburban area are always in demand and developers will often pay a premium to acquire such properties. Buy-in-prices for commercial properties are substantially higher and are usually purchased by wealthier groups or corporations.

- **Valuation**

  – Probably the most significant difference between commercial and residential properties is in assessing its value. The value of residential property is based predominantly on supply and demand and is therefore calculated by comparing the market price of similar residential properties in that location.

  – For commercial properties, their value is determined by an inverse proportion to the degree of risk inherent to the continuance and stability of the income stream from the property. This means that no matter how attractive the commercial building may look or how much it cost to build, the bottom line in assessing its value will depend on the leases and the net income stream the building produces.

- **Market research**

  – When undertaking market research for a residential development, the market is more localised, meaning the study is generally conducted within the suburb and the adjacent suburbs and involves assessing the price point of similar homes for the general demographic profile.

  – With commercial property, market research would cover a broader area and need to be reviewed on a macro or regional level. As an example, for a shopping centre development, the research would consider the spending power not only within the specific suburb of the development but several suburbs beyond.

- **Type of purchasers**

  – Residential purchasers entering this market are not as sophisticated as seasoned investors operating in commercial spaces. An offer on a residential property is generally completed on a standard offer and acceptance can be executed by a real estate agent, whereas with larger commercial properties a solicitor is usually required to formalise the purchase as the purchase contracts are more complex.

  – Being more sophisticated, commercial property buyers will generally negotiate strongly on a number of issues, therefore potentially delaying the settlement that in turns affects the developer's profit.

- **Tenants and leases**

  – Tenants for residential property look for residences where location and local amenity are at the forefront of their minds. Even if the rent for a high-quality residential property is comparatively low, the investor will be compensated by good capital growth. A residential lease is less detailed and less complicated. The lease period for a residential property is short, ranging from a few months to three years, leading to the possibility of more periods of vacancy. The annual rent escalation is low and is dependent on the demand for rental property in the specific location.

  – In contrast, commercial property leases are often based on the precise requirements of business tenants and are generally longer than residential leases – typically from 3 to 10 years with escalation related to CPI (Consumer Price Index) and rent reviews at an agreed interval. During tough economic times or in situations of intense competition, investors will have difficulty finding commercial tenants and will offer generous lease terms. This could be in the form of rent-free periods or significant expenditure to meet the tenant's specific planning requirements. One of the key benefits of a commercial lease is that the tenant is responsible for all outgoings such as rates, land taxes, insurance and so on, whereas with residential these costs are the responsibility of the landlord.

- **Rental yields**

  – Most residential tenants have a variety of properties to choose from which means that if they do not like your property or the rent offered, they can just as easily find another, creating competition between landlords. Most yields in residential properties range from 3% to 5%.

  – With commercial properties, on the other hand, the rental yields are much higher ranging from 5 to 8% or higher, depending on the location and the demand for the commercial space. Most business owners come to view a commercial property would have done their homework and evaluated whether the location and traffic are suitable for their business.

- **Capital growth**

  – Housing prices fluctuate according to supply and demand. Quite often during a boom period, housing prices peak and set the benchmark for future pricing. The capital growth in this period can be quite significant.

  – Prices on commercial buildings, on the other hand, are governed by the leases they have in place and only increase in value relative to the escalation clause in the lease. This escalation in a lease is generally linked to the consumer price index (CPI). With commercial leases over five years, a rent review clause may be added so that the rent is adjusted to market value.

- **Adding value**

  – Many investors or homeowners in residential property can enjoy the prospect of enhancing the value of their properties, through the construction of a second storey, a renovated kitchen or a new garage.

  – A negative aspect of commercial property is the owner's relative inability to enhance the value of the property through renovation or extension. On the positive side, however, the owner, by renovating the building, could change the lease to encompass more favourable terms thereby improving the returns and capital value of the building.

- **Rental growth**

  – House rentals are determined by comparable market rates of similar houses in the area. Tenants pay their rents on a weekly or fortnightly basis. Although rental growth can vary according to location, commercial property offers greater opportunities for rental growth than those achieved by residential properties.

  – Most commercial leases link rental growth to the Consumer Price Index (CPI). With commercial properties, it may be possible to negotiate a specified annual rate above the CPI. Rent reviews are also quite common with commercial leases where the landlord reviews the rent currently paid by the tenant. This review takes into account any economic growth and the state of the market in that specific sector and locality.

- **Vacancy rates**

  – Residential tenants are always available regardless of the economic condition at the time because most people want to live and rent in places close to their friends, families, job location, educational institutions, and so on.

  – Commercial properties can be harder to lease due to the precise requirements of commercial tenants. Sometimes, owners who are pressed to find a commercial tenant will offer generous lease terms to make sure that the property is vacant for as little time as possible.

- **Summary**

Residential	Commercial
– Easier to finance	– Complex to finance
– Larger purchaser base	– Smaller purchaser base
– More development land available	– Land for development limited
– Valuation based on supply and demand in a specific area	– Valuation based on the net return of the property
– Market research localised	– Market research at the macro or regional level
– Less sophisticated purchaser – shorter negotiations	– Sophisticated purchasers – longer negotiations
– Shorter lease periods	– Longer lease periods
– Lower yields: 3% to 5%	– Higher yields: 5% to8% or higher
– Greater capital growth in boom times	– Capital growth limited by CPI
– More opportunities for building improvements	– Fewer opportunities for building improvements
– Shorter vacancy periods	– Longer vacancy periods

OFFICES

The advancement of computer and telecommunications technology has made the present day office a complex and unpredictable environment. With the daily introduction of new technology, office planning is in a constant state of flux, expanding in one area, streamlining in another, with ongoing replacing and redefining of responsibilities and procedures. Today, 75% of office workers are knowledge workers.

Retention of these assets has become increasingly important. Alternative office planning strategies, more collaboration, use of unassigned space and encouragement of telecommunications are commonly being employed by businesses large and small. These increases in corporate efficiencies have a direct impact on space needs and real estate costs as fewer square metres are being allocated per employee.

Types of office developments

Office developments can range from a small to a large building, accommodating a small one-person business to a multi-disciplinary corporation and can be broken into the following categories:

- **Renovated house**

  In more recent times and due to zoning changes we have seen many homes in older suburbs and along major arterial roads being renovated and converted to professional offices. These conversions are generally undertaken by owner-occupiers such as real estate agents, doctors, dentist, or by smaller investors.

- **Strata title offices**

  These are smaller office units within an office block that is managed by a body corporate. Generally, these strata office blocks are developed on the fringes of the central business district. The units are either rented out by investors or used and owned by smaller businesses that may have been part of the original development syndicate.

- **Business parks**

  Over the last decade, business parks have become more popular and are generally developed in decentralised suburban areas where land is less expensive. The developments are made up of smaller, two to three storey office blocks, which are surrounded by well-landscaped gardens and open areas.

- **Multi-storey office blocks**

  A city's population density and economic well-being are in part identified by the size and scale of its office towers. Over the years, commercial ego and identity have seen developers and large corporations attempting to build taller and more attractive office blocks, better known as skyscrapers.

Office developments can be classed as:

- **Class A:** The buildings are in excellent locations and are able to attract the highest quality tenants. The quality of the building is of superior construction and finish, relative to new or competitive with new buildings, and it provides professional on-site management. Rents are competitive and in line with new construction.

- **Class B:** These buildings are in good locations, with sound management, construction and tenancy. The construction and physical condition are reasonable and meet all building codes. Class B buildings may suffer some physical deterioration or functional obsolescence. Rents are lower than those for Class A buildings and new constructions but may be able to compete at the low end of the Class A market.

- **Class C:** This class consists mainly of older buildings (typically at least 20 years old) and have some degree of functional and economic obsolescence. The buildings may not meet new building codes and would usually require renovation to attract tenancy. Reasonable rents offered are generally lower than Class B buildings.

The demand for office space

The demand for new office space is generally determined by the economy of the country, where there are new business start-ups and the expansion of operations by existing tenants. However, this demand is highly cyclical and is prone to the effects of supply and demand. Compared to residential buildings, office space tends to be more reactive to these fluctuations. In a market where there is an undersupply of office space, there tends to be a reduction in the vacancy rate, whereas in an oversupplied market, the vacancy rate is higher and prospects for steady rental growth are a lot slimmer. Economic factors have a significant impact on the demand for office space, but economic reasons do not drive other influencing factors such as:

- *Business growth*

  In addition to the economic cycle, either the movement of businesses from other areas or the expansion of a multi-national company seeking a presence in new areas can generate the demand.

- *Outdated buildings*

  Older buildings do not provide an environment conducive to

productive office work. Poor ventilation and low lighting levels are not ideal working conditions. In addition, older buildings do not have the ducting and facilities to accommodate infrastructure for new technology.

- *Transport pressure*
  With mounting transport pressure on the CBD, decentralised office space such as business parks have been created to alleviate traffic congestion in the city centre, thus reducing the wasted travelling time of long commutes.

- *Supportive environments*
  Tenants in a similar industry such as finance or the legal fraternity tend to congregate in the same precinct. In addition, businesses supporting these industries also tend to find premises close by, thus creating complimentary services.

Rewards in office development

The major benefits of developing office buildings over other real estate asset classes include:

- *Higher potential returns*
  Compared to residential developments, the returns can be better if developed in the right location. Renting or selling office space is based on a rate per square metre and calculated on existing or proposed leases. Because of this, the construction or replacement cost does not hold much value when compared to the locality and rental agreements.

- *Economy of scale*
  If designed correctly, not much space is wasted, and the leasable area can be maximised. External finishes and structural elements are standardised, bringing economies of scale into play.

- *Relatively efficient use of land*
  With inner-city office developments, developers build to the maximum allowable plot ratios to maximise their returns. Office

parks and renovated home offices, which are generally located on the outskirts of the city, are more liberal in their planning.

- *Anchor tenants can provide cash flow stability*
  Securing a blue chip company or a government department as a long-term tenant can provide a stable income. With residential tenants, the leases are much shorter. Therefore, the returns are reduced by temporary vacancies and the cost of advertising.

- *A multi-tenant building can offer cash flow diversification*
  Larger office developments can provide diversification in lease negotiations. To attract a major blue chip tenant, the developer may have to reduce the asking rental. However, the return can be made up from smaller tenants who want to locate close to the blue-chip company.

- *Rental escalation provides additional inflation protection*
  With all leases in office developments, there is a built-in annual rental escalation. This escalation can be linked to either the CPI or a negotiated percentage. The rental return does not fall or lag behind regular inflationary figures.

- *Leaseback-sale opportunities*
  Some custom-built office developments can be sold to a group of investors and leased back for a fixed term. This frees up a developer's cash reserves, which may be needed for another development. In other cases, speculative developers secure prime tenants and sell the development to cash-rich investors.

Risks in office development

While office developments may show higher returns and be more sophisticated than residential developments, there are more risks involved, namely:

- *Larger financial capital required*
  The building and land costs need more capital investment compared to residential developments. The price of land is

generally higher for an office development unless a well-located piece of land is bought as residential and later rezoned to commercial. Building cost can be higher especially if lifts and the number of storeys increase.

- *The supply and demand for office space is highly cyclical*
  Office vacancy statistics brought out by the ABS are a guide used by the property industry as they help to forecast the supply and demand for office space. After a building boom, there is generally a surplus of office space, and rentals are very favourable. Higher demand and premium rental rates follow this just before the peak of the cycle.

- *Tenants are more sophisticated in negotiations*
  The majority of tenants seeking office space are business-people and therefore take a business approach when negotiating a lease. The developer and their agent or real estate broker will require robust negotiation techniques.

- *Alterations to suit tenant requirements*
  At times and to secure a tenant, a developer may be required to make some alterations, which may not be suitable for other future tenants. If you have to undertake such alterations, ensure that the tenant signs a long-term lease so that you can secure a return on the additional investment cost.

- *Management cost higher*
  Larger office buildings will require efficient management and accounting facilities. Depending on the size of the development, a full-time property manager may be necessary to ensure the smooth operation of the building.

Opportunities and strategy

Opportunities in office development will be dependent upon the market demand and the state of the economy. Development opportunities will be dependent on the short or long-term goals of the developer. For example, if a developer is looking for a quick return then small scale strata titled office developments would be preferable with profits generated by selling smaller office units to smaller business operators. On the other hand, with a long-term strategy, the developer would look for an opportunity in a larger-scale project, seek to lease the primary area to an anchor tenant on a long-term lease, and offer the naming rights to such tenant.

Another short-term strategy to achieve an immediate return is for the developer to build, lease and sell to an institutional investor. Some institutional investors prefer office developments as an investment compared to retail or other forms of real estate. The reason for this is that the management and investment security is better and safer. With office developments, the design is more straightforward and less varied compared to retail developments where tenants have significant and diverse requirements. Whichever approach or strategy the developer takes, they may find themselves developing the following:

- *Custom-built offices*

  These offices may be built for the government or large institutional corporations, which are broken into a number of departments ranging from two people to several hundred. These departments may have to be connected through central cores or service links. In developing a custom-built project, the developer should seek a very long-term lease with the minimum being ten years. Care should also be taken not to risk building deep, air-conditioned space, which will reduce the possibility of sub-letting should the tenant fail or when the lease is terminated.

- *Multi-tenancy offices*

  When a developer decides to develop and lease office space in small parcels, the need for deep offices and single access is less pronounced. The appropriate building is subdivided into a variety of different sized areas each having its own access. While this approach may have less risk, it will require more management.

- *Business parks*

  The developer would secure a larger tract of land, create a masterplan with smaller independent offices built at a lower density, well-landscaped areas and plenty of parking all within a secure site. The smaller office blocks can be sold to investors or leased to independent businesses but would be under the control of the park's management.

Recommendation

If you are thinking of entering the commercial property with a 'develop and hold' strategy, small office projects would be less complex of commercial property development structures. You could consider buying an existing house in a recently rezoned commercial area, renovating it and then leasing it out, or starting a syndicate to develop a strata office building. My first commercial development was an eight strata title office block which I syndicated together with five other businesses owners. Each syndicate member paid for their share of the total development cost (wholesale) and then either owned or operated their business within their strata held space. The other two strata offices were sold at retail, and the profit was shared between the six syndicate members.

RETAIL

Shopping is one of the major activities in which most people in an enlightened society take part. The building of shopping centres, like housing and education facilities, is a requirement for all communities. Shopping can be a chore, a social outing, or a much-needed stimulus, depending on the person. Interestingly, when tourists arrive at their destinations, they often go shopping as a leisure pursuit. Developing commercial retail outlets has many more requirements and risks than other development projects. However, they can produce greater income and growth prospects if analysed correctly and cautiously.

The other major point of difference from some other forms of development is the long-term involvement of the owner/developer. Unlike residential buildings, there is no sizeable short-term profit in large shopping centre development. The majority of owners are there for the long term. Therefore, they have a greater interest in ensuring profitability on an ongoing basis.

Types of retail outlets

Corner convenience stores, strip shopping and neighbourhood shopping centres can be developed by individuals or small syndicates without a great deal of expertise, whereas the development of the larger centres is usually undertaken by experienced, knowledgeable and financially able development groups. These larger centres involve complicated research analysis, smart planning, correct financial structures, various leasing options and expert management. While each of these categories has its characteristics, there are similar basic principles that apply to each when developing and financing. Retail properties can be divided into the following categories:

- *Corner shop convenience store*

  The traditional corner convenience store is typically found in older suburban areas. These are unfortunately becoming obsolete.

- *Strip shopping*

  This can be described as a continuous line of shops usually found along major arterial routes.

- *Neighbourhood shopping centre (1000m2 – 5000m2)*

  This centre usually has one major anchor tenant such as a supermarket together with a number of smaller line shops.

- *District shopping centre (5000m² – 20,000m²)*

  This centre has an anchor tenant, which is generally a junior department store, and may include banks and professional offices.

- *Regional shopping centre (20,000m² plus)*

  Developed with one or more major department stores, this centre includes general merchandise, apparel and service establishments.

- *Festival retail*

  This type of retail is also known as flea markets. The design and construction consist of economic lightweight or removable structures and are at times under cover of a large shed.

- *Discount warehouse centres*
  A typical complex would consist of a number of warehouses grouped together offering retail goods at factory prices. The rental per square metre is relatively comparatively lower than other centres because of the less sophisticated warehouse construction.

Rewards and risks

Developing a retail outlet can be exciting and rewarding, and the major benefits are:

- *Monopoly opportunities*
  This situation is created if there is no other land within the neighbourhood available for another competing retail centre.

- *Greater capital growth*
  As with most commercial property the value of the buildings increases in direct relationship to the escalation in rent. In addition, having longer leases, the potential long-term growth in commercial properties is generally higher than in residential properties.

- *Cash flow potential*
  Tenants generally pay the major portion of the operational and promotional cost together with outgoings.

- *Care by tenants*
  As tenants have to create ways to maintain or grow the standards of their business, they generally take care of the property.

Like all the other developments, retail centres involve many risks and also have unique problems such as:

- *Inefficient use of land*
  Because of parking requirements in retail centres, a considerable portion of development land cannot be used for building.

- *High land cost*

  Many factors contribute to this, including the shortage of developable land within an established neighbourhood and the inefficient use of land due to parking requirements.

- *A large scale of development finance*

  The large-scale building with high quality finishes to attract consumers to the centre requires a greater financial capital commitment.

- *Tenant business failure*

  Statistics reveal that a high proportion of new businesses tend to fail in their early years and new shopping centres seem to attract these types of tenants.

- *Risk of new centres opening*

  New nearby centres create new competition and could attract your consumers and key tenants by offering favourable leases.

- *High level of management required*

  Tenant requests, high levels of maintenance, security and promotions require a specialist, full-time management.

- *Higher exposure to tenant problems*

  Business problems, rental increases and tenant competition within the same centre creates an environment for tenant complaints.

- *Risk of obsolescence*

  In order to attract consumers, retail buildings have to continually keep up with new architectural trends and modern finishes, especially in high traffic areas of the building.

- *Online shopping*

  There is a growing concern that demand for retail space will wane due to online shopping and new technology eliminating the need for consumers to leave their homes to shop.

Recommendation

Developing and owning a shopping centre can be fun, creative and very stimulating but it is not for the faint-hearted as there are strict deadlines to meet, unrealistic demands by tenants, huge capital commitments and so on. A great deal of devotion to, and expertise in, this type of project is necessary. If you would like to add a retail asset under your portfolio and if you do not have the expertise or knowledge on how to develop one, then it is advisable to join a syndicate or a developer seeking investors. Alternatively, you can consider a strip-shopping scenario such as strata showrooms, which can be syndicated to other investors or owner-occupiers.

INDUSTRIAL

Industrial buildings are known as the least glamorous of the commercial property sector. The buildings have no elaborate architectural design features, resort-like amenities or high-profile addresses. Instead, industrial property is purely developed to provide practical and efficient space for users who consider its function over form. However, over the long term, industrial properties are steady performers, which is why they merit inclusion in a real estate investment portfolio.

Industrial property offers practical and efficient spaces that comes in all shapes and sizes serving requirements such as manufacturing and storing goods, logistics and distributions, R&D, labs, showrooms, and telecom buildings. Some developers specialise only in this sector and hold onto the building as long-term investments due to the following reasons:

- The demand for properties such as fulfilment centres for Amazon, distribution warehouses and self-storage facilities withstand market downturns better than other commercial properties.
- Compared to residential properties, industrial tenants typically sign longer leases ranging between 3 and even up to 10 years providing a stable investment.
- Due to the longer leases, fewer market fluctuations, and

less turnover, investors may see a greater return on their investment which lead to higher yields.

- Industrial buildings are relatively easy to maintain compared to other commercial spaces as the tenants that lease are typically handy, and unless there is a major issue, will quickly resolve maintenance issues themselves.

Types of industrial buildings

Industrial developments fall under the same category as other commercial developments but through the nature of their function, require less sophistication than shopping centres and offices, and at times may have different development principles. Industrial property consists mainly of factories and warehouses of varying sizes and can be broken down into the following categories:

- Single occupier/operation
- Strata title factories/warehouses
- Industrial parks
- Distribution centres

The zoning of industrial buildings falls into two main sectors:

- Industrial 1 - toxic, manufacture, special uses
- Industrial 2 - warehouses, light manufacture

Most industrial buildings are simple in design and are generally not architectural masterpieces. Large spaces are required, and therefore, for economic reasons, construction is repetitive and as simple as possible. Industrial real estate investments enjoy a higher rental return, but this is subject to the welfare of the particular business and the location of the property. Due to the high capital cost and investment required by most tenants to set up the internal plant in factories, tenants tend to be more stable and take out longer leases.

Demand Drivers

There are many factors to consider when analysing industrial development opportunities. Among these are location, proximity to customers and workers, transportation, access to land and financial incentives that can offset building costs.

- *Transportation:*

  Industrial property depends on easy access to major freeways, intermodal rail, ports and air freight and, as a result, serves as a significant driver for industrial demand.

- *E-commerce:*

  E-commerce acts as a substantial demand driver for industrial property, particularly in larger format buildings such as warehouses. The growth of e-commerce is omnipresent and gaining momentum.

- *Incentives:*

  Locating large industrial facilities often involves working closely with local or state governments to negotiate incentives that can influence location decisions. Large industrial properties such as a manufacturing plant, distribution centres or data centres can have a significant tax benefit, and state governments compete aggressively for bigger projects that will boost their tax base with jobs and property taxes.

Benefits and risks

Developing industrial buildings can be rewarding from an investment point of view, for the following reasons:

- *Stable form of revenue*

  If the development is designed, built and rented to suit a prime tenant, it is done mainly on the basis that a long-term lease is contracted and will bring a stable form of income to the investor for a reasonable period.

- *Less management required*

  As there are fewer tenants and at times only a single tenant that occupy industrial buildings, the management is less intense compared with other forms of buildings.

- *Potential monopoly*

  Industrial property is generally planned and zoned within a specific limited area. This usually creates a monopoly in pricing if there is no additional land left for further industrial development.

- *Reduced sensitivity to neighbourhood problems*

  Industrial land usually is zoned early and as part of an overall urban structure plan. The town planners who plan these zonings typically take into consideration that there should be no problems with future adjacent neighbours.

- *Fewer landlord and tenant problems*

  Most industrial businesses on average take great care in their business, and there are generally fewer problems with these tenants compared to other forms of real estate.

- *Less construction time*

  Because less time is required to construct industrial space, the industrial market tends to adjust supply to meet demand more efficiently than other property types. Given that factor, an influx of speculative development can influence the market quickly.

The risks in developing and investing in industrial buildings are:

- *Large capital investment required*

  Although costing less per square metre than other buildings to construct, industrial buildings are much larger in floor area with long roof-spans, so they require more capital investment.

- *Greater exposure to government regulations*

  Due to the number of people that occupy these buildings and especially if they are processing plants, the building of these developments has to comply with several stringent government regulations and government inspections.

- *Changes in technology*

  With manufacturing and assembly technology changing at a rapid pace to increase production, industrial buildings are exposed to the possibility of becoming obsolete.

- *Less escalation potential*

  As most leases are long term, the escalation clauses are at times fixed and not in line with the consumer price index, therefore not allowing the escalation to be adjusted if inflation increases.

- *Tenant more sophisticated*

  Tenants that occupy these buildings are generally established businesses and are therefore experienced negotiators when the lease is being drawn up.

- *Custom built problems*

  In some cases, a developer has to build to a tenant's specific requirements only to find that it does not suit the general market when the term of the lease has expired.

Recommendation

The long-term demand for industrial buildings is expected to stay healthy as a function of the same factors that drive the market today. Should you have an interest in this sector, the strategy for an industrial project would be worked out with the objective of maximising the market potential while minimising development costs. This applies whether you intend to sell or hold onto the completed project as a long-term investment. Most developers would fall into the latter category, especially if they have signed a long-term lease with a credible corporate tenant. In the case where your planned project is a set of smaller industrial strata units aimed at the small businesses, you may sell some of these units to owner-operators and investors to better your equity and gearing position and retain the balance as a long-term investment.

CONCLUSION

As mentioned earlier, commercial property is complex but potentially offers a better return than residential. If you do not have the experience and do not want any of the headaches associated with commercial property development or if you are starting in commercial real estate investment there is an alternative way through a group structure such as a syndicate, partnership or joint venture. Some of these group structures are made up of professionals, expert managers and investors. It is ideal, and if you do not have the required experience or capital for direct real estate investment, group structures can be a very viable alternative. Through this system, one can also take advantage of the superior leverage and greater diversification across a wide range of property sectors, including property development. Alternatively, should you have the knowledge and experience in the commercial sector you can start your group structure.

CHAPTER 12

ALTERNATIVE INVESTMENT PROPERTIES

INTRODUCTION

Adding to the traditional residential and commercial development and investment projects where a 'develop and hold' strategy can be applied, there are alternative properties that you could accumulate in your portfolio. Some of these properties have been created by imaginative property developers looking for better returns while specialist developers undertake others because they are too challenging for most developers.

In this chapter, a list of properties have been selected that can be developed and managed by individuals or a small syndicate rather than complex projects that require expertise and resources of larger corporations or experienced developers. Each selected property explores the details on how these alternative properties function and the risk and rewards in participating in the development of these alternative properties.

In this Chapter, the following alternative properties that could slot into a real estate portfolio include the following classes:

1. Dual-key property:
2. Retirement homes:
3. Student accommodation:
4. Childcare centres:
5. Serviced apartments:
6. Medical centres:

DUAL-KEY PROPERTY

A dual-key property is one which has a shared common entrance with access to two self-contained living units. The two units fall under one title but can be rented or leased to two separate tenants rather than one, therefore, providing an additional income to the owner. The application initially started with hotel room suites, where two adjacent hotel rooms had an inter-leading door to the other. This allows the two rooms to be utilised by two individual persons separately or by a family of four using both rooms. This concept developed further where a shared entrance hall was created but still provided access to the two separate rooms. Today, numerous developments are incorporating the dual-key concept. It can be found in both single homes and apartment developments.

- **Dual-key homes:**
  Unlike duplexes, dual-key homes enable a single space to be shared by two separate parties or tenants. The property may have only one entrance or front lobby, through which all residents enter. Some dual-key properties have only the entrance space as a common area while others have a shared lounge, dining and kitchen. Usually, each tenant will have separate keys that unlock only their own bedroom and bathroom spaces. See the sample drawings at the end of this section.

- **Dual-key apartments**
  Often called twin-key apartments, dual-key apartments provide a stand-alone studio apartment with an adjoining one- or two-bedroom apartment. There are separate entries for each apartment and no shared facilities, but they can be sold under a single title. See the sample drawing at the end of this section.

The pros of a dual-key property

- *Two income producing properties on one title*
  As there are two properties under one title, there is the option to rent out both properties, providing property investors with a higher rental return.

- *Only one set of outgoings to pay*
  If the dual key is a home on a single title, the rates and taxes are applied to a single lot. If the dual key is an apartment, there is only one strata fee to pay. Essentially you are getting two properties for the price of one.

- *Elderly residents*
  Families who have elderly relatives can benefit from a dual-key property if they need to look after their relatives. A dual-key home provides the ideal solution for this while giving each resident with their own space to go about their day-to-day activities.

- *Student accommodation*
  A dual-key home can provide a low-cost lifestyle to suit both students and first-time renters. A small family can live in the main house, while the other section of the home can be rented to a student.

- *Early payment of a mortgage*
  With the increase in rental yields in dual-key homes with two rental incomes, the owners have an opportunity to pay off the mortgage on the property earlier and therefore receive a passive income.

The cons of a dual-key property

- *A dual-key property may not be as in high demand*
  The dual-key property concept is relatively new in Australia. It is therefore difficult to evaluate the market demand this property type. However, if you buy a dual-key home in an area that is close to transport, schools, retail and work then you are more likely to attract tenants. Ensure that you do your homework first and study the local demographics.

- *Difficult in securing a loan*
  As this is a relatively new real estate investment type, some banks or home loan lenders may have reservations when it

comes to approving mortgages for dual-key properties. You should, therefore, speak to a reputable broker beforehand and find out what restrictions you could potentially encounter.

- *Splitting the cost*
  As a dual key falls under one title whether it is a green title, vacant strata title or strata title, there is the question of splitting the cost of utilities such as water and electricity as there is generally one meter of each service to the dual key. This requires additional management to work out the proper amounts to each tenant to ensure that there are no disputes.

- *Cannot sell separately*
  As the property is under one title, the two dwellings must be sold together and not separately which could cause problems when selling. However, to get around this, a dual-key home can be re-converted into a single property to create a larger property.

Recommendation

Although dual-key properties have their pros and cons, they can make a great investment property in your real estate portfolio. However, you need to ensure that you do your thorough research beforehand to make sure you develop in a good location and have the right target demographic that you can tap into to make renting out your property far easier. Furthermore, check with your local council that their planning laws allow developments of this nature especially on single lots.

Figure 12.1 The floor plan of a typical dual-living property

RETIREMENT HOMES

The number of older people living in Australia is rapidly increasing due to an ageing population, lower birth rates and immigration. In June 2015, there were 3.5 million people aged 65 years or older equating to 1 in every 7 Australians. Population projections by the ABS are that by 2056, around 1 in 4 Australians will be 65 years or older. If you are considering adding this asset class to your portfolio, here are some of the key investment drivers:

- *Low proportion of workers to retirees*

  As the number of older people in Australia grows, the relative number and percentage of working age residents aged 15 to 64 are falling. In 1985 there were 6.4 workers for every retiree, but by 2055 this corresponding number will more than halve to 2.8 workers per retiree.

- *Life expectancy increasing as the population ages*

  As a result of medical improvements and low fertility rates, the population of Australia will age. In 2015 life expectancy averaged at around 80 years for a male and 84 years for a female. This is projected to increase to between 87 and 88 years for males and females respectively by 2055 based on

ABS projections. As more people are living longer this means a higher demand for healthcare and retirement living with the related services that this sector requires.

- *Government spending on the older generation*

  Retirees and senior citizens place a more significant financial burden on government spending than other age groups on a per person basis. For example, the Government spends an average $31,690 per person per annum for the 5 – 9 age group, mainly as a result of educational spending, before declining through secondary education and stabilising during working age. By the time residents reach the age of 70 – 74, Government spending per person per annum rises to $32,568, and by 90 – 94 it is $72,630. This is almost 4.7 times greater than spending on a person aged in the 20 – 24 age group.

Size and types of retirement homes

Retirement homes can be split into the following categories, namely:

1. *Self-contained dwellings*

   – These are a group of units or villas without a supervisor for the daily care of its residents and developed in small groups of up to 20 units that integrate into the local community. They provide little on-site service, maximum privacy and assume a high degree of independence.

   – The units have at least two bedrooms with the second bedroom used for guest accom-modation. In some cases, a study is incorporated which can act as an additional bedroom. The location of the site will determine car parking provision.

2. *Grouped units with supervision*

   – These developments consist of grouped units, which include a supervisor's dwelling. Each unit is provided with an emer-gency alarm system connected to the supervisor's residence. Smaller schemes are provided with a shared lounge, a laundry and a guest room facility. Larger projects may include space for hobbies, hairdressing rooms and separate lounges.

– In providing a supervisor and communal facilities, the size of development is determined by economics and resources. The most cost-effective size, where a resident supervisor is to be employed, is 25 to 35 units. In schemes of 35 to 70 units, two resident supervisors would be required, working in, shifts.

3. *Grouped Units with supervision and health care*

– Similar grouped units but with extra health care on-site services such as 24-hour frail care for the elderly with additional rooms for the preparation of meals and dining, provision for assisted bathrooms, extra-care units for temporary use and extra staff provision.

– Developments of approximately 40 dwellings are found to be the most viable. These schemes may adopt either the 'hotel' or 'grouped-unit' model. In the hotel model the supervisor, kitchen and dining room provision are centralised, with public space more akin to a hotel foyer where social intercourse is optional.

4. *Residential aged care*

– These buildings have a very high level of service content with nursing as the prime function, and there is little privacy apart from private bedrooms.

– The residential aged care home is a specialised provider for the elderly where the residents surrender their self-reliance. Meals are provided, and nursing staff are brought in to care for residents.

Types of occupancy

There are several types of resident arrangements that give residents occupation rights in a unit. Below are examples of the more common structures used in Australian retirement villages.

Lease:

Several lease variations exist across Australia with similar characteristics. Residents are provided with a long-term lease, either for life or 99 years, which grants them use of a home of their choice and the right to use the common areas and other village facilities. The more common lease is the 'lease for life' but with a deferred management fee (DMF). The resident would purchase a lease similar to a strata unit but would be charged the DMF when they sell or leave the village.

Strata Titled Units:

Under strata title, the senior resident has direct ownership of their unit. There is common property, which residents have a right to use. Unit owners are members of a strata corporation that administers and maintains the property. The owners pay a quarterly fee to cover the cost of strata management, maintenance of the common areas and building insurance.

Company Title:

Senior residents buy shares in a company that owns a village, which entitles the resident to occupy a particular unit in the village and the use of common areas and facilities. The management of the company is governed by its constitution, and the Corporations Act regulates the company.

Unit Trust:

A Unit Trust is similar to a Company Title structure, but instead of shares, the residents buy units in a unit trust. This entitles the resident to occupy a particular unit in a village and the right to use the common areas and facilities of the village. The trustee of the trust owns the village. The trust deed under which the trust was created contains the terms and conditions of the trust

Conventional Lease:

Residents sign a lease and pay rent that entitles the use of a unit and the use of the common areas and facilities of a village. When lease term expires the resident either leaves or exercises options to renew. The resident also often has a right to terminate the lease on reasonable notice.

Manufactured Homes / Residential Parks:

This is a ground lease only where the resident pays rent for the site which also entitles them to use the common areas and facilities. Either a new or used transportable home already occupies the site, or a new home is erected which the residents pay for. The main difference is that the manufactured transportable home can be dismantled and re-erected elsewhere.

The pros of retirement homes

- *Growing demand*

  There is a growing demand for retirement accommodation especially in the affordable sector – whether for sale or rent.

- *Government subsidies*

  Rental income underpinned by the Federal Government can play a part given that most residents are eligible for rental assistance.

- *Largest market*

  The baby boomer market is the largest, fastest growing target market within the seniors living spectrum.

- *Less competition*

  There are very few options that exist for retirees to rent accommodation which give specialist developers more opportunities.

- *Lack of supply*

  Due to the high demand for affordable retirement accommodation in this growing sector, there is a lack of new supply coming onto the market.

The cons of retirement homes

- *Funding more complex*

  Funding from banks is not as secure as regular residential, and most lenders do not have a good understanding of this sector.

- *Limited secondary market*

  The secondary resale market is limited and generally only open to other retirees as most retirement projects have a specific age bracket of residents who can reside within its premises.

- *Limited rental options*

  Rental units located in retirement villages are currently the only viable option for the average investor to access direct property exposure to the retirement sector which poses a higher risk than standard residential property.

Recommendation

The ageing population in Australia will increase the demand for affordable housing options and astute developers are well positioned to capture demand from retirees. As with all asset classes, however, there are risks as well. If you are considering having a retirement home as part of your asset portfolio, your option would be to develop and invest in a self-contained dwelling(s) which could be leased out to retirees. If you have the capital, you could consider owning an entire village that is leased out to residents on a 'lease for life' arrangement. The latter provides a significant return and could be sold late to a larger corporation or investment fund as a going concern.

STUDENT ACCOMMODATION

The scale of the Australian education export market is well above the size relative to our population and economy. Australia is the third most popular destination for international students, attracting nearly 7% of the world's international students. This $15 billion industry is Australia's fourth largest export, behind iron ore, coal and gold. This fact, coupled with an overall increase in the number of places being offered by universities, has resulted in higher demand for student rental accommodation in Australia's university cities and towns.

Investing in student accommodation is effectively a yield play for investors. With student apartments, there is usually on-site management to handle the day-to-day chores. At the time of writing some student apartments are showing a 7.5 to 8.5% yield. With standard residential properties located in university precincts, instead of renting a house to a family you could enhance your yield significantly by renting room-by-room and fully furnished.

Types of student housing

Student housing can be split into two main categories namely On-campus and Off-campus with some sub-categories.

On Campus

- Institutional: These are traditional buildings developed are by a university or college and are part of the campus. The administration and management of these buildings are under the control of university or college.
- Leasing: Under this scheme, a university or college leases land within the campus to a private developer who will build, operate and administer the buildings for the term of the lease.

Off-Campus

- Shared Housing: This is where students group together to rent a property or go into an established household offered by investors, other students or families. The bedroom provided may be furnished or unfurnished with use of the other household areas and facilities. The cost of utilities may be shared between household members or already built into the room rent costs.
- Renting: Vacant properties vary from one to four or more bedrooms. The majority of vacant apartments and houses are unfurnished except for fully self-contained 'granny flats' or bungalows and holiday houses.
- Off-Campus Residences: There are many residences in the community operated by private providers. Residences offer furnished bedrooms and fully equipped common areas. Rent typically includes all expenses such as gas and electricity unless rooms are separately metered.
- Full Board 5 and 7 days: Usually includes a fully furnished room, breakfast and dinner and utility costs included in a set price. Lunch, laundry and other services may be nego-tiated or offered by the provider.

If you are considering adding student accommodation to your portfolio, there are mainly two types of student accommodation in the residential property market:

- Designated student accommodation apartment blocks that are purpose-built and used only for student accommodation;
- Investment properties located within a university precinct, which are rented to students on a room-by-room basis.

The pros of student accommodation

- *Growing demand:*

  Strong demand as universities expands the number of places on offer, and interest from overseas grows. Accommodation provision by the higher education institutions has not increased commensurately with student numbers.

- *Reliable income:*

  Students are known to be reliable paying tenants, and in particular as being good at paying the rent on time. Many students are subsidised by their parents, with some able to pay six months in advance, therefore reducing the arrears risk.

- *Higher yields:*

  Unlike other parts of this sector, the student rental market appears to be robust. Developers and investors can achieve higher returns from leasing a shared house for several students than can be obtained from leasing to other types of household.

- *Less sophistication:*

  As most students are itinerant and are on usually short-term leases, they do not develop an emotional attachment to their accommodation. They evaluate their place of residence as a means to an end. Therefore, developers do not have to provide sophisticated finishes to attract the student market.

The cons of student accommodation

- *Oversupply:*
  The student accommodation market can be subject to over-supply, leading to empty properties that are not readily available to other renting groups. Competition between investors for student leases could push up standards of amenity as well.

- *Short leases:*
  Some students only want a short-term lease or rental option for nine months or less, particularly from rural, interstate and international students who often prefer to return home for the summer break between December and February, leaving you with a vacancy period.

- *Limited market segment:*
  Unless the local housing market was pressurised because of high demand, other groups such as young professionals and low-income households tend not to compete for the same properties as students.

- *Management cost:*
  In student apartment blocks, the on-site management fees can be expensive and will eat into your rental return. It is crucial that you check out all the management fees associated with the management of the building.

- *Lower capital growth:*
  While the yields are higher, the capital growth is more moderate in student accommodation. However, this may mean that it works in your favour to pay it off the mortgage faster leading to a faster passive income.

- *Students problems:*
  Students love to party as they are young and have plenty to celebrate. However, this is not great for the investor, who might find themselves on the blacklist of neighbours due to noise issues. Also, maintenance could be costly, as young students may not be as responsible.

Recommendation

Having student accommodation as part of your portfolio has both its pros and its cons, but the key driver here is a yield game. You may not generate huge increases in capital growth. It may remain stagnant in its value for some time until the rental escalation kicks in. However, you will see reliable and robust yield results. If you want to test the water, look out for a house within an education precinct and do some internal alterations to suit the student market.

CHILDCARE CENTRES

Child care, otherwise known as day-care, is the care and supervision of a child or multiple children aged from six weeks to thirteen years. Some strong trends are driving growth in the childcare centre industry, which includes strong government funding, growing demand for locations and an increase in workforce participation. A significant part of the cash flow of childcare centres is government sourced, and the move from the current rebate/benefit system to the new subsidy system will increase the funding available for lower-income families. Currently, the Australian Government spends almost $7 billion a year to support families to access quality and affordable childcare. Below are key points child care in Australia. Other facts in this sector include:

- There are around 1.6 million Australian children currently attending childcare centres.
- The rate of child care use in Australia increased by 77% between 2000 and 2015.
- Overall, families cover 37% of the cost of childcare. The rest comes from the government.
- The federal government spends $7 billion on child care each financial year, of which over $6 billion is allocated to the childcare rebate and the childcare benefit.
- The childcare rebate covers 50% of out of pocket childcare expenses of parents up to a maximum of $7,500 per child per year, regardless of income.
- The childcare benefit is additional assistance paid to low

and middle-income earners, progressively declining to zero for families with income over $149,597 and only one child. The thresholds for families with more children are higher.

- In Australia, 86% of mothers returning to work use flexible working arrangements to care for their child, including working part-time (65%), flexible hours (35%), and working from home (26%).

Types of childcare centres

The size and facilities of a childcare centres varies according to the number of children attending and the type of services offered by the operator. The majority of child care centres in older suburbs are home conversions whereas new centres are being developed in either newly established suburbs or part of a mixed-use development. The services offered by most operators include:

- *Long Day Care:*
  This service provides all-day care or part-time care for children, usually below school age. This is the most popular form of childcare; it has had steady growth over the last five years. There is a heavy reliance for this service by parents particularly for children aged 0–4 years.

- *Family Day Care:*
  Individuals provide a flexible care arrangement and developmental activities in their own homes for children on behalf of an approved Family Day Care service. This segment is popular within regional areas and has seen growth since 2013 after a stagnant period.

- *Occasional Day Care:*
  This mainly caters for the needs of families who require short-term care for their children, which are usually non-school aged. The service is flexible according to community needs by providing care at short notice and in emergencies. Used intermittently, this segment accounts for approximately 6,670 children nationwide and is the least popular service.

- *Outside School Hours Care:*

  This care is for school-aged children providing care before or after school during the school term. As parents are working longer, the number of children in this segment grows. This also includes vacation care (child care services during school holidays) which is becoming more popular adding further demand for outside school hours' care services.

The future of child care

With population growth forecast over the next five years and maternal participation rates in the workforce, the demand in the child sector will grow further. The demand for new centres will grow exponentially in keeping with the Government's focus on providing affordable and accessible child care services. On the other hand, operating costs will likely experience some inflationary pressure due to imposed regulatory standards. However, this isn't expected to impact the sector's trajectory.

Recent history and forward projections indicate that child care will continue as a sector of sustained growth, primarily supported by social trends. It's unlikely that it will retreat to its previous fragmented nature as institutions have aggressively taken opportunities to enter a performing market, growing market share and gaining economies of scale. Accordingly, industry consolidation will continue as an acquisition and merger activity is expected to increase.

The pros of developing childcare centres

- *Long term lease:*

  Childcare centres offer long-term leases with most terms ranging from 15 to 20 years with options and 3% annual rental increase.

- *Strong yields:*

  The childcare industry has historically recorded higher yields than the office, retail and industrial sectors. Yields range from 6% to 10%, which has outstripped all other real estate asset classes.

- *Payment of outgoings:*
  Under the lease agreements, the operators are responsible for paying the property taxes, insurance but maintenance items and repairs are the landlord's responsibility.

- *Government support:*
  The Australian Government aims to incentivise families to return to work by increasing access to childcare services. For example, as approved on 1 July 2018, the childcare packages provide families earning less than $65,000 per annum with an 85% rebate, tapering off to 20% for households earning $250,000 - $340,000.

- *Steady demand:*
  The increasing demand is underpinned by steady population growth as well as female workforce participation rates, which have been on a consistent upturn since the 1980s.

- *Tenant investments:*
  Tenants invest heavily in their properties, leading to fewer relocations, longer-term leases, and higher levels of income stability.

The cons of developing childcare centres

- *Poor location:*
  The success of a childcare centre is highly dependent on its location and the catchment area. Selecting a site in the wrong address can lead to business failure.

- *Poor operator:*
  As an owner of the childcare centre building, you want to ensure that the operator you contract to lease the property has a good track record. Poor performance by the operator may lead to the delay in lease payments or finding a new operator should their business fail.

- *Low capital growth:*
  Like most commercial real estate investments, capital growth

is lower than that of residential property as the value is linked to the lease agreement between the building owner and the tenant/operator.

Recommendation

With strong yields and excellent lease conditions, childcare centres have become Australia's fastest growing and most desirable new real estate investment class. The rental range is between $1,500 and $6,000 per childcare centre each year, with metropolitan centres averaging $3,000 per place. Like any good thing, more investors and developers are starting to look at this market opportunity. If you are considering tackling one of these projects, you first need to find a great location and secondly a good operator with recommended credentials. From a financial perspective, the entry level must not be too high if you have to find an existing residential building that can be converted into a childcare centre through renovation. However, building new would require more capital, and it may be worthwhile bringing in a financial partner.

SERVICED APARTMENTS

Compared to traditional hotels or motels, serviced apartments can be a convenient and cost-effective accommodation option for leisure and business travellers looking for extended-stay ac-commodation. Guest are provided with a self-contained apart-ment-style unit together with private cooking facilities such as a kitchenette, living and sleeping areas that are larger than most standard rooms, and often access to gyms, restaurants, meeting space, concierges and other hotel-like services.

Success in developing and investing in serviced apartments will largely depend on their location and the tourism market. If you are contemplating entering this sector, it will be vital to undertake thorough market research. Depending on your financial position you could develop on your own or form a syndicate, find a rep-utable operator and hold the building as an investment. Alterna-tively, you could sell off some of the apartments under a strata title to reduce debt. Finding a good operator, and one that can provide a lease or guaranteed return, is ideal as this will help in securing funding for your project. As an owner of serviced apartments, the agreement with the operator may take many different forms, but there are two general models of serviced apartment agreements.

- *Long-term lease:*

  A long-term lease allows the operator to offer the apartment for short- or long-term accommodation and to operate it in much the same way as a hotel room. In this model, the owner of the apartment does not use it as a residence, but solely as a rental property.

- *Short-term lease:*

  A short-term lease allows the owner intermittent use of the property, while the operator can let it out for short-term accommodation when it is not in use by the owner. This is often the case with resort style properties, where the owner may use the property as holiday accommodation for part of the year and allow the operator to rent it out for short-term accommodation for the rest of the year.

Types of serviced apartments

Serviced apartments come in all shapes and sizes, and they are a cost-effective alternative to hotel accommodation. Generally, they are cleaned once a week and provide home comforts for longer-term stays, while allowing guests a degree of independence by providing cooking facilities. Below is a list of various offerings by operators.

- *Apart-hotels:*

  This is a blend of a serviced apartment and a hotel. It offers the best of both worlds. They generally provide hotel-style facilities such as breakfast, room service, gyms and even swimming pools, as well as a living area and kitchen facilities. Sometimes apart-hotels are part of a standard hotel and share on-site amenities with the rest of the hotel, such as the bar or restaurant.

- *Dedicated apartment buildings:*

  These buildings often have on-site concierge during office hours, and usually, offer a self-check-in facility or a meet-and-greet service. There are emergency phone numbers provided for assistance outside office hours.

- *Individual apartments within a residential development*

  These are serviced apartments in a development that may include privately let or privately owned apartments. With these properties, it is unlikely that on-site reception or staff will be provided, and the focus is on privacy and independence for the guest.

- *Individual apartments (owned by a serviced apartment company)*

  These apartments usually do not have any on-site staff and use self-check-in facilities or a meet-and-greet service. An emergency out-of-hours number is provided. Individual apartments are perfect for privacy.

The pros of serviced apartments

- *Guaranteed rental income*

  With most serviced apartment agreements, the risk of vacancy is placed upon the operator. This means that the operator leases each individual property from its owner for a fixed price and then rents the apartments to people seeking accommodation. This alleviates the risk of long periods of vacancy that often comes with other investment properties.

- *Good rental returns*

  Because many serviced apartment agreements offer a fixed price to the property owner, the rate of returns can often be much higher than it is for other types of residential property. Historical evidence shows serviced apartments offer a net rental yield more than 6% compared to other residential rents which average between 3% to 5% return.

- *No maintenance or repairs*

  In most service apartment agreements, the operator is responsible for the ongoing maintenance and repair of a serviced apartment. This means that you don't have to worry about dealing with maintenance requests from property managers or repair complaints from tenants. In many serviced apartment agreements, the operator is your tenant and carries out repairs themselves.

The cons of serviced apartments

- *Lower capital growth*

  If your investment strategy is geared towards capital growth, then you may want to think again whether to invest in a serviced apartment. Serviced apartments typically have poor capital growth because they are offered solely to investors, which therefore dampens demand.

- *Difficult resale market*

  If you decide to sell your serviced apartment, you may encounter difficulty in finding a buyer as these properties attract a particular type of investor with a specific strategy of investment and risk profile, limiting the market for resale.

- *Poor management*

  In the serviced apartment industry, some large operators have a high degree of stability, offer brand recognition and have transparent and trustworthy agreements with property owners. However, this industry also includes many smaller operators. While some may be excellent operators, there are others who are incompetent and have poor management protocols.

- *Difficult to finance*

  The financing for serviced apartments can be more difficult to obtain. Most lenders may require a larger deposit as they consider this sector as a risky business. Some have stringent criteria around the size and use of serviced apartments and will seldom be willing to lend for items like furniture, which owners must pay for themselves.

- *Competition from other operators*

  While serviced apartments used to be the only style of accommodation that offered a well-priced, self-contained and more independent option, Airbnb has proven to be a disruptor in this sector. Before considering a development of this kind, it would be a good idea to do your research into the number and success of Airbnb properties in the area.

Recommendation

The short stay accommodation industry is typically a very cyclical business and is impacted by many external events beyond one's control. However, serviced apartments can offer investors some unique benefits from an investor's perspective. A service apartment project carries a higher risk and projects of this nature are more substantial in dollar value. Should you decide to undertake a serviced apartment project, it is best to analyse your financial risk and maybe consider spreading this risk through a syndicated model.

MEDICAL CENTRES

Australia has one of the best health care systems in the world based on the health results of its population, and Australian investors are starting to move into the healthcare sector. There are several benefits of investing in the healthcare sector, one of the biggest being the baby boomer population. This generation will be requiring significant amounts of healthcare in the near future. Investors that choose to get involved on the front end of this trend could potentially realise substantial returns on their investment.

The first baby boomers turned 65 in 2011, starting the swell in Australia's senior population. This population expansion will create a vast pipeline of customers for medical providers, increasing the demand for hospital stays, outpatient treatments and doctor visits. Also, there will be a need to develop new outpatient facilities including on-campus medical office buildings, off-campus integrated outpatient centres, urgent care centres and freestanding emergency departments, health villages (medical fitness and wellness centres), retail primary care clinics, and a variety of post-acute care facilities.

Adopting a 'develop and hold' strategy, most developers would look at projects in primary healthcare which is generally housed in well-located medical centres. For more than 30 years, primary healthcare has been a catalyst and a leader in providing affordable, accessible healthcare for all Australians. These businesses are strategically positioned in the affordable and accessible market with quality national brands, a substantial footprint and no capacity constraints.

Types of Medical Centres

A major shift in workplace dynamics is happening in the Australian healthcare general practice. Medical centres are getting larger, and ownership is becoming concentrated into fewer hands, thanks to the era of corporate ownership and the rise of the GP super clinic. The number of doctors working in solo practice in Australia has halved over the past decade, and over half of all GPs now work in medical practices with five or more practitioners. The premise is that a group of doctors and allied health professionals can share common resources more efficiently while collaborating to improve the care of people living with chronic conditions. In the Australian context, medical centres have two scales of operation, namely:

1. *Small practice*

    These practices would have either one doctor or a few partners operating their business in a suburban area. The advantage of working in a smaller privately owned practice is autonomy. Doctors who work in small practices have more control over the way patients are managed and the way they practise.

2. Large practice

    Similar to GP Super Clinics, these practices have several doctors and specialists under one roof together with nursing staff. The increased number of practitioners makes support staff and equipment more affordable, which unshackles doctors from routine administrative and practice management tasks. These are either owned by private investors or a corporate. Some of these larger practices incorporate a pharmacy as well.

The pros of medical centres

*   *Higher returns*

    The average rental return for residential property across Australia's capital cities is 3.6%. In contrast, it's not uncommon to get anywhere between 8% and 12% gross rental yield for a medical centre.

- *Longer leases*

  A medical centre tenancy can be anywhere between 10 to 15 years. Doctors tend to stay longer especially when they've invested some capital customising the premises.

- *No outgoings*

  Similar to a commercial lease, tenants within a medical centre are liable for paying rates and taxes, land tax, water, insurances and body corporate fees if applicable.

- *Secure tenants*

  Having a lease with professional doctors provides secure tenants which ensures the stability of cash flow and fewer vacancies

- *Social need*

  Medical centres can be considered as social infrastructure where the services provided by the tenant doctors are essential for the functioning of a society.

The cons of medical centres

- *Regulatory interference*

  The medical industry is highly regulated, and policy changes can be initiated by a new government coming into power, which may, in turn, affect the businesses operating in the medical centre.

- *Development approval*

  Most sites for medical centres require commercial zoning. If not and if the proposed site is zoned residential, the rezoning and development approval process could be a long drawn out process.

- *Sophisticated tenants*

  With the tenants being professional doctors, they would seek better terms and conditions when negotiating the agreement.

Recommendation

Medical centres have several unique characteristics that make them attractive investments, but opportunities are few as most corporates are entering this sector. Most new opportunities would be in greenfield suburban land subdivisions, but this comes with higher risk in the short term, as the required population has not been established to support a medical centre. Unless you have deep pockets, you may consider land banking and wait for a while before building.

CONCLUSION

If you are considering having any of the kinds of properties considered in this chapter in your investment portfolio, thorough research and understanding of the type of property are essential. While there are similarities between the various types of properties from both a development and investments perspective, there may be variations due to local market demand, local market understanding of the product.

One way of overcoming risks and understanding more about the kind of property you are interested in developing is to speak to experts who have knowledge and experience working in the sector of interest. It is also important to appoint a designer or architect who has experience in the specific sector. Appointing one who does not have full knowledge of the particular type of development could lead to mistakes and you don't want to be paying for their education at your cost.

CHAPTER 13

MANAGING YOUR REAL ESTATE PORTFOLIO

INTRODUCTION

Managing a property development is a short-term exercise but if the properties are held as a long-term investment, the management of these assets is quite different, and you need to consider how you will be protecting them. As a landlord you will be taking on responsibilities and certain tasks such as securing tenants, chasing rental payments and coordinating maintenance and repairs, which can be time consuming.

The success of your real estate portfolio will depend mainly on your management skills and how your tenants – who are your customers – are treated. Unfortunately, landlords have a poor reputation because the majority of them do a terrible job because they do not see they are renting a property as a business. In other words, they treat their investing like a hobby. However, a real estate portfolio is an investment and should be treated like any other business venture through effective management systems and structure. If you follow this, the results will generate revenue and ensure success.

While the basis of renting a property is to produce an income to a landlord, the management and investment of commercial property has some differences when compared to a residential property. For instance, the latter rent is paid weekly or fortnightly whereas with commercial rent is paid monthly. Residential leases are much shorter compared to long commercial leases which require more advertising for tenants and additional management. The comparison of the two assets types is described further in this chapter.

You can choose to manage the properties in your portfolio

yourself, or you can outsource your management to a professional. Alternatively, you can choose to practise a mix of both, but this will depend on your circumstances and your time available to undertake the management. Managing the properties in your real estate portfolio yourself is undoubtedly achievable and may seem appealing from a cost point of view, but being a landlord comes with a lot of stress and responsibilities. Therefore, a good quality and respected property management agent or company can often justify their fees when you look at the service and facilities they can offer you.

LANDLORD RIGHTS AND OBLIGATIONS

Being a landlord is not just a matter of collecting rent and maintaining the property. As a landlord, it is also your responsibility for you to understand your rights and obligations so that you do not fall foul of the law. If you employ a property manager, they will be able to advise you and act on your behalf. Unfortunately, many landlords who manage their rental properties are not familiar with these regulations and become disillusioned with owning an investment property because of difficult tenants or problems with maintenance issues.

By law, landlords have a duty of care to the tenants who are renting your property and their affects kept onsite. It is of utmost importance that no injury or damage is caused to the tenants, visitors, neighbours or members of the general public as a direct result of landlords neglecting their duties and responsibilities. Landlord responsibilities include:

- Maintaining the structure and exterior of the building in good order;
- Ensuring all services such as gas, electricity and air-conditioning are working;
- Installation and appliances provided are safe and well maintained;
- Treating potentially health-threatening issues such as rising damp; and
- Any other terms and conditions that is stipulated in the tenancy agreement.

State tenancy laws

In addition to the standard landlord responsibilities, each Australian state and territory has specific requirements. As the laws relating to tenancy agreements may vary between Australian states and territories, and change over time, it is recommended that you check with the relevant state or territory government department. It is also recommended that you obtain independent legal advice about matters relating to landlord obligations and tenant rights in order to avoid a legal dispute with a tenant.

Discrimination

As a landlord, you have the right to choose the type of tenant you consider the most suitable for your property, but the equal opportunity legislation in each state makes it unlawful to discriminate against or harass people. This means is that you cannot choose a tenant based on their age, race, religion, sex or a whole host of other discriminatory reasons. If you do, you could be liable to for damages or fines.

The bond

It is recommended that all landlords acquire a bond from their new tenants. The bond is there to protect the landlord or their property manager if the tenants fails to keep the premises orderly, damage the property or don't pay rent. In this instance the landlord or their property manager can claim some or all of the bond at the end of the tenancy. In both commercial and residential properties, the bond is usually the equivalent of one month's rent but it can be more than that for some expensive properties. At the end of the tenancy, any cost incurred by the landlord to bring the property into the same condition as it was at the beginning of the tenancy can be claimed against the bond, but 'fair wear and tear' cannot be claimed. Below are some items that can be claimed against the bond:

- Damage caused by the tenant or their visitors
- Cleaning expenses
- Landlord being forced to pay tenant's bills
- Loss of landlord's goods

- The tenant abandoning the premises
- The tenant leaving unpaid bills
- Loss of the landlord's goods
- Unpaid rent

If there is a disagreement about the bond, or the landlord wants to claim compensation over and above the bond, each state has a tribunal to adjudicate on these matters. For this reason, it is essential that a comprehensive property condition report is completed at the beginning of the tenancy together with photographic evidence.

Leases

It is important to understand that commercial leases and residential leases are quite different. Here are the main distinctions between them:

- *Residential leases:*

  A residential lease agreement is a contract between a tenant or tenants and the landlord to use property for their living arrangement. A standard residential lease for housing covers the renting of a house, townhouse or an apartment. The property is primarily used for a residence and not for running a business. Residential leases are subject to consumer protection laws and there are a number of standard lease agreement forms.

- *Commercial Lease:*

  A commercial lease is a contract between a business tenant and landlord for the use of the commercial property to generate a profit through the sale of goods, services or the manufacture of a product. The commercial property can be defined as a warehouse, retail shops in a shopping mall or office space in an industrial or commercial building. Unlike residential leases, most commercial leases are not based on a standard form or agreement; each commercial lease is customised to the landlord's needs. The term of the lease is typically for a set number of years (much longer than a residential lease) and close to the end of the term, the tenant has an option to renew for another set term. The negotiations of a commercial lease between a business owner and a landlord can be extensive and pro-tracted. Most businesses often need special features in their leased premises, and these and other conditions need to be included in the lease.

The rent

- *Residential Rent*

  Residential leases are typically 'gross' leases in that the tenant pays a fixed rental price. The landlord pays out all outgoings such as rates, land tax, insurance and so on except for utilities such as water, gas and electricity used by the tenant. Residential rent can be paid weekly, fortnightly or monthly. If rent is paid weekly, the landlord cannot ask for more than 14 days rent at the beginning of a tenancy. The rent is based on the quality and size of the home and the current market rental in its location. The conditions of rent increases vary from state to state so these should be checked with your relevant state authority.

- *Commercial Rent*

  Commercial leases can be described as 'net' leases whereby the tenant pays a base rent plus outgoings plus the use of utilities. With commercial property leases, rent is usually paid monthly. The rent is typically based upon the amount of square meterage occupied by the tenant. In some instances, such as retail outlets, a base rate and outgoings plus a percentage of the gross turnover received by the tenant can form the basis of the rent charged by the landlord. Rent increases are annual and are typically based on the CPI (Consumer Price Index) with rent reviews every 3 to 5 years or as agreed between the tenant and the landlord.

Property condition report

Once the lease agreement has been agreed upon or signed, a property condition report must be completed between the landlord or his or her agent and tenant. This report will record in detail the condition of the premises at the start of the lease, and any past damages. It is important to have photographic evidence with the report as it may be used as evidence if there is a disagreement regarding the bond claim in the future. It should also state if anything within the property is broken or in poor condition. Both the lessor and the tenant should sign the report when it is completed. If either party won't sign the document, an independent person can do it. Should photographs be taken at the time the property inspection is carried out, it is recommended that all photographs be dated and signed by all parties.

Maintenance and repairs

As a landlord, you are obliged to provide a rental property in good clean operating condition. This means that you have to provide maintenance to the property and to repair items that need urgent attention. So what is the difference between maintenance and repairs?

- Maintenance is work that prevents deterioration, e.g. painting your property
- A repair is usually partial and restores something to its original state, e.g. repairing a leaking pipe.

Maintenance relates directly to normal wear and tear of a property. The following are examples of typical maintenance items:

- servicing fixed appliances such as gas and air-conditioning
- internal and external painting
- replacing rusted gutters
- replacing or repainting fences

Repairs should be dealt with immediately, to provide the tenant with a secure and habitable building. Urgent repairs are those that are needed to fix a severe problem or fault, which may harm the tenant or damage the property such as:

- blocked or broken plumbing, e.g. burst water pipes or blocked drains;
- physical damage to the property causing compromised

living conditions e.g. roof leaks, broken windows or flooding;

- failure of services for water, gas, or electricity; and
- faults or damage to the property rendering it unsafe or not secure, e.g. gas leaks, fire damage or broken locks.

If these repairs are not dealt with, the tenant has the right to organise a qualified tradesperson to complete repairs up to the value specified in the lease agreement. As the landlord, you will then be liable to reimburse the tenant for the cost incurred.

ROLE OF A PROPERTY MANAGER

A property manager can be a person or company who acts on behalf of a landlord to maintain the value of his or her property while generating income. Managed properties include residential and vacation homes, commercial retail space or industrial warehouse space. Property management involves seeking out tenants to occupy the space, collecting rent, maintaining the property, and upkeep of the grounds.

There are various types of property management companies ranging from those that manage large apartment complexes, to those that manage single-family homes. Some even specialise in managing serviced apartments or commercial retail units only. It is also not uncommon to find real estate agents who manage a few properties for their clients. Property managers are typically paid a fee or a percentage of the rental of the property while under management.

The property manager is responsible firstly to the landlord and secondly to the tenant. The relationships the property manager establishes with the landlord and with the tenant are crucial in forming the expectations of both parties to the lease since both parties will seek and expect certain rights and benefits out of it.

If you decide to use a property manager to lease and manage an investment property on your behalf, check that they have a license to operate. Under the law, all property managers must either hold a licence or have a certificate of registration and work under the supervision of a licensed agent. You can also do a licence check on the fair trading website.

Property manager's duties

A property manager's typical duties include the following tasks:

- Marketing for, and finding prospective tenants
- Screening of an applicant's credit, criminal history, rental history and ability to pay
- Preparation and signing of lease agreements
- Lodging the rental bond
- Collection of rent and maintaining rent records
- Paying necessary expenses and taxes
- Attending to repairs requested by tenants
- Undertaking regular property inspections
- Making periodic reports to the owner
- Paying the rent to the landlord, less any costs and agency fees
- Dealing with and eviction of bad tenants.

Property management fees

Property management fees can vary between residential and commercial, so it is important to negotiate this upfront. Fees are not regulated and are therefore negotiable (except any fixed by statute) and must be recorded on an agency agreement, including any GST liabilities. Below are typical formats in which fees can be charged.

Residential fees:
- Leasing fee: This fee covers the initial set-up cost for vetting and securing a tenant. Leasing fees are negotiable and usually charged at the start of each tenancy agreement. Some property managers also charge a re-leasing fee (also subject to negotiation) if current tenants sign a new tenancy agreement. Most managers charge a letting fee (e.g. one week's rent)
- Management fee: This is an ongoing fee that is deducted from the rent received from the tenant. If this fee is calculated as a percentage, ensure it is also displayed as a dollar

amount on the agency agreement. The management fee is based on a percentage of the gross weekly rental which is usually between 5% to 12% plus other fees set out in the agreement for residential properties.

- Marketing expenses: Marketing costs could be spent when the property manager advertises your rental property. Costs will vary depending on the advertising methods you choose.
- Other expenses: Examples of other expenses include statement fees, administrative and postage costs, tribunal appearances and warrant of possession.

Commercial fees:

- Leasing fee: In a typical commercial lease contract, the leasing company charges between 4% and 7% of the gross rent over the life of the lease. The leasing fee is usually paid when the new tenant moves in. Also, they could charge around 2% of gross rent when the lease is renewed.
- Management fee: The fee varies between 3% to 6% of the base monthly rent for commercial property, depending on the amount of work required to manage the property. For example, it takes much less time to manage a small commercial property with just a single tenant than a large commercial property with more than ten tenants. So, for the property with many tenants, you may have to pay a higher percentage to motivate the property manager.
- Marketing expenses: It takes longer to find a commercial tenant than a residential tenant therefore marketing cost are likely to be higher. These include the cost of site signs and media marketing, which will be at your cost.
- The property manager will charge other expenses similar to residential fees, such as disbursement and administrative costs.

Selecting a property manager

A good property manager will aim to maximise the rental income and source high-quality tenants. If you have decided to engage a property manager to act for you and your property, it is crucial to choose wisely. It is worth putting some time and effort into finding the right manager. Speak to at least three different agents before you decide. Don't base your decision on who is the cheapest. It will help if you consider what services they are going to provide and how well your investment will be looked after. Choosing the wrong agent may cost you money if they do not do their job correctly.

Once you have shortlisted a few potential property managers, it is essential to meet with them and consider asking the following questions before you decide:

- Are they able to provide a written comparison on rental values in the market? An experienced and knowledgeable manager will be able to offer comparable rental properties and advise on the optimal rental return on your rental property.

- How long have they been a property manager? Experienced property managers can attract the best tenants and deal with difficult problems.

- How many properties do they currently manage? More significant numbers are not always better, and you may become a number without getting the service and attention required.

- How long has the property manager been with that particular agency? Larger companies have many property managers and could have a high turnover of staff.

- How do they review potential tenants? A good manager will conduct police checks, or checks regarding their past rental history, current employment, and so on.

- How do they handle repair request from tenants? Do they have contacts with good tradespeople that will attend immediately to urgent repairs and keep the tenants happy?

- Do they check repairs once they have been carried out? It is essential that the manager ensures that the repairs have been done correctly and are not wasting your money.

- What steps would they take if the tenant is late with the rent? Your cash flow is important, and a good manager would know this and take immediate steps to collect late payments.

- How many times have they been to the tribunal and what is their success rate? Problems with difficult tenants may lead to a court to resolve issues costing time and money. A good manager tries to address the problems before going to court.
- How much are the management fees and what is included? Ask them about management fees as well as any other costs a property manager may charge.
- Are they able to provide references or contact details of their clients? These references are relevant and should be followed up to give you peace of mind that you will be in good hands.

Management agency agreement

When you engage a property manager a management agency agreement needs to be agreed upon and signed by both parties. The agency will usually have a standard agreement but bear in mind that the fees, terms and conditions of the agreement are negotiable. Ensure that all matters you want the agent to undertake and any specific conditions are listed explicitly in the agreement to avoid any misunderstandings should problems occur during the contracted period. Some questions you should consider are:

- How quickly do you wish to be told if your tenant is behind with the rent?
- How often should property inspections be carried out on your property?
- What is the period of the contract with the manager?
- Do you want to be involved each time a tenant is selected?
- Do you prefer to be consulted before any repairs or maintenance are carried out, no matter how small? Alternatively, would you prefer to be contacted only when the amount exceeds a set limit?

The agreement also requires you to specify whether or not you agree to pay separate marketing and advertising costs. An agreed letting fee and management fee schedule should also be defined. An agent may claim expenses from you that are related to their duties, such as photocopying and faxing costs, or reimbursement for repairs paid on your behalf. It would help if you discussed these expenses with the agent before signing the agreement.

The agreement that you sign appointing a property manager to manage your property is a legally binding contract. This means that both you and the property manager are obliged to fulfil the requirements of the agreement. Management agency agreements can vary between agencies, so it is vital that you read the contract carefully.

SELF-MANAGED VERSUS MANAGEMENT CONTRACT

The decision of whether to manage your investment property yourself or to appoint a property manager is dependent on your circumstances which should be carefully considered. There are advantages and disadvantages in each case. The points listed below are important to consider.

Property Manager	Owner–Manager
Advantages • **Time:** As the manager will take care of all the weekly duties it will give you more time to deal with your matters. • **Industry knowledge:** As is an expert in all areas of property management, the manager can best advise you on the best return based on current market conditions. • **Tradespeople contacts:** As they manage a range of properties, they will have access to reputable tradespeople to perform maintenance. • **Emotional attachment:** When it comes to difficult tenants or problems with the property you won't be emotionally involved.	**Advantages** • **Management fees:** You will save on property management fees. • **Management:** You will manage the property more diligently than anyone else as you will be emotionally attached to the investment you have made. • **Top priority:** As it is your investment, it will be your top priority to ensure it is tenanted, whereas a property manager may have many properties to manage, meaning yours may not be a top priority.

Disadvantages	Disadvantages
• **Agent fees:** You will have to pay the agent who is representing you and your property an ongoing fee. • **Management:** A property manager may not manage your property as you would. They may have several properties to manage so yours may be just a number.	• **Time:** Self-management of an investment property can be very time consuming and stressful due to ongoing management. • **Emotional attachment:** You could become emotionally attached to the property when dealing with problematic tenants. • **Industry knowledge:** You will have to familiarise yourself with up-to-date information on the current market, tenant history, etc. • **Marketing:** You will not have access to all of the tools and websites needed to market your property effectively.

ONGOING COST IN REAL ESTATE INVESTMENT

Estimating ongoing costs is essential to ascertain your cash flow on your investment property. However, it can be confusing as costs can vary from month to month and annually. Below is an outline of the potential cost and frequency of payment:

Cost	Frequency	Consideration
Mortgage Repayments	Monthly	The rental income may cover most of your monthly mortgage repayments, however, ensure that you have an allowance for any shortfall which could be affected by an interest rate rise.
Property Management	Monthly	If you have appointed a property manager to take care of your property, their commission or fees will need to be considered. Their fees vary but are negotiable.

Utilities	Monthly / Quarterly	Depending on your lease agreement with your tenant, you may be responsible for the cost of any services which do not have separate metering devices like water.
Body Corporate Fees	Quarterly	If your investment property is part of a strata title such as a townhouse, unit or apartment, it is likely to incur body corporation fees which covers maintenance of common areas as well as building insurance and council rates.
Council Rates	Quarterly	Council rates or shire rates are imposed by local government authorities and is usually based in some way on the value of the property. These valuations are typically determined by a statutory body and are subject to periodic revision.
Insurance (Building & Landlord)	Annual	Depending on the policy taken, building and landlord insurance will cover you from unforeseen building repairs (e.g. storm damage) and tenants damage, not paying rent, abandoning the property before the term of the lease, etc.
Mortgage Fees	Annual	A mortgage loan may attract a yearly loan account fee. Check with your lender if this will be applicable.
Land Tax	Annual	This cost is the annual tax levied on the owners of the land. States and territories levy land tax. Contact your relevant state authority to confirm the cost of your property.
Maintenance and Repairs	Ongoing	Depending on the age of the property these costs can vary. Maintenance of a property can be partly tax deductable, however, it is essential to check what is claimable.

It must be noted that the above costs that you are responsible for are mainly applicable to a residential property. With commercial property, the outgoings are commonly paid by the tenant. These outgoings are the landlord's reasonable expenses associated with the premises but have to be adequately documented in the lease. These outgoings include:

- Taxes, charges and fees such as council rates, body corporate levies and audit fees;
- Day to day premises costs paid by the landlord, such as cleaning, garbage collection, security services, fire protection equipment etc.
- Maintenance and repair services paid by the landlord and not for fair wear and tear (e.g. air-con servicing).

PROPERTY MANAGEMENT SOFTWARE

Selecting the best property management software will depend on many factors such as the type and number of properties being managed. Property management software continues to grow in popularity in Australia and to find one that suits your needs is easier said than done. With hundreds of software packages on the market, selection of the best one for you can become a minefield. Greater affordability of property managing software has allowed smaller companies and amateur property managers to adopt some of the same best practices and efficiencies as larger companies. Online asset management software or online property management software has been a significant cause of the price drops.

Before purchasing software that is suitable for your specific needs, it is advisable to read online reviews or talk to people who are currently using a particular program. Some of the companies promote their software by allowing you to have a trail run. Below are some points to consider when selecting software; make sure you check that it has the following capabilities:

- Ease of use
- Flexibility (the process can be modified by a user to meet individual needs)

- Reporting capabilities (e.g. rental areas statements, financial statements)
- Technical support (help service)
- Security procedures
- Communication capabilities (e.g. sending rent arrears to tenants by text message)
- Scalability (ability to handle an increase in the number of properties managed)
- Track record of the software supplier
- Data storage and retrieval (e.g. storing previous landlord details etc.)
- Maintenance activities (e.g. sending work orders to contractors etc.)
- The cost of the software fits your budget
- On-line integration (the ability of software to communicate with a website and be backed up in the cloud)
- Completeness of software (integration with other property software)

SUCCESSFUL PROPERTY MANAGEMENT TIPS

Owning and managing an investment property comes with a great deal of responsibility, which could become a stressful task if not handled properly. Most property investors can only see real estate investment with dollars in mind, instead of looking at the job as a business which means keeping your customers (tenants) happy. After all, they are the ones paying for the use of your product (property). By treating property management as a professional business you will find that the investment can be financially rewarding. Below are tips on how to approach property management. Even if you do not undertake the tasks yourself and appoint a property manager to do them instead, these pointers are essential to ensure that your property manager follows these guidelines.

1. Understand the laws

Whether you own residential or commercial property, it is essential to understand the laws applicable to leasing a property to a third party. Each state and territory has a landlord and tenant act that covers rent, security deposits, landlord and tenant obligations, tenant's rights, and evictions. With residential property you can get a copy of the landlord and tenant act from the Department of Housing in your state – this can generally be found on their website.

2. Tenant Screening

Understand the importance of running credit checks. A credit report is not just a number or a pass/fail test; it is a measure of how a person handles his or her financial obligations. The credit report also can reveal evasive answers on a rental application and save you the nightmare of renting to a tenant from hell. Also do not look for the 'perfect' tenant but focus on the tenant qualifications. Preconceived notions about the type of person you are looking for not only give rise to costly discrimination claims, but they also hamper tenant screening, mainly because the 'ideal' person gets a pass on credit checks, while the better applicant goes somewhere else. Don't turn away perfectly good tenants because you have a different image in your mind.

3. Customise the Lease

For residential leases, you can get a standard lease form at any office supply store which will cover basic things like rent, security deposit costs and any legal tenant rights in your state. You can use these basic documents as the framework to customise your lease by adding in any special conditions you have for your property, such as late payment fees or a maximum number of occupants and so on. Most commercial lawyers would have standard leases for small commercial properties. However, for larger commercial properties leases are generally negotiated between the tenant and the landlord. Hiring a property lawyer to draft up an agreement can save you a lot of money in the future. A good lease agreement clearly states the rights and responsibilities of both parties in detail to help avoid any future disputes.

4. Attend to repairs promptly

By attending to repairs in a prompt, professional manner, you will keep your tenant happy. When a tenant calls with a repair problem, set up a time to come and inspect the problem. If the repair is not an emergency such as a leaking tap or electrical fault, set up a time that works best for the tenant. Tenants will respect you more if you let them know ahead of time when you have organised a tradesperson to attend to the problem. Furthermore, avoid major costly repairs by attending to minor repair and maintenance items. When it comes to repairs and maintenance, a little expenditure today can save a lot tomorrow. Good quality properties attract good tenants.

5. Don't become emotionally attached

Although sometimes difficult, it is wise not to become emotionally attached to your investment property. Investment property should be treated as such. The relationship between you and your tenant should be kept at arm's length as a close relationship can lead to difficulties down the track, especially in situations where the parties have a falling out. To overcome this, treat the relationship with caution by establishing the rules early in the lease. By making up the rules as you go, you are opening yourself up for problems. Tenants will know if you are making rules up on the spot so having written rules will make life much easier. People tend not to question 'rules' even if you are the one who created these rules. Once the rules are set, do not deviate from them.

6. Keep the lines of communication open

While you do not want your tenant calling you at all hours of the day, you do not want to cut yourself off from your tenant completely. As a landlord, you still need to ensure that you or your property manager are always readily accessible and have the time to deal with situations when they arise. Tenants will feel more comfortable when they know how to get in touch with their landlord or property manager.

7. Conduct inspections but respect the tenant's privacy

While it is essential to conduct regular inspections of your property, it is equally important that you respect your tenants' privacy. Tenants like their privacy and most states require that you give a tenant notice before you enter the rental property. So let the tenant know ahead of time when you or your manager plan to visit and limit your visits to business hours or the early evening wherever possible.

8. Ensure that rent is paid on time

Late rental payments will impact on your cash flow and repayments to your lender so ensure that rent is paid on time. One option is to request that your tenant pay electronically though Internet banking. Most tenants prefer it, and many landlords have learned that automatic payments, electronic cheques and credit card payment options are key to having rent paid on time, which keeps cash flow healthy. A deterrent in a tenant paying late is to charge a late payment fee. By being strict with late payments, you place 'rent' higher on the priority scale than their other financial obligations. However, if there is real or compelling reason for late payments show a bit of human compassion and understanding. If a tenant is hospitalised, loses their job, or has a tragedy in the family, helping them to sort out the rent money can be a godsend.

9. Resolve disputes

Always try to resolve any disputes with your tenants without getting lawyers involved if you have a conflict with a tenant over rent, deposits, repairs, your access to the property, noise, or some other issue that does not warrant an eviction, meet with the tenant to see if the problem can be resolved informally. If that does not work, consider mediation by appointing a neutral party, who are often available at little or no cost from a publicly funded program. If the dispute involves money, and if all attempts fail to reach an agreement then try the small claims court, where you can represent yourself.

10. Keeping records

Keeping records on hand is essential for many financial and legal reasons. Keep any papers that you have your tenant sign, plus any other relevant documents related to your rental business or property. It is handy to keep electronic copies of these as well. You never know when that one incredibly important document will go missing. Whether it is for taxes, future loan applications, or legal issues with a tenant down the line, you always want to be sure that you have access to the information you need at any future point. The types of records that should be kept include:

- Tenant's information, lease agreements
- Financial transactions (both rents received and payments made)
- Property-related information (inspections, photographs, maintenance etc.)
- Insurance
- Legal documentation
- Accounts and audit documentation

Taking the above tips into consideration, you can make sure that that you and your tenant have a harmonious business relationship. Always maintain a professional relationship with your tenant, to avoid any misunderstandings and potential communication issues that may arise. Remember, they are the ones paying the rent, and you want to keep them paying the rent.

PROTECTION AND YOUR REAL ESTATE PORTFOLIO

If you have created a substantial real estate portfolio, it is crucial that you know how to protect your assets. You do not want to see the hard work you have undertaken from the development stage to the investment stage on several projects go to waste. Below we look at several fundamentals that require attention to keep your prized portfolio safe.

1. Take out landlord's insurance

Even though you may have the best property management team, there is still that something could go wrong such as tenants not paying rent or damaging property, an accident and so on, which can be entirely outside a landlord's control. A standard landlord insurance policy should cover:

- Malicious or intentional damage to the property by the tenant or their guests
- Theft by the tenant or their guests
- Loss of rent if the tenant defaults on their payments
- Liability, including for a claim against you by the tenant, and
- Legal expenses incurred in taking action against a tenant.

Most premiums for this type of insurance are not significant and they a small price to pay for peace of mind and mitigating the risk of potentially thousands of dollars in out-of-pocket expenses. As it is an investment expense, it is fully tax deductible.

2. Take out income protection insurance

If you are self-employed and don't have a monthly salary, it will be worthwhile to have an income protection insurance policy in place. This ensures you continue to receive a certain amount of income if you suffer a health issue or have an accident and are unable to work. Income protection insurance covers you for such an eventuality. Similar to the landlord's insurance, the premiums paid for income protection insurance are deductible for tax purposes.

3. Establish a cash contingency

A cash contingency is helpful for a couple of reasons. The cash flow from a real estate portfolio can fluctuate depending on circumstances. If you suddenly find one of your properties untenanted or have a tenant who runs into hardship and cannot make their rent payments, you could find your cash flow significantly reduced. If you have a cash contingency built up, you can weather periods when rental income reduces or dries up entirely. Another reason to build up a cash contingency is to have a cash reserve plan in place if you need to make unexpected repairs. If any repairs have to be made as a result of damage to your property, you may be able to claim on your landlord's insurance. However, a cash contingency can help get repairs underway while you wait for a claim to be processed. Another way of having a cash buffer is to set up a 'line of credit' with your lender that allows you have cash on hand when needed.

4. Lock in your interest rate

Talk to your mortgage adviser about whether to fix the entire loan or split the loan and fix a portion for flexibility. Such is the game of interest rates. When interest rates are at the market bottom then lock them in. Of course, there's always the possibility that interest rates will drop below your fixed rate. However, the risk lies in your ability to meet your loan repayments. A fixed rate gives you the certainty of your loan repayments for a set period.

5. Don't cross-collateralise your loans

Some developers use cross-collateralisation to finance another project. The problem with this is that if repayments fall short on one of the loans, it endangers your entire portfolio because it is all financed with the same bank. The best strategy is to separate your property loans. Smart investors know that to accumulate a secure and robust investment real estate portfolio it is best to ensure that each loan is individual and financed by separate banks. By using this strategy, you will be protecting yourself, and your other properties, in the event one of your properties sustain a loss.

6. Use a trust structure

When you place your real estate portfolio in a trust, the trust owns your portfolio and not yourself personally. Should something happen to you or you sustain bankruptcy, your properties are protected. A trust is a recognised legal entity and can own one or more properties. A trustee oversees the trust and distributes returns to the beneficiaries, which can include you personally. Another important aspect is that only the creditors of your trust have a claim upon the trust's assets. The creditors of trusts have no claim against the beneficiaries and can only claim against the trust entity itself. Similarly, if there is a claim against you personally even though you are a beneficiary, your creditors cannot claim against the trust or its assets.

7. Consider a pre-nuptial agreement

It is never a happy topic to consider, but if you're getting married or in the early stages of a long-term relationship and want to ensure that your property assets stay in your hands in the event of the breakdown of the relationship, a pre-nuptial agreement may be suitable. A pre-nuptial agreement stipulates how assets will be divided should your marriage or relationship dissolve. If the worst should happen and your relationship ends, your partner has a legal claim to your real estate portfolio. If you believe your relationship will last the distance or that your partner won't take your assets in the event of a breakdown, then don't get a pre-nuptial agreement.

8. Ensure you have an up-to-date will

Often viewed as a morbid subject, your will is essential as it is your final statement of who gets what when you pass away. Your real estate portfolio is your life's work, and you want to ensure that your portfolio goes to the right person or people, such as your children. If you don't have a will, your properties may pass to those you would not have chosen or cause disagreements among your beneficiaries. So keep your will current.

CONCLUSION

Whether you decide to manage your properties yourself or employ a third party property manager will depend on your circumstances and the size of your portfolio. Making a choice either way is only part of the picture in protecting and growing your real estate investment portfolio. If you are applying a 'develop and hold' strategy to grow your portfolio, you will have to think about delegating certain duties to others. Property development and its processes and stages will take up a considerable amount of your time both mentally and physically, and as property development is the riskier part of the 'develop and hold' strategy, it is advisable that you consider outsourcing the management of your rental properties within your real estate portfolio.

CONCLUSION

I hope that after reading this book that you are inspired and enlightened by the concept of the 'develop and hold' strategy and that you will start planning your pathway to a future passive income. During the course of your journey, you will be facing many challenges but do not let these bumps in the road stop you from achieving your goals. The development phase of the journey will be the bumpy road with many bridges to cross, but once you have completed this part, the investment stage is your reward where you can enjoy the financial fruits of your labour.

One strong piece of advice I would like to make is: please do not take short-cuts during your journey as you may end up in the wrong direction. Remember that the product you are developing is for you to keep and nurture, and if you do this it will take care of you financially in your retirement. It is also an asset for your future generations to enjoy should you pass your assets to your children. Let greed not get in your way with a focus on purely making money. Money is essential as you are taking a high risk but try and find a balance between making money and developing great sustainable buildings that can be appreciated by others as well.

Plan your journey

Before starting on your journey to financial freedom, it is important that you map out your route with an effective strategy set out in a well thought out business plan. The property development and investment industries have seen many wreckages and financial disasters as a result of bad planning. However, there have been equally as many successful journeys by those who planned well according to sound business principles. Embarking on a 'develop and hold' strategy, requires both short and long term planning with the short term being the development phase and the long term being the building up of your portfolio. Each person's planned journey will be different as our needs, and personal circumstance are different, so plan your journey according to what suits you and not according to others as if you get this wrong it will make the challenges more difficult.

Set your goals

Goal setting plays an integral part in establishing a passive income producing a real estate portfolio. However, your goals have to be practical with a degree of flexibility. From a practical viewpoint, establish what you will need to be financially comfortable during your retirement years. This gives you an idea of how many rental properties you should target and the level of passive income you would need to maintain your future lifestyle. After completing your end goals, then break these down into mini-goals and goals you would like to achieve every year. As each year passes look again at your goals and see if you have met your targets or need to revise or amend your objectives and dates. Allow for flexibility when establishing your goals as circumstances will certainly change along the way. With the property and investment game being cyclical, your goals will have to adapt according to the conditions that prevail at the time. However, this should not divert your attention from your ultimate dream. It is simply a matter of formulating another strategy so you can reach your targets.

Be socially aware

As property developers, we are the creators and decision makers of the environments we build that determine the social fabric that people will live or work in when completed. It is therefore crucial that we develop buildings and environments that are ecologically sustainable not only for the short term but for future generations as well. We have to be socially aware of how we go about our developments as we are at the forefront of social structuring through the control of the design and planning of these new environments. Even though we employ a professional team who have active social ethics, we as the developer have the final say the project's outcome.

We have all seen developments that appear overbuilt, claustrophobic and lacking in any form of ambience thus becoming a hindrance to its neighbours and an unhealthy living and working space for its occupants. The developer has maximised or pushed the limit to its allowable plot ratio meaning that the occupants live too close to each other, lose their privacy, are angered by noise created by adjacent units, which ultimately leads to bad karma within the development. As a socially orientated developer, brief your development team to design your project so that it blends with its neighbouring buildings and surroundings and creates a pleasant ambience within the development. This can be achieved by careful design and planning, the creation of open and green spaces and a ensuring a reasonable distance between units.

Be concerned about the environment

As a developer, you should strive for economic well-being, environmental protection, and overall quality of life for people without compromising the ability of future generations to meet these needs. By adopting this policy, we all benefit from an environmentally sensitive approach to growth and development. By following this principle, you will benefit from competitive advantages from building green, an improved image and public goodwill, a reduction in land and infrastructure costs, fewer consumer complaints and healthier construction conditions.

Those of us that adopt these principles will attract a growing market and will assist in creating desirable communities that are sustainable. For those of us who are responsible for carrying out developments, we should ask of ourselves some simple questions:

- Does the development maximise the use of existing infrastructure and minimise new infrastructure?
- Does the development reduce dependence on motor vehicles and promote other forms of transport?
- Does the development form a livable and long-lasting community?
- Does the design encourage social interaction and places for random encounters?
- Are natural habitats, wetlands and fertile soil resources preserved during and after construction?

- Are homes and other buildings in the development energy efficient?
- Can building materials be used efficiently?
- Can renewable building resources be used?
- Can construction waste products be recycled during construction?
- Can the buildings be sturdy, adaptable, and of high quality?

Be quality conscious

If you are building a portfolio of investment properties that you will hold and lease out for many years, then you have to develop a passion for excellence and attention to detail. These buildings will have to last the wear and tear of a variety of people who will be living or working in them. Not only does the built form have to be of quality and low maintenance materials, proper design and planning ensure that the building is functional, fit-for-purpose and visually appealing in line with design excellence. A commitment to producing excellent design and construction in your development is the safest and the most likely strategy for achieving business success. Therefore, the key is to develop a passion for excellence in everything you do. Develop a reputation for being a person who is always seeking ways to do things better. Never accept sub-standard work or service from anybody associated with your development project. It is imperative to set out and inform team members the standards and quality you want to achieve.

Enjoy the ride

By adopting the 'build and hold' strategy and adhering to the strategies, policies and ethos outlined in this book, you are well on your way to building not only a wealthy portfolio but one that includes buildings that you can be proud of. The process can be compared to a roller-coaster ride. There will be many ups and downs but at the same time it will be very exciting. It is a risky business, but the rewards can be immense if you are developing and investing with a cautious approach. Anything can change without warning, and sometimes these changes are beyond your control. Be prepared to take some risks and learn from the experience. If you are an overcautious person and a pessimist, then this business is not for you as you will be too afraid to take that first step to enrich yourself both mentally and financially. However, if you have money available and some knowledge of property and are prepared to tolerate an occasional attack of nerves, then tackle your first project. Do your homework and be cautious, and you will sleep well at night knowing that your money, through the 'build and hold' strategy, can appreciate faster than most other investments or businesses.

WISHING YOU SUCCESS

www.ingramcontent.com/pod-product-compliance
Lightning Source LLC
Chambersburg PA
CBHW060328200326
41519CB00011BA/1874